THE AGON IN EURIPIDES

The Agon in Euripides

MICHAEL LLOYD

CLARENDON PRESS · OXFORD

Oxford University Press, Walton Street, Oxford OX2 6DP
Oxford New York
Athens Auckland Bangkok Bombay
Calcutta Cape Town Dar es Salaam Delhi
Florence Hong Kong Istanbul Karachi
Kuala Lumpur Madras Madrid Melbourne
Mexico City Nairobi Paris Singapore
Taipei Tokyo Toronto
and associated companies in
Berlin Ibadan

Oxford is a trade mark of Oxford University Press

Published in the United States by
Oxford University Press Inc., New York

© Michael Lloyd 1992

All rights reserved. No part of this publication may be reproduced,
stored in a retrieval system, or transmitted, in any form or by any means,
without the prior permission in writing of Oxford University Press.
Within the UK, exceptions are allowed in respect of any fair dealing for the
purpose of research or private study, or criticism or review, as permitted
under the Copyright, Designs and Patents Act, 1988, or in the case of
reprographic reproduction in accordance with the terms of the licences
issued by the Copyright Licensing Agency. Enquiries concerning
reproduction outside these terms and in other countries should be
sent to the Rights Department, Oxford University Press,
at the address above

British Library Cataloguing in Publication Data
Data available

Library of Congress Cataloging in Publication Data
The agon in Euripides / Michael Lloyd.
Includes bibliographical references and index.
1. Euripides—Technique. 2. Debates and debating in literature.
3. Rhetoric, Ancient. 4. Tragedy. I. Title.
PA3978.L6 1992   882'.01—dc20
ISBN 0–19–814778–3

3 5 7 9 10 8 6 4 2

Printed in Great Britain on acid-free paper by
Ipswich Book Co. Ltd., Suffolk

PREFACE

THE English word 'agon', like its Greek original, can refer to various kinds of contest or conflict. The present work is concerned with a type of formal debate, common in Euripides, in which two hostile characters make conflicting speeches. I have concentrated on the agon, rather strictly defined, in Euripides' extant plays, and have not attempted to rival the comprehensive coverage given by the still-useful book of J. Duchemin (1968; 1st edn. 1945). This has left me free to discuss the specific issues of individual agones as well as offering a more narrowly formal study of the agon itself.

This book has its origins in my Oxford D.Phil. thesis, submitted in 1983, which included discussion of the agones in *Alcestis*, *Electra*, and *Troades*. Colin Macleod was an exacting supervisor, and, whatever its inadequacies, the present work is both shorter and better because of my worries about what he would have thought of it. I discussed the agon in general, and the agon in *Troades* in particular, in 'The Helen Scene in Euripides' *Troades*', *CQ* 34 (1984) 303–13; some material from that article reappears here, by permission of Oxford University Press. I am grateful to Dr M. J. Cropp and Prof. W. G. Arnott for reading earlier versions of the chapters on *Electra* and *Orestes* respectively, and for giving me the benefit of their perceptive comments. The Clarendon Press reader, whom I am permitted to identify as Prof. C. Collard, read the whole book in draft form and made many helpful suggestions about both structure and content. My greatest debt remains that to Tom Stinton, both for his generous encouragement as my tutor at Wadham College and for the example afforded by his wide learning and fine feeling for Greek poetry.

M.A.L.

Dublin
June 1991

CONTENTS

1. The Nature and Function of the Agon — 1
2. Rhetoric and Euripides' Agones — 19
3. Early Agones: *Alcestis, Medea, Hippolytus, Andromache* — 37
4. *Electra* — 55
5. Political Debates: *Heraclidae, Supplices, Phoenissae* — 71
6. *Hecuba* and *Troades* — 94
7. *Orestes* — 113
Conclusion — 130
Bibliography — 133
Index — 141

1

The Nature and Function of the Agon

GREEK tragedies are representations of human action, but also formal structures with internal rules of their own.[1] The possibilities of tension between these two aspects of tragedy are especially evident in the plays of Euripides, which combine realism with a marked formalism of structure.[2] This formalism is most apparent in the construction of his plays as sequences of distinct formal units. These units tend to be strongly demarcated within the individual play, and to contain formulaic elements which recur in many plays. *Electra*, for example, can be analysed as a series of set-pieces: prologue speech, actor's monody, formal *rhesis*, stichomythia, messenger speech, agon, and *deus ex machina*. The formality and distinctness of these set-pieces is emphasized, but the play is also, in some respects, realistic in its depiction of human behaviour.

Most of Euripides' plays have some kind of conflict as a central theme, and he characteristically expresses this conflict in a type of set-piece which is normally referred to as the agon. The agon basically consists of a pair of opposing set speeches of substantial, and about equal, length. Other elements are often present, such as angry dialogue after the speeches, or a judgement speech by a third party, but the opposition of two set speeches is central to the form. The earliest extant examples of this dramatic form occur in the *Ajax* and *Antigone* of Sophocles, plays of uncertain date but usually thought to be earlier than the earliest extant play of Euripides, the *Alcestis* of 438 BC. Unfortunately, too little is known about the earlier plays of Sophocles and Euripides for it to be clear which of them, if either, established the form of the agon as it appears in their extant plays. This form is favoured especially by Euripides, with his liking for set-pieces, and

---

[1] See Taplin 1977: 49–60 for some useful remarks on the whole question of formal structure in Greek tragedy.
[2] 'Realism' here refers to a literary mode, and does not imply any straightforward reflection of the world. On Euripides' formalism, see Schadewaldt 1926: 104–8; Ludwig 1957; Strohm 1957: 3; Gould 1978: 51; Michelini 1987: ch. 4.

it appears throughout the period of his extant plays, from *Alcestis* to *Iphigenia in Aulis*.³

Verbal conflicts of a more or less formal kind were no doubt a feature of Greek life from an early period, and appear in literature as early as the first book of Homer's *Iliad*. The surviving plays of Aeschylus contain a number of scenes of confrontation and argument, but not even the trial scene in *Eumenides* has the balance of substantial speeches which characterizes the agon in Euripides. Euripides' agones clearly owe a great deal, both in form and in content, to a variety of situations in contemporary Athenian life which provided a formal context for the conflict of arguments.⁴ Prominent among these were the lawcourts, but political and diplomatic debates are also relevant. Sophists and rhetoricians concerned themselves with the theory and practice of argument, and there was a sophisticated audience in late fifth-century Athens for every kind of debate.

Euripides' formalism makes it both possible and necessary to give a fairly strict definition of the agon in his plays. It is almost always marked as a distinct and separate section within a play, and there are many resemblances between the agones in different plays. The basic form remains constant from *Alcestis* to *Iphigenia in Aulis*. Studies of the agon in Euripides may have tended to concentrate excessively on dry categorization, and the present work deals mainly with the agones in the context of the various individual plays, but it is nevertheless necessary to make some general observations about the form of the agon. This form is part of Euripides' dramatic language, and it must be grasped if any individual example is to be understood. Variations can be understood only in terms of the norm. The agon in Sophocles is rather different, in that he avoids formality and incorporates agones into his plays in a more naturalistic way. It is often difficult in practice to decide whether a given scene in Sophocles is or is not an agon, and where an agon begins and ends. Few such problems arise with Euripides.

In Euripides' extant plays there are thirteen scenes which are generally recognized as agones.⁵ There are a number of other scenes which are related to the thirteen undisputed agones, and scholars differ in their

---

³ The term 'agon' is used here in a specialized sense, but it can also apply to a wide variety of verbal (and other) contests. For a comprehensive account, see Froleyks 1973 (reviewed by D. M. MacDowell, *CR* 26 (1976), 277). Cf. Duchemin 1968: 11–37.

⁴ Cf. Goff 1990: 78–80. W. Burkert, *Griechische Religion der archaischen und klassischen Epoche* (Stuttgart, 1977), ii. 7. 5 (Eng. tr. as *Greek Religion*, Oxford, 1985).

⁵ Cf. Nuchelmans 1971. Various other scenes, in addition to the undisputed 13, are treated as agones by Graf 1950, Epke 1951, and Senoner 1960. Even wider definitions are given by Duchemin 1968: 39–41; and Collard 1975a: 60–1.

The Nature and Function of the Agon 3

readiness to regard some or all of these scenes as being themselves agones. The question of terminology is of limited interest in itself, and what is needed is to find some appropriate and useful way of describing the agon and the scenes which are related to it. The method adopted in this chapter will be to take the thirteen undisputed agones in Euripides' extant plays, and to examine both their common features and the ways in which they are marked off as separate scenes. The principles thus established will be applied to marginal cases in Euripides and to possible agones in Sophocles. Finally, some general observations will be made about the function of the agon in Euripides.

THE NATURE OF THE AGON

The following thirteen scenes in Euripides' extant plays are generally recognized as agones:

1. *Alcestis* 614–733
2. *Medea* 446–622
3. *Heraclidae* 120–283
4. *Hippolytus* 902–1089
5. *Andromache* 147–273
6. *Andromache* 547–746
7. *Hecuba* 1109–292
8. *Supplices* 399–580
9. *Electra* 988–1138
10. *Troades* 895–1059
11. *Phoenissae* 446–635
12. *Orestes* 470–629
13. *Iphigenia in Aulis* 317–414

Agones in Euripides are almost always distinct scenes, and the line numbers given above for the limits of the various agones indicate, for the most part, the entrance or exit of one of the main contestants. Normally the hostility between the two opposed characters is such that the agon clearly continues for as long as they are on stage together. It is much less common for the agon in Sophocles to be a clearly defined scene, with its beginning and end marked by entrances and exits. In four of Euripides' plays, in fact, the agon occupies all, or almost all, of an act and it frequently either begins or ends with an act division. The only agon whose end is not clearly marked is that in *Iphigenia in Aulis*, which seems to end (at line 414) without an exit. The only other agones which do not end at, or very near, the end of an act are those in *Heraclidae* and *Orestes*.

The agon in Euripides is not only a clearly defined scene, but it is also usually made clear when an agon is in progress. Eight of the thirteen agones are thus announced, more or less formally, in advance. In *Heraclidae* the Herald states that the argument will be with Demophon (116), and he begins his speech after Demophon's arrival with a formal headline (134 f.). When the Herald has finished, there is a choral comment of an almost formulaic type (179 f.) which stresses the balance of speeches and leaves no doubt that an agon is in progress. The comparable agon in *Supplices* has explicit markers at every stage to show what is happening (403 f., 409 f., 427 f., 456 f., 465 f., 515–17). The agon in *Hecuba* is explicitly announced in advance by Agamemnon (1129–31) with reference to the forthcoming balanced speeches. In *Electra*, Clytaemestra's speech has an elaborate introduction (1013–17), and the end of her speech and the ensuing dialogue make it clear that there is to be a balance of speeches (1049–60). The formality is even more marked in Euripides' later plays, with explicit statements in advance that there will be a balanced pair of speeches at *Troades* 906–9 and *Phoenissae* 465–8, and a headline at *Orestes* 491. There is nothing quite as explicit in the agon of *Iphigenia in Aulis*, but the formal beginning of Menelaus' speech (334–6) indicates that an agon is in progress; this impression is confirmed by the corresponding introduction to Agamemnon's speech (378–80). In these eight plays the agon manifests itself as such almost from the start. In three other plays the first speech consists of an impassioned attack without formal indications of an agon, while the second speech begins with elaborate gestures which make it clear that an agon is in progress (*Med.* 522–5, *Hi.* 983–91, *An.* 186–91).[6] Only in *Alcestis* and in the second agon of *Andromache* is there no indication, by the beginning of the second speech at the latest, that an agon is in progress.

The agon, in the narrower dramatic sense, is part of a wider category of verbal contests for which the terms in Euripides are ἀγών or ἅμιλλα λόγων. These are not technical terms with a specifically theatrical connotation, and they are applied in Euripides to scenes which are not agones in the sense defined above (e.g. *Hec.* 271, *Su.* 195, *HF* 155, 1255, *Pho.* 930).[7] This is not surprising, since Euripides could not use these terms

[6] Cf. Finley 1967: 30–1.
[7] Notable uses of agonistic terminology in fragments are fr. 189 (*Antiope*), fr. 334. 3 (*Dicte*), and fr. 812. 1–3 (*Phoenix*). Cf. generally Duchemin 1968: 11 f.; Collard 1975b on *Su.* 195–6a.

The Nature and Function of the Agon 5

at all if their only application were to a specific aspect of the theatrical performance.[8] Nevertheless, such terminology does occur in seven of the thirteen agones. The agon in *Heraclidae* is twice stated or implied to be an ἀγών (116, 161); that in *Medea* is described as an ἅμιλλα . . . λόγων (*Med.* 546); at *Hi.* 971, Theseus asks τί ταῦτα σοῖς ἀμιλλῶμαι λόγοις; (cf. 1023); Hermione criticizes Andromache, after her speech in the agon of *Andromache*, for engaging in an ἀγὼν λόγων (*An.* 234); Theseus uses the terms ἀγῶνα ἀγωνίζομαι and ἅμιλλα λόγων to describe the proceedings in *Supplices* (427f.) while the Herald refers to τῶν ἠγωνισμένων (465); Eteocles describes the agon in *Phoenissae* as ἀγὼν λόγων (588); and Tyndareus introduces the agon in *Orestes* with the term ἀγών (491).

It is thus clear that Euripides normally gives formal indications when an agon is in progress, and also that he often uses agonistic terminology in the course of his agones. These two features of the agon combine to mark its formality, but it is interesting that they rarely coincide (partial exceptions to this are *Hcld.* 116, *Su.* 427 f., and *Or.* 491). A statement, in so many words, that an agon is imminent would thus be too explicit even for Euripides and would be in danger of referring too overtly to a formal feature of the play as a play.

Central to the structure of the agon is the opposition of two speeches of substantial length, separated by two or three iambic trimeters from the chorus.[9] There is always subsidiary material of various kinds, but only in *Phoenissae* are the two main opposing speeches not predominant. Undue importance should not be attached to a mere computation of line numbers, but it is striking that 14 of the 26 speeches are between 45 and 54 lines in length.[10] Only three of the speeches are below 30 lines in length, which suggests that a certain minimum length is necessary to make the appropriate impact. Two of these three speeches are in *Phoenissae*, where the speeches of Polynices and Eteocles are overshadowed by Jocasta's long and impressive arbitration speech, while Agamemnon's speech in *Iphigenia in Aulis* is explicitly said to be short (378, 400).

One of the most striking features of the agon in Euripides is the way in which the main speeches tend to balance each other. Not only is it regularly stressed that there are to be speeches on both sides of an issue, or that the second speech will answer the first, but the two main opposing

---

[8] On this somewhat controversial point, see Taplin 1986: 168–70; Bain 1987: 8–14.

[9] On choral comments, see Graf 1950: 165. The agones in *Supplices* and *Electra* have some slight variation in the material between the speeches.

[10] This calculation is based on the Oxford Classical Text (vols. i and ii ed. J. Diggle, vol. iii ed. G. Murray).

speeches are also normally about the same length. Few scholars would now emend speeches in order to achieve an exact balance, but it is significant that in five of the thirteen agones the speeches are within three lines of each other in length (*Medea, Hecuba, Supplices, Electra,* and *Phoenissae*). Five other agones have speeches of approximately equal length in contexts where the balance of speeches is also made clear in other ways: *Alcestis* (42 lines to 31 lines), *Heraclidae* (45 : 51), *Hippolytus* (45 : 52), *Troades* (49 : 64), and *Orestes* (50 : 61). In only three scenes does there seem to be a significant difference in the length of the speeches: *Iphigenia in Aulis* (42 : 25 trochaic tetrameters), where Agamemnon does, as was remarked above, comment on the shortness of his speech; and in the two agones in *Andromache* (33 : 49 in the scene between Hermione and Andromache, and 52 : 36 in that between Peleus and Menelaus). These two scenes are, in fact, irregular in other ways and *Andromache* also contains another scene (discussed below) which has agonistic features. In this play, unusually for Euripides, the distinctness of the agon form is blurred, and he is clearly being careful to maintain variety in a series of scenes of confrontation and argument.

The two main opposing speeches are the most regular and striking element in the agon, but there are always other elements. The material that precedes the two main speeches varies from nothing at all in the first agon of *Andromache* to 70 lines in the agon of *Supplices* (which some scholars have treated as a separate agon). The material that follows the two main speeches is rather more regular. The conflict is always continued in a less formal style, sometimes after a judgement speech, and stichomythia is a regular feature of this section. Sometimes this dialogue is rather short, but in eight of the thirteen agones it is about the same in total as one of the main speeches and there seems to be some sense of balance here.[11]

NEAR-AGONES, SUPPLICATION SCENES, AND EPIDEIXIS SCENES

A pattern has emerged from this examination of the thirteen undisputed agones in Euripides' extant plays, and the next question to consider is how this pattern applies to related scenes in Euripides. There are, in the first place, two scenes in which the agon form is present in the background but is not fulfilled in all its details.

---

[11] On stichomythia in the agon, see Schwinge 1968: 33–56.

In the first of these scenes, *Med.* 1317–414, Medea makes a formal invitation to Jason to speak (1320). He then makes a speech which is rather short for an agon (28 lines), and is not really formal or argumentative. The first speech of an agon is, however, sometimes an impassioned outburst, and Jason's speech here is clearly comparable in some ways to Medea's speech in the earlier agon. Medea then explicitly refuses to make a speech (1351–3) and the scene concludes with angry dialogue of the usual sort. In other words, this scene would be a fairly regular agon if Medea had made the formal speech that she explicitly rejects. The reason for the abbreviation of the agon form is clear. There has already been one full agon between Jason and Medea and it would be repetitive to have another. The shortness of the speeches is to some extent compensated by the long stichomythia which, unusually for an agon, dominates the main speeches. There is minimal stichomythia in the earlier agon, and Euripides seems to have spread the elements of the agon over two scenes.

The other interesting borderline case is *Hcld.* 928–1055. This scene is a regular agon in every respect except that Alcmene's prosecution speech is cut short. There is, as she explains (952), much that she could have said, but instead of continuing the speech she engages in dialogue with a servant. This dialogue does, as it were, make up the missing part of Alcmene's speech in the structure of the scene.[12] Eurystheus makes an entirely regular defence speech, and there is angry dialogue after it. The scene is an interesting variation on the agon form and, as in *Medea*, the near-agon at the end of the play balances the full agon earlier.

This is perhaps the appropriate point at which to discuss the episode involving Hector and Rhesus at *Rh.* 379–526. This scene demands consideration as an agon, but it is unusual in some important respects. Rhesus arrives and greets Hector (388–92), prompting a speech by Hector which criticizes him for coming late and showing ingratitude (393–421). This speech is, at 29 lines, on the short side for an agon, but the structure of the scene so far does in general conform to the pattern of the Euripidean agon. (Compare *Alcestis* and *Medea* for the arrival of a character provoking an outburst about ingratitude.[13]) There is no choral comment and Rhesus' reply is, at 32 lines, rather short. What is really unusual about Rhesus' speech, however, is that it does not escalate the dispute and has neither the intention nor the effect of antagonizing Hector further. Rhesus is not exactly apologetic, but he does seem to offer a quite acceptable explanation of his delay which contrasts sharply with the infuriating defences of Pheres

---

[12] Cf. Duchemin 1968: 76, 121, 146.   [13] Cf. Ritchie 1964: 91 f., 244 f.

and Jason. He concludes with some provocative remarks, but the main body of his speech is conciliatory enough.[14] This means that, uniquely for an agon, there is no angry dialogue after the two main speeches. What happens is that, after an unusual choral strophe,[15] Hector and Rhesus have a long dialogue in which they may have some differences of opinion but which is in no sense an angry argument, and which ends on a fairly harmonious note. This dialogue is also, at 60 lines, longer than that at the equivalent stage of any agon, and it overshadows the two rather short speeches. In conclusion, this scene diverges markedly from the normal Euripidean agon.

The near-agones in *Medea* and *Heraclidae* may deviate from the norm in various ways but there is no doubt that they are to be understood against the background of the agon form. A number of other scenes in Euripides which have been treated as agones by some scholars are really quite distinct from the agon form, and are liable to be misunderstood if they are treated as agones. In fact, all the other scenes in Euripides which could remotely be regarded as agones fall into two categories, which might be termed supplication scenes and epideixis scenes. The former can come close to the agon in their overall structure but are distinct in content,[16] while the latter often have the contentiousness of the agon while being different in structure.

A good example of a supplication scene is *Alc.* 244–392. This scene is, in form, exactly like an agon, with introductory dialogue, two balancing speeches separated by a choral distich, and concluding stichomythia. In content, however, it could not be more different. There is no sense of hostility or contentiousness as Alcestis pleads with Admetus not to remarry (αἰτοῦμαι 308), and he replies by expressing enthusiastic assent. Few scholars treat this scene as an agon, but it does in fact come closer to the agon in form than any other supplication scene. It is more usual for the difference of content to lead to corresponding differences of form. The scene between Odysseus and Hecuba at *Hec.* 218 ff. does have balanced speeches but lacks the angry dialogue after the speeches which is normal in the agon. Hecuba's speech is a plea (ἀπαιτῶ 276, ἱκετεύω 276, οἴκτιρον 287) which Odysseus rejects without any personal hostility to Hecuba. There is thus no angry dialogue, and the direction of the scene changes without either character

---

[14] V. J. Rosivach, 'Hector in the *Rhesus*', *Hermes*, 106 (1978), 54–73, at 59 f, does, however, argue that Rhesus' explanation is not satisfactory, and that Hector shows self-restraint in not reacting angrily.

[15] Cf. Ritchie 1964: 328–33.

[16] Strohm 1957: 47 f. distinguishes *Bittrede* from *Streitrede*. Cf. Solmsen 1975: ch. 2.

leaving the stage. This almost never happens in the agon (*Iphigenia in Aulis* is an exception) because hostility normally reaches such a pitch that at least one contestant must leave the stage before anything else can happen. There is, similarly, no angry dialogue after the speeches in the supplication scene at *Su.* 87–262, and no exit at the end of it. The lack of initial hostility between Theseus and Adrastus means that they can have a conversation before the two main speeches which is of a length unparalleled in the agon. A comparatively minor point is that Theseus' speech is nearly twice as long as Adrastus', a greater disparity than in any of the thirteen genuine agones. The difference of content between this scene and the agon is summarized by Adrastus' comment that, while he sought benefit, Theseus replied as a δικαστής (253–6).

An agon has sometimes been detected somewhere in the first episode of *Cyclops*, although there has been no agreement about which lines are to count as such.[17] There are indeed balanced speeches by Odysseus and the Cyclops, but this is clearly a supplication scene (ἱκετεύομεν 287) and not an agon. The informality of structure is unusual in Euripides, and may owe something to *Cyclops* being a satyr play, although it should be noted that supplication scenes tend to be looser in structure than agones.

There are two supplication scenes, *Hel.* 857–1031 and *IA* 1098–275, in which a pair of pleas is addressed to one character who then responds. The scene in *Helen* never at any stage resembles an agon, as the suppliant status of Helen and Menelaus is made abundantly clear (ἱκέτις 894, ἱκετεύω 939). The supplication scene in *Iphigenia in Aulis*, however, does evoke the agon form to some extent. Clytaemestra's speech (1146–208) is highly contentious and argumentative in tone (ὀνειδίσω 1148) and, far from being a plea, challenges Agamemnon to refute her (1206–8). This speech is just like the first speech of an agon, and raises expectations of a contentious response by Agamemnon followed by angry dialogue. What actually happens is that Iphigenia intervenes with a supplication speech (ἱκετηρίαν 1216, ἱκέτευσον 1242, κατοίκτιρον 1246), and it is to this that Agamemnon replies. We thus have a scene which begins by looking like an agon but turns into a supplication scene, and Euripides manipulates these distinct types of scene in a skilful and surprising way. Even more complex is the second episode of *Orestes*, where an agon between Tyndareus and Orestes is placed in the middle of a supplication scene between Orestes and Menelaus.

---

[17] Seaford 1984: 46 treats lines 285–346 as an agon; Graf 1950 thinks that the agon occupies lines 275–355; Duchemin 1968 regards lines 222–74 and 275–355 as separate agones.

A second type of scene which has often been confused with the agon might be termed the epideixis scene.[18] In this type of scene, one character makes a long speech in response to some provocative behaviour or proposal. The tone of the proceedings might or might not be contentious, but what all these scenes share is that they lack the balance of speeches which is so characteristic of the agon. A straightforward example is *Ion* 510–675, where Ion makes a long speech (585–647) rejecting Xuthus' proposal that he come to Athens. This speech is a general exposition of the disadvantages of going to Athens, and it is not forensic in manner. There is no balance of speeches, since Xuthus merely repudiates the idea of argument (650). The end of *Heracles* has a scene with a somewhat similar structure, if very different tone, when Heracles is provoked by Theseus to make a long speech (1255–310) in which he argues that his life is unendurable. This speech is an epideixis (1256 f.), in no way forensic (despite the agonistic terminology in 1255), and there is no question of Theseus replying in a contentious spirit. Another epideixis is Tiresias' defence of Dionysus at *Ba.* 266–327, which is provoked by Pentheus' entry speech (215–62). This scene has some superficial resemblance to the agon, but Pentheus' speech is not at all agonistic. He does not, in fact, even notice Cadmus and Tiresias until line 248 when his speech has only 15 lines left to run.[19] The structure of this scene is somewhat similar to *An.* 309–463, where the outrageous words and actions of Menelaus provoke a series of outbursts from Andromache.

These examples of epideixis scenes may shed some light on the formally puzzling first episode of the *Heracles*, in which Amphitryo makes a long speech (170–235) in reply to a speech by Lycus (140–69). The scene differs markedly from the normal agon form.[20] Amphitryo's speech is more than twice the length of Lycus', a disparity without parallel in an undisputed agon, and there is no choral comment between the speeches. There is no introductory dialogue, which is unusual but not unparalleled, no angry dialogue after the two main speeches, and no exit at the end (if 251 is the end). Lycus' speech is not a normal prosecution speech, but a series of threats and insults, and Amphitryo's reply has a variety of content unparalleled in any genuine agon speech: defence of Heracles' reputation (18 lines), a discussion of archery (18 lines), a plea to Lycus (11 lines), reproaches to the Thebans and to the Greeks generally (10 lines), and

---

[18] Cf. Wilamowitz 1895 on *HF* 138, 139.
[19] See Bain 1977: 64 f.
[20] Bond 1981: 101 f. argues that lines 140–251 are an agon, while Hamilton 1985 treats the whole act as a double agon. Schwinge 1968: 33 n. 1 points out that the scenes in *HF* and *Ba.* both lack the stichomythia which is usual in the agon.

a pathetic address to the children (9 lines). These irregularities are decisive in view of the consistency of the agon form throughout the extant plays, and this is clearly an epideixis scene. The epideixis scene in *Bacchae* provides a parallel for the defence of someone who is not present (which never happens in the agon), and the second episode of *Andromache* for the overall dramatic situation. *Bacchae* and *Heracles* are Euripides' only tragedies (excluding for present purposes *Iphigenia in Tauris, Ion,* and *Helen*) not to have an agon, and these epideixis scenes evidently stand in for agones in plays where the conflict would not appropriately be expressed by balanced speeches.

Thus, apart from the thirteen agones themselves and the two near-agones in *Medea* and *Heraclidae*, the scenes which could remotely be considered as agones fall into the category either of the supplication scene or of the epideixis scene. Supplication scenes can come close to the agon in their structure but are essentially distinct in content, while epideixis scenes have the contentiousness of the agon but lack the characteristic balancing of speeches. The justification for a fairly strict definition of the agon is partly that the thirteen agones do, in practice, have a striking number of features in common, and partly that supplication and epideixis scenes tend to diverge from the agon in several ways and not just in one. Furthermore, they have a distinct pattern of their own, and can better be treated in terms of that than by being treated as deviant agones.

THE AGON IN SOPHOCLES

The characteristic features of the Euripidean agon can be further highlighted by means of a comparison with the agon in Sophocles. The scene between Electra and Clytaemestra (S. *El.* 516–633) is Sophocles' most Euripidean agon. The beginning is strongly marked, with Clytaemestra entering at the beginning of an act and launching straight into her speech (compare Hermione in Euripides' *Andromache*). Her speech is in distinct sections, like a Euripidean speech (516–24, 525–33, 534–47, 548–51). Electra begins her speech with elaborate gestures which indicate that an agon is in progress, and her speech is also in distinct sections, which answer Clytaemestra in detail (558–62, 563–76, 577–83, 584–94, 595–609). The scene continues with angry dialogue, but concludes, in a typically Sophoclean style, without an exit by either character. This agon is very much in Euripides' manner, and was probably influenced by him, although not necessarily by his *Electra*.[21]

---

[21] Cf. Graf 1950: 202 f.; Strohm 1957: 97 f.; Duchemin 1968: 100.

Sophocles does, however, use the agon in a characteristic fashion to point up the heroic obstinacy and isolation of Electra. Clytaemestra follows the chorus and Chrysothemis in criticizing her behaviour, and Electra again justifies herself. Her isolation is completed in the next scene when Orestes' death is announced.

The two agones at the end of *Ajax* in which Teucer confronts first Menelaus (1047–162) and then Agamemnon (1226–315) are also more or less regular by Euripidean standards. The first is defined by the entry and exit of Menelaus, and has two balanced speeches (Teucer's, at 25 lines, is rather short) followed by angry dialogue. The beginning of the second coincides with the arrival of Agamemnon at the beginning of an act, and has balanced speeches of fairly substantial length. There would certainly have been some angry dialogue but for the intervention of Odysseus which changes the direction of the scene. This is a sophisticated variation on a standard form, and the shortness of Teucer's speech in the first agon can readily be explained in terms of the fact that he has another speech to make in the second.

The scene between Creon and Haemon at *Ant.* 631–765 is completely regular in form, being defined by the entry and exit of Haemon and having two substantial speeches of equal length followed by angry dialogue, mostly stichomythia (note also the lawcourt allusion at 742 f.) But this Euripidean form has most unEuripidean content. In all of Euripides' agones the hostility between the contestants is evident from the start, and they make their speeches on that basis. Here, in response to Haemon's conciliatory opening remarks, Creon makes a speech which is not at all agonistic but which consists mainly of moralizing and advice. Haemon replies in a rather similar vein, showing general good will, but Creon is not going to take this from his son and open hostility then emerges for the first time in the stichomythia. Sophocles thus uses a superficially rigid agonistic form to express a hostility that develops only gradually.

These four scenes have some basic similarity to the Euripidean agon, at least in form. Elsewhere in Sophocles the agon is treated with such flexibility as hardly to be distinguished as a separate form at all. Agonistic confrontations are incorporated into larger structures. A good example of this is the confrontation of Antigone and Creon (*Ant.* 441–525). This scene comes in the middle of an act, and is demarcated only by the exit of the Guard before it and the entry of Ismene at the end of it. The two main participants, however, are on stage both before and after and this gives a fluidity that is more characteristic of Sophocles than of Euripides. There are conflicting speeches followed by angry stichomythia, but the speeches are very short by the standards of the Euripidean agon; this contributes to reducing the impression of a set-piece.[22]

It is a short step from this scene in *Antigone* to a type of scene, common in Sophocles, which one might term the mini-agon (e.g. *Ant.* 1–99, 988–1114; *El.* 328–471; *OT* 300–462, 531–633; *Phil.* 50–134). These scenes contain confrontation and argument but lack full-scale speeches, and it does, in fact, mean very little to define them in terms of the agon at all.[23] Sophocles' most elaborate agonistic structure is *OC* 720–1043, a complex episode of confrontation and struggle which has none of the formality of the Euripidean agon. Sophocles' avoidance of the set-piece is nowhere clearer than here.[24]

THE FUNCTION OF THE AGON

The agon in Euripides has its own formality as a purely dramatic structure, but it also evokes a variety of situations in fifth-century Athenian life in which conflicting *logoi* competed with each other. The lawcourt provides the most relevant parallel to the Euripidean agon. Quarrels are not normally conducted through the medium of set speeches, but that is exactly the form that they took in the Athenian courts. Euripides evidently adapted the form of the trial in order to obtain a dramatic form in which opposing characters have the opportunity to state their cases in a systematic way. There is a pair of speeches on each side in the agon between Peleus and Menelaus in *Andromache*, but more often there is angry dialogue after a single set speech on each side. This gives the speakers the opportunity to react to each other's points, but in a more dramatic way than the necessarily more rigid forensic structure. The term ἀγών did indeed include, among other things, both actual trials (e.g. Lysias 3. 20) and the dramatic trial in Aeschylus' *Eumenides* (677, 744).[25]

The trial in Aeschylus' *Eumenides* contrasts interestingly with the Euripidean agon. On the one hand, it takes place in a court and has a jury

---

[22] Cf. Long 1968: 155–60; Gould 1978: 53 f.

[23] Cf. S. *Phil.* 974–1080, where Odysseus disdains (1047 f.) to reply to a long outburst by Philoctetes, and there is a general resemblance in structure to the near-agon at the end of E. *Med.*

[24] Duchemin 1968 also includes as agones four supplication scenes in Sophocles: *Aj.* 430–595; *El.* 938–1057; *Phil.* 1308–408; *OC* 1254–446.

[25] See LSJ, svv. ἀγών, ἀγωνίζομαι. On the question of the number of speeches on each side in an Athenian trial, see D. M. MacDowell, *The Law in Classical Athens* (London, 1978), 249.

which decides the issue by voting. It is related explicitly, as a paradigm, to actual Athenian procedure.[26] No Euripidean agon has such an explicitly forensic context. On the other hand, Aeschylus' trial differs from actual practice in that there is no balance of speeches. The chorus, invited to speak first (582–4), questions Orestes in stichomythia (586–608). Orestes then calls upon Apollo as a witness, who expounds his case in four short speeches (of 8, 15, 8, and 17 lines, although there are lacunae in two of them), partly prompted by interjections from the chorus (of 3, 4, and 5 lines). Athene then moves the vote, and the contest as such is explicitly contained between her introduction (582–4) and her conclusion when both parties have had their say (674 f.).[27] There are certainly parallels for cross-examination in Athenian forensic practice,[28] but the absence of set speeches is clearly irregular. Part of the reason for this is that the chorus cannot make a set speech (συντόμως 585 seems to signal or prepare for this), and the need for balance means that Orestes cannot make one either.[29] Aeschylus no doubt also preferred the more flexible interchange, and we may compare the stichomythia between Clytaemestra and Orestes at a similarly vital stage of his *Choephori*.

Aeschylus thus stresses the framework of the trial, but adapts the content to his dramatic needs. The whole trilogy has treated the various conflicts in legal terms,[30] and a trial is an appropriate culmination to the specific legal concerns of the trilogy. It is part of the point that due legal process is being carried out. In Euripides, on the other hand, no agon has a setting that remotely resembles an actual court, but the content of his agones is much more like an actual trial, with set speeches used to state the case in a formal way. What Euripides wants, then, is the formal statement of conflicting cases, for which the courts offered a compelling parallel, rather than any impression of due legal process.

The lawcourts may offer the closest parallel to the Euripidean agon, but not the only one, nor does every agon equally resemble a trial of any sort. Some agones (e.g. those in *Alcestis* and *Iphigenia in Aulis*) are more like quarrels than trials, while others (e.g. the agon in *Medea* and the scene between Hermione and Andromache in *Andromache*) begin like quarrels

---

[26] Cf. Sommerstein 1989: 13–17.
[27] On *Eum.* 674–80, see R. P. Winnington-Ingram, *Studies in Aeschylus* (Cambridge, 1983), 219–21.
[28] See E. M. Carawan, '*Erotesis*: Interrogation in the Courts of Fourth-Century Athens', *GRBS* 24 (1983), 209–26.
[29] Cf. Dale 1969: 212 f.
[30] Cf. Daube 1938; Fraenkel 1950 on A. *Ag.* 41.

and only develop into trials with their formal defence speeches. The agon in *Heraclidae* is furthest from a trial, and does in fact resemble quite closely a diplomatic episode like the Corcyrean Debate (Thuc. 1. 32–43). The same is true, to a rather lesser extent, of the agones in *Supplices* and *Phoenissae*. There may be regularities in the form of Euripides' agones, but there is certainly no rigid uniformity in the uses to which he puts them.

Real court cases end with victory for one side or the other, so that one party at least gains their ends even if hostility persists. The agon in Euripides rarely achieves anything.[31] In only two agones does either side clearly gain its ends by means of what is said. In *Hecuba*, Hecuba successfully defends herself against the charge of Polymestor while, in *Heraclidae*, Iolaus persuades Demophon to accept his supplication. In two other cases it appears, though rather less clearly, that one character gains his ends by means of the agon. In the second agon of *Andromache* it is fairly clear that Peleus succeeds in driving off Menelaus (despite the latter's comment at 744), and it is perhaps futile to try to distinguish the effect of what he says from the force of his personality and the possible appeal to military force (759 f.). In *Iphigenia in Aulis* the angry stichomythia that follows the two main speeches by Menelaus and Agamemnon is interrupted by the arrival of a messenger before there is any sign of agreement.[32] After the departure of the messenger, and a self-pitying speech by Agamemnon, Menelaus has a change of heart.[33] This is unique in the agon, and leads to the unusual structural feature of its being unclear when the agon ends. Normally, at least one participant leaves the stage with the conflict still unresolved. How far is Menelaus' change of heart due to the agon? It seems at first sight that it is due primarily to pity for the tears that Agamemnon sheds after the agon (477–82), and later that the messenger speech also played its part (e.g. 491–4). But Menelaus' explanation of his new attitude seems at least to reflect, if not to be caused by, Agamemnon's arguments in the agon. The idea that it is wrong for Menelaus to be happy while, or because, Agamemnon is unhappy (482–4) recalls the latter's arguments in the agon (396–9); and the idea that it is wrong for Iphigenia to be killed in order to recover the bad wife Helen (485–94) recalls Agamemnon's similar point (381–90).[34] Thus, even in a case where the agon might uniquely have been shown to lead not just to victory but to agreement, Euripides obscures

---

[31] Cf. Strohm 1957: 37 f., 45 f.; Mastronarde 1986: 205 f.
[32] There are some grounds for regarding the messenger scene as an interpolation. The scene is discussed by Foley 1985: 69 f.
[33] Cf. R. Bogaert, 'Le Revirement de Ménélas', *LEC* 33 (1965), 3–11; Knox 1979: 244 f.
[34] Cf. Foley 1985: 95 f.

the causal connection, if there is one, between the arguments advanced in the agon and the agreement. What is more, Agamemnon himself then changes his mind.

In no other agon in Euripides does any character gain a meaningful victory in the sense of achieving his ends by means of what he says. The other agones do not, in fact, have any impact whatever on their plays in the narrow sense of actually affecting the ensuing action. This statement is uncontroversial in the cases of the agones in *Medea*, *Hippolytus*, *Andromache* (first agon, between Hermione and Andromache), *Supplices*, *Electra*, and *Phoenissae*. In all these plays the characters continue in their original course of violent action. It has been suggested that the agon in *Alcestis* has some effect, if only on the attitudes of Admetus, but there are reasons to think that this is not the case.[35] The agones in *Troades* and *Orestes* present rather similar problems, which need careful discussion, about what effect, if any, the arguments have on a weak and indecisive Menelaus.

It could be objected that the definition of victory discussed above is unduly narrow, and that characters can be victorious in the sense of getting the better of the argument or by being generally more sympathetic. Such victories would undoubtedly be hollow if no benefits followed from them, but it could be significant dramatically that one character proved his case. In the four cases mentioned above, in which the characters were victorious in the sense of gaining their ends (Iolaus in *Heraclidae*, Hecuba in *Hecuba*, Peleus in *Andromache*, and Agamemnon in *Iphigenia in Aulis*) it seems fairly clear that the winner also has the better of the argument and is the more sympathetic character. There is thus no clear-cut case of a villain gaining his ends as the result of an agon. There are three other cases in which one side is undoubtedly in the right, namely Medea in *Medea*, Andromache in *Andromache*, and Theseus in *Supplices*. The other six agones raise problems of various kinds. In *Hippolytus*, for example, Hippolytus is obviously innocent of the charge of raping Phaedra, but his actual arguments are not especially strong and different views can be taken of how sympathetic he is as a character. *Phoenissae* is somewhat similar, in that Polynices is clearly right on the narrower issue of the agon but open to criticism about his general behaviour in the play. In *Alcestis*, *Electra*, *Troades*, and *Orestes* there are strong arguments on both sides of the case and it is at least not obvious which side is right.

It is not surprising that the agon usually fails to achieve anything, since these are tragic conflicts which cannot be resolved merely by talking about

[35] See M. Lloyd 1985: 122, 125 f.

them. Euripides thus sometimes makes a point of the tragic futility of rational discussion. More often, however, he seems positively to avoid engaging the agon in the action of the play, even in cases where it might seem actually easier to do so. The agon in *Iphigenia in Aulis*, discussed above, is a case in point. In *Troades* and *Orestes* it is left obscure whether the agon has an effect or not, and Euripides does not seem even to make a negative point about its lack of effect. The same is true of the agones in *Hippolytus* and *Electra*, where they seem to be detached even from the possibility of practical effect. The crucial thing in these cases is the conflict of attitudes itself, and not the details of the expression of that conflict on a given occasion. The agon does, indeed, normally expound the central conflict of the play.

The whole question of victory in the agon is thus more complex than is sometimes supposed, and this has some bearing on the order of speeches in the agon. It is often alleged that the speaker with the stronger arguments or the more sympathetic character speaks second.[36] This is clearly false in *Medea*, in the agon between Peleus and Menelaus in *Andromache*, and in *Phoenissae*, and this rule is further undermined by the cases in which there is no obvious winner in any sense. The rule is, in fact, that the plaintiff or claimant speaks first. This is dictated by common sense, was the practice in the lawcourts, and is stated as the rule by Jocasta (*Pho.* 465–8; cf. A. *Eum.* 583 f.). The only exceptions to this rule are the agones in *Electra* and *Troades*, where the natural defendants have already been so much criticized in the play that a further prosecution speech would be superfluous. Clytaemestra also speaks first in the agon of Sophocles' *Electra* (516 ff.), where she gives as a reason for this that she has been criticized by Electra in the past (520–4). This also shows her nervous insecurity, as she defends herself, on this occasion at least, before she has actually been attacked. Electra seems more sympathetic for not starting the quarrel (552–5). It is always clear in Euripides' agones who the plaintiff is, although in one or two cases the roles could easily have been reversed. In *Alcestis*, for example, Admetus prosecutes Pheres for not sacrificing himself, and it is significant that Euripides does not organize the scene in such a way that Pheres prosecutes Admetus. In *Hecuba*, Polymestor prosecutes Hecuba for blinding him, but the issues would not have been very different if Hecuba had prosecuted Polymestor for killing Polydorus.

The agon is thus identifiable in Euripides' plays as a distinct dramatic form. There are thirteen scenes in the extant plays which are undeniably

---

[36] Cf. Strohm 1957: 44; Dale 1954 on *Alc.* 697 ff.; Page 1938 on *Med.* 465 ff.; Collard 1975*b*: 132 f.

agones, and two further scenes (in *Medea* and *Heraclidae*) in which the agon form stands in the background but is not fulfilled in all its details. Numerous agones have no doubt been lost, most notably the agon in *Antiope*, and Duchemin assembles some information about them.[37] The present study, however, will concern itself mainly with the thirteen agones in the extant plays, where they can be studied in their full dramatic context, and fragmentary material will be used only for purposes of comparison.

The agones in the extant plays have many features in common, and the essence of the form is the confrontation of a balancing pair of substantial speeches. The formality of the agon is emphasized rather than concealed and there are various ways in which it is marked out as such within the individual play. Recurrent formal structures of this kind are far less evident in Sophocles, who tends to avoid set-pieces and to favour a more fluid and continuous style of action. The agon in Euripides is distinct from two other types of scene which also involve formal speeches, the supplication scene and the epideixis scene. Euripides uses it to express, in a concentrated form, what is usually the central conflict of the play. The relationship of the agon to the action is often obscure, and Euripides often seems to go to great lengths to detach it from its immediate dramatic context.

[37] Duchemin 1968: ch. 3.

2

Rhetoric and Euripides' Agones

EURIPIDES' agones evoke the lawcourts not only in their structure but also in their style. The opposing set speeches which are characteristic of the agon are often, although by no means always, composed in a rhetorically sophisticated and self-conscious manner. This serves further to identify the agon as a distinct dramatic form, since this rhetorical style is much more common in the agon than in other parts of the play, and the manner that a character adopts in the agon is sometimes strikingly at variance with his or her manner elsewhere (e.g. Hippolytus in *Hippolytus*, Hecuba in *Troades*). Different views have been taken of the influence of rhetoric on Euripides, and some discussion of this topic is necessary if the style and function of his agones is to be understood.[1]

Ancient authors, at least from the time of Aristophanes, were certainly in little doubt about Euripides' rhetorical sophistication. At *Peace* 534 there is a reference to Euripides as ποιητῇ ῥηματίων δικανικῶν, and in *Frogs* he is regularly accused of making his characters argue and debate and teaching his audiences to do likewise (e.g. 89–91, 771–8, 954, 1069, 1083–8). It is in his agones that these features are most prominent, and at *Frogs* 775 skill in ἀντιλογίαι is explicitly attributed to him. His expertise in rhetoric is often praised by later authors.[2]

The problem remains that, while a general forensic flavour cannot be denied, it is extremely difficult to determine the precise extent of rhetorical influence in particular cases. One problem is that rhetorical devices often emerged gradually out of natural modes of self-expression. Many devices which were later thought of as rhetorical developed in poetry and can be found as early as Homer.[3] Secondly, there are many gaps in our knowledge of early rhetorical theory and practice, where we depend to a great extent on late and often conflicting sources. Very little forensic oratory from Euripides' lifetime is extant.

---

[1] 'Rhetoric' refers here, and in what follows, either to the systematic study of the art of speaking or to speeches containing features associated with such study.
[2] Cf. Xanthakis-Karamanos 1979: 66 f.
[3] See Kroll 1940: col. 1048; Radermacher 1951: A IV; Dover 1968: 185–7.

On the other hand, the style and meaning of Euripides' agones cannot fully be understood without some knowledge of their relationship to contemporary rhetoric. Furthermore, Euripides himself seems to furnish important evidence for the development of rhetoric, which is a subject of some interest in itself, and he may indeed have had some influence on it.[4]

The solution to this problem, in so far as a solution is attainable, lies in a judicious use of the various kinds of evidence for the development of rhetoric which are available. In the first place, we have indirect knowledge of early rhetoric, and especially of its concern with the structure of a speech and with the argument from probability. Secondly, there is the evidence of the earliest surviving orators, especially Antiphon, who practised during Euripides' lifetime, and Lysias, whose career began shortly after Euripides' death. There is uncertainty about the dates of Gorgias' *Palamedes* and of the *Tetralogies* attributed to Antiphon, works which are of obvious relevance to Euripides' agones. Thirdly, there are two fourth-century rhetorical treatises, Aristotle's *Rhetoric*, and the *Rhetorica ad Alexandrum* which has come down to us among Aristotle's works. These works must be used with the greatest caution in discussing Euripides, but they can provide valuable support for other evidence. Finally, there is the evidence of Euripides' plays themselves, where repeated use of formulaic expressions in rhetorical contexts seems occasionally to indicate rhetorical influence.

THE ORIGINS OF RHETORIC

Rhetoric traditionally originated in Syracuse after the fall of the tyrants in 467 BC, where it was invented by Corax and Tisias.[5] The new ideas would have been designed for both deliberative and forensic use, since the fundamental principles of rhetoric would have applied equally in the courts and in the assembly. The deliberative and forensic functions are, in any case, difficult to separate, since political disputes would have found their way into the courts as they were later to do in Athens.[6] Corax and Tisias were credited by later authors with two inventions, the argument

---

[4] Cf. Ludwig 1957: 41. For a similar point about Thucydides, see Hornblower 1987: 48 f., 112. On Aristophanes, see C. T. Murphy, 'Aristophanes and the Art of Rhetoric', *HSCP* 49 (1938), 69–113.

[5] Evidence in Radermacher 1951: 11–35. Cf. Kennedy 1963: 58–61; Martin 1974: 52–60.

[6] See Dover 1968: 50.

from probability and the formal organization of speeches. These two features are hallmarks of speeches influenced by the new rhetoric, and a further distinguishing feature is self-consciousness about the whole process of making a speech. It is this self-consciousness, as much as anything, which distinguishes Euripides' more rhetorical speeches from speeches in Homer, Herodotus, and Sophocles.[7]

The early rhetoricians were evidently interested in the formal division of speeches, although their precise recommendations are difficult to establish.[8] The most troublesome parts of a speech are the beginning and the end, and the handbooks seem to have given particular attention to proems and epilogues. We hear of various works devoted specifically to the proem, and in extant speeches it is here that formulaic elements are most clearly visible.[9] The classic four-part division of a speech into proem, narration, argument, and epilogue seems to be well established by the time of Antiphon, whose extant speeches were apparently delivered in the 410s.[10] The *Tetralogies* contain very little in the way of narration, but these hypothetical cases naturally concentrate on argument and there is no reason to suppose that the distinction between narration and argument had not yet been made.[11] Various refinements were possible. Antiphon's forensic speeches have a προκατασκευή in addition to the usual four parts, while Gorgias' *Palamedes* has an elaborate and ostentatious disposition.[12] The pseudo-Aristotelian *Rhetorica ad Alexandrum* adds a section of προκατάληψις to the basic four parts (1443^{a}7–^{b}14), while Aristotle himself focuses on the two main parts of a speech, statement and proof, although he does mention proem and epilogue (*Rh.* 1414^{a}29–^{b}18). Speeches could,

[7] Cf. Kerferd 1981: 78. Some rule-proving exceptions are cited by Hutchinson 1985 on A. *Se.* 1–9.

[8] Pl. *Phdr.* 266d5 ff. comments on the concern of the early handbooks with structure. Cf. S. Wilcox, 'Corax and the Prolegomena', *AJP* 64 (1943), 1–23; Kennedy 1959: 169–78; Goebel 1983: 238–55. Conflicting evidence about the recommended division of speeches: Radermacher 1951: A V 16; B II 8, 23.

[9] There is a collection of proems in the Demosthenic corpus, fragments of a similar collection by Antiphon (on his attention to proems and epilogues, see Navarre 1900: 132–4; Edwards 1985 on 5. 1–7), and evidence of one by Critias (Radermacher 1951: B XVII 1). On formulaic elements in proems, see Radermacher 1951: C 25, 26, 29. One conventional proem device is parodied by Cratinus, *Pytine* fr. 197 K.-A. (423 BC).

[10] On the date of Antiphon's extant speeches, see K. J. Dover, 'The Chronology of Antiphon's Speeches', *CQ* 44 (1950), 44–60. On the 'Antiphon problem', see Ostwald 1986: 359–64. For a judicious discussion of early rhetorical disposition, see Goebel 1983: ch. 3.

[11] Thus Caizzi 1969: 15 n. 13, criticizing Kennedy 1963: 130.

[12] (1) introduction 1–5, (2) argument 6–21, (3) attack on opponent 22–7, (4) defence of his own character 28–32, (5) exhortation to judges 33–6, (6) summary 37. There is no need for a narration.

therefore, be analysed in different ways, but the important point is that this interest in formal disposition was one of the main distinguishing features of the new rhetoric.

The other invention which our sources agree in attributing to Corax and Tisias is the argument from probability.[13] This argument is the most striking kind of 'artificial' (ἔντεχνος) proof which Aristotle distinguished from 'natural' (ἄτεχνος) proofs such as witnesses or oaths.[14] An influential model of the development of forensic argument is that it progressed from reliance on natural proofs (such as the oath challenge at *Iliad* 23. 581–5) to a greater use of reasoned arguments. This development can be overstated, as it is difficult to imagine that reasoning was ever wholly absent from trials, while natural proofs will always have some relevance. Solmsen argued that Antiphon represents a transitional phase in which natural proofs are still fundamental, but artificial proofs cluster round them. This theory has been criticized by scholars who have pointed out that artificial proofs are in fact of central importance in Antiphon, and that even natural proofs are fitted into complex reasoned arguments.[15] As early as the trial in Aeschylus' *Eumenides* there is a contrast between crude reliance on oaths (429) and μαρτυριά τε καὶ τεκμήρια (485).[16] Apollo's speech thus puts forward an argument, which is supported by witnesses and logical deductions (τεκμήριον 662, μάρτυς 664). The crucial element in Antiphon, as contrasted with the arguments in *Eumenides*, is the stress on probability which reveals the influence of the new Sicilian rhetoric.

There is no clear evidence about the date when the new Sicilian rhetoric reached Athens. The visit of Gorgias in 427 clearly made a great impact, but there can be little doubt that rhetoric was studied in Athens long before that date.[17] Athenian democracy provided vast scope for public speaking, both deliberative and forensic, and the Athenians were famously receptive to new ideas. Opportunities for public speaking may well have been increased by the reforms of Ephialtes (462 BC).[18] Contacts between Athens and Sicily were sufficiently close for any developments in rhetoric to have

---

[13] See Pl. *Phdr.* 267a6–7. Plato (*Phdr.* 273a–c) attributes to Tisias an argument from probability which Aristotle (*Rh.* 1402^{a}17–20) attributes to Corax, but G. H. Goebel, *Mnem.* 42 (1989), 41–53, argues that their accounts are in fact consistent. General discussions of probability: Ar. *Rh.* 1357^{a}34–^{b}3; [Ar.] *Rh. Al.* 1428^{a}27–^{b}11.

[14] Ar. *Rh.* 1355^{b}35–9. Cf. Martin 1974: 95 ff.

[15] Solmsen 1931, criticized by Scheidweiler 1966; Due 1980; Goebel 1983: 49–55; Gagarin 1990.

[16] On τεκμήρια, see Finley 1967: 9, 74; Goebel 1983: 55–73; Hornblower 1987: 100–7.

[17] Cf. Finley 1967: chs. 1 and 2.

[18] Thus Kennedy 1963: 27–9; Hornblower 1987: 40 f. Doubts in Dover 1968: 180–5.

reached Athens soon after their invention. It is thus very likely that rhetorical theory and teaching had reached Athens by the mid-450s at the latest.

Some scholars have played down the question of Sicilian influence and stressed the part played by the early sophists, especially Protagoras.[19] He certainly seems to have been a key figure in the development of rhetoric, whatever his relationship to the Sicilian rhetoric which traditionally preceded him. His training in the art of speaking on both sides of a case is highly relevant to Euripides' agones. Even if we stress the influence of Protagoras, rather than that of the Sicilian rhetoricians, the date of the impact of rhetoric on Athens will be much the same, since Protagoras seems to have been active in Athens from around the 450s.[20]

Euripides was more or less contemporary with the older sophists, Protagoras and Gorgias, and he first competed at the Dionysia in 455. The beginning of his career thus coincides with the beginning of formal rhetoric in Athens, but his relationship with contemporary rhetorical theory and practice is obscured by lack of evidence. His earliest extant play is *Alcestis* (438), while the earliest extant forensic speeches (those of Antiphon) are twenty years later still. Euripides himself does, in fact, provide the best evidence for the development of rhetoric between 438 and 418. Several scholars at the end of the nineteenth century argued that Euripides' speeches followed the rules laid down in the rhetorical handbooks.[21] The most ambitious of these scholars, Miller, thought that Euripides followed a lost ancestor of the *Rhetorica ad Alexandrum*. The problem here is that no treatises on rhetoric survive from Euripides' day and that, while the *Rhetorica ad Alexandrum* does seem to preserve some fairly well-worn advice, it remains very likely that rhetorical theory had developed considerably since Euripides' day. In particular, many devices will have become formally rhetorical that had not been so earlier. Miller was thus criticized by Tietze who, generally influenced by Solmsen's view of the development of rhetoric, denied any influence of Sicilian rhetoric on Euripides.[22] He argued that early rhetoric had an expository, non-rational style, and that this style is to be seen in *Alcestis*, *Medea*, and *Heraclidae*. Tietze argued further that any increase in rational argument from *Hippolytus* onwards was due

---

[19] e.g. Kroll 1940: col. 1043. Evidence in Radermacher 1951: B III. Cf. Navarre 1900: 45–66; Hudson-Williams 1950: 156–69; Kerferd 1981: ch. 6; de Romilly 1967: ch. 3.

[20] See Morrison 1941; Guthrie 1971: 262–4; Kerferd 1981: 42 f.

[21] Lechner 1874; Miller 1887; Lees 1891. These scholars were largely independent of each other.

[22] Tietze 1933, who was in turn criticized by A. Lesky in his review of Tietze, *Gnomon*, 13 (1937), 595–7; Kroll 1940: col. 1042; Ludwig 1957: 41 f.; Strohm 1957: 5 n. 2.

to the general intellectual atmosphere rather than to any specifically rhetorical influence. Tietze's argument is unconvincing in several respects, not least because he fails to consider *Cretes*, an apparently early play which shows definite signs of rhetorical sophistication.[23] There is clearly need for a fresh examination of rhetorical features of Euripides' agon speeches, taking particular account of the ways in which he organizes a speech, his use of arguments from probability, and the extent to which his characters show rhetorical self-consciousness.

RHETORICAL DISPOSITION

Lees and Miller tried hard to find the traditional four-part structure in Euripides' speeches, with separate narration and argument as in Antiphon and Lysias. Their attempts were conspicuously unsuccessful in the great majority of cases, not least because there is rarely any need in Euripides' agones for a straightforward narration designed merely to inform the judge of the facts.[24] In Euripides' agones, as in Antiphon's *Tetralogies* and Gorgias' *Palamedes*, the emphasis is on the speaker's manipulation of his argument.

Euripides twice seems to evoke the four-part structure, in both cases for specific poetic purposes. Medea's speech in *Medea* has a formal proem followed by a distinct section of narration (476—87), but she then launches into an emotional outburst against Jason and the strict rhetorical form breaks down. This contrast between self-control and passion is an important theme in the play.[25] Polynices' speech in *Phoenissae* also has a clear four-part structure which includes a section of narration (473—83), and the clarity of this structure gives an impression of simple truthfulness. The third section of his speech, however, is not a section of argument in any rhetorical sense but a proposal of what he wants to happen now (καὶ νῦν 484). He does not regard argument as being necessary at all, and thinks that a plain statement of the facts is enough to make his case. There is something very similar in the first prosecution speeches of Antiphon's second and third *Tetralogies*. Other speakers in Euripides who rely on a plain statement of the facts are Polymestor in *Hecuba* and Menelaus in *Iphigenia in Aulis*, although neither of those speeches hints at the four-part structure.

[23] Cf. Goebel 1983: 271—5. On the date of *Cretes*, see M. Cropp and G. Fick, *Resolutions and Chronology in Euripides: The Fragmentary Tragedies* (BICS Suppl. 43, London, 1985), 82.
[24] Cf. Duchemin 1968: 170—3.
[25] See below, Ch. 3.

There are thus only traces of a distinction between narration and argument in the speeches of Euripides' agones. What usually happens is that, after a rhetorical proem, the speech is divided into a series of more or less self-contained blocks, each of which makes a particular point. These sections are often distinguished from each other in a self-conscious way, and some speakers are especially explicit about their rhetorical procedures. A section might convey a certain amount of information, which could be termed a fragment of narration, but it is always linked closely to the argument. The speech then concludes with a rhetorical epilogue.

Rhetorical formulae and conventions are most clearly visible in the proems of Euripides' agon speeches.[26] Early rhetorical theory seems to have devoted particular attention to this section of a speech, and extant forensic speeches reveal formulaic elements here from an early date. The formal proem is a distinctively rhetorical feature, as comparison with speeches in Homer, Herodotus, or Sophocles will readily reveal. Actual orators need to gain the attention of audiences which may be large, unruly, or unsympathetic. Speakers in tragedy do not have to cope with audiences which are large and unruly, but often with listeners who are hostile or unsympathetic. Euripides uses proem formulae in a subtle way, either to underline the difficulties or disadvantages that a speaker may face or to show a speaker creating prejudice against his opponent.

Almost all of Euripides' agon speeches have a more or less formal proem. The two exceptions are Hecuba's speech in *Troades* and Polymestor's speech in *Hecuba*, both of which are preceded by an elaborate invitation to speak which renders a proem unnecessary.[27] The proems to the other speeches can be related to rhetorical theory and practice. Ancient rhetorical theory agreed on three main purposes of this part of a speech: exhortation to the audience to pay attention, summary of the case, and *captatio benevolentiae*. These are the three purposes summarized at *Rhetorica ad Alexandrum*, ch. 29, and they can readily be inferred from the practice of the early orators.[28]

There is little or nothing in Euripides' agon speeches in the way of exhortations to attend. Large juries are not being addressed, and the audience usually has every reason to pay attention. Several speeches have proems which are little more than headlines, making clear the basic subject of the speech or attitude of the speaker (*Hcld.* 134–8; *Su.* 465 f.; *Or.* 491; *IA*

---

[26] On the term προοίμιον (cf. *Hec.* 1195, *El.* 1060), see Wilamowitz 1895 on *HF* 538; Martin 1974: 60; Goebel 1983: 370 n. 7.

[27] On λέγοιμ' ἄν at the beginning of Polymestor's speech (cf. *Su.* 465, *El.* 1060, *IT* 939, *Or.* 640), see Fraenkel 1950 on A. *Ag.* 838.

[28] Cf. Ar. *Rh.* 1414[b]19 ff.; Lechner 1874: 10–13; Navarre 1900: 213–39.

334–6, 378–80). It is in the *captatio benevolentiae* that Euripides shows most subtlety and variety. *Rhetorica ad Alexandrum*, ch. 36, advises the orator to praise his client, run down his adversaries, praise the jury, deal with areas where his client is at a disadvantage, and try to get rid of prejudice. The same general recommendations are given at Aristotle, *Rhetoric* 3. 14. Many of Euripides' proems can be related to these recommendations, and seem to be positively rhetorical and not just natural pieces of self-expression.

Proems of this type tend to be either aggressive or defensive, and sometimes a combination of the two. The most obvious kind of aggressive proem is that which consists largely or entirely of abuse (often in the form of a generalization).[29] Proems of this kind are to be found at *Med.* 465–74; *Hcld.* 941; *Hi.* 936–45; *An.* 184 f., 590 f., 645 f.; *El.* 1060 f.; *IA* 334. Some of these proems show no particular evidence of formal rhetorical influence. Abuse is natural enough in such contexts, although the regular use of generalization might suggest some more artful principles at work. A more specific type of abuse is directed particularly against the opponent's manner of speaking, stressing his verbosity and cleverness with words, and frequently contrasting this with the speaker's own plain honesty.[30] This line of attack, which is most common in proems but also appears in other parts of the speech, does seem to be more specifically rhetorical. Some examples in Euripidean proems are *Med.* 522–5, *Hi.* 983–5, *Hec.* 1187–94, *Su.* 426–8, *Pho.* 469–72, *Ba.* 266–71. The similarity of the basic method suggests by itself that a stock device is being used, and there is no shortage of rhetorical parallels.[31] This rhetorical move does, in fact, seem to have ossified at quite an early stage of Euripides' career, and three of the above proems (those in *Hecuba*, *Phoenissae*, and *Bacchae*) are very nearly interchangeable and could have come straight out of the handbook. The same is true of a passage from an even earlier play, *Med.* 579–87, which is not actually from the proem to a speech although it does occur in a rhetorical context.

Other proems are predominantly defensive. One of the commonest types is that in which the speaker mentions the disadvantages under which he labours. The earliest example of this kind of proem in Euripides is *Hi.* 986–91, a comparatively early play in which the rhetorical form is not

---

[29] Ar. *Rh.* 1415ᵃ29–34 advises the prosecutor to put διαβολή in the epilogue, but Euripides' prosecutors often have it in the proem. On διαβολή in the orators and in Euripides, see Süss 1910: 245–56.

[30] Jouan 1984 discusses the paradox that there are many passages in Euripides on the dangers of clever speaking. Cf. Lechner 1874: 16 f.; Dodds 1960 on *Ba.* 266–71; Dover 1974: 25 f.; North 1988.

[31] Cf. Macleod 1983: 117 f.

only fully developed but seems almost to be parodied. This kind of defensive proem can come close, as it does here, to the aggressive proem in which the opponent's cleverness with words is criticized. Normally the speaker stresses his inexperience and lack of skill at speaking,[32] but sometimes he needs to insist on the necessity for clever speaking, as at *Med.* 522–5, *Pho.* 499–502. The defendant in Antiphon's second *Tetralogy* is aware that his arguments are unusually subtle, and apologizes for this in advance. Some speakers in Euripides know that they will cause offence and try in some way to counteract this, if only by showing awareness of the fact. Examples of this type of proem occur at *An.* 186–91; *Or.* 544 f., 548–50 (with Hartung's transposition); *Tro.* 914 f.; *El.* 1013–17. The essence of this type of proem is that it tries to establish the speaker's right to speak and to be heard. In tragic situations this is regularly in doubt. Thus at *Hcld.* 181–3 Iolaus observes that it is unusual for him to have the right to speak that he has in the present case.

Euripides thus shows considerable sophistication in his use of proem formulae. It is possible to doubt that there is any specifically rhetorical element in a proem which consists entirely of abuse, but in the other cases it is hard to deny that Euripides is using rhetorical devices. Even when he provides the earliest extant example of a particular device, we can be fairly confident that it is rhetorical if it is used in rhetorical contexts and in a formulaic manner by Euripides himself, and then appears in the early orators. When the existence of a device is established, we are in a position to appreciate subtle uses of it by Euripides, and also to use him as evidence for the early development of rhetoric.

Speeches in Sophocles' agones are, by contrast, notably lacking in formal proems. Two speeches begin with insults in the form of generalizations (*Aj.* 1093–6, *Ant.* 473–9); Odysseus begins a speech by saying that although he could say many things he will say just one (*Phil.* 1047 f.); and Creon has a kind of proem at *OC* 728–39, stating his business and encouraging the chorus. Polynices' speech (*OC* 1284 ff.) is unusually rhetorical by Sophocles' standards, but it still does not have a proem as such.

In discussing the way in which Euripides ends speeches in his agones, the distinction needs to be made between the agones in *Heraclidae, Hecuba, Troades, Phoenissae*, and *Orestes*, in which there is a third party to whom the speeches are directed, and agones which are essentially between two persons with no third party effectively involved. It is obviously likely that

---

[32] Cf. Solmsen 1931: 65 ff.; Lavency 1964: 71 n. 2; Barrett 1964 on *Hi.* 986–7; Edwards 1985 on *Ant.* 5. 1; Due 1980: 27 n. 3.

different types of conclusion will be needed in the two cases, and that three-person agones will be more comparable to actual forensic speeches. Aristotle, *Rhetoric* 3. 19, suggests that the epilogue should be used for making the judges favourable to oneself and unfavourable to one's opponent, for amplification or diminution of the gravity of the case, for exciting the passions of the judges, and for recapitulation.[33] *Rhetorica ad Alexandrum* advises, more simply, that the epilogue should be used for recapitulation and emotional effect (1443^b15-21, 1444^b22-35). This is generally what happens in Euripides' agones, making allowance for the fact that the absence of a mass jury makes some of the usual forensic techniques unnecessary.

Eight out of the ten speeches in three-cornered agones end with summaries and appeals, in keeping with rhetorical theory and practice. The exceptions are Eteocles, who ends with a generalization and completely ignores the arbitrator Jocasta (*Pho.* 524 f.), and Polymestor, whose speech has a gnomic ending because it also serves as a messenger speech (*Hec.* 1177–82).[34] There are also six speeches in two-person agones which end with summaries: *Alc.* 703–5; *Hi.* 1032–5; *Su.* 560–3; *El.* 1049 f., 1093–6; *IA* 400 f. Almost all of these summaries and appeals, in both two-person and three-person agones, contain heavily loaded moral language such as δίκαιος, σοφός, φίλος, and κακός, and make reference to the gods and to the laws.[35]

Speeches in agones where there is no third party tend to conclude with γνῶμαι: *Alc.* 669–72; *Med.* 516–19, 573–5; *An.* 177–80, 230 f., 639–41; *Su.* 506–10; *IA* 373–5.[36] The γνῶμαι in these cases are usually preceded by threats or insults, while both the speeches not so far mentioned conclude with threats and insults but no γνώμη (*Hi.* 971–80, *An.* 688–90). Sophocles has nothing so formalized in the conclusions to the speeches in his agones.

METHODS OF ARGUMENT

Rhetorical elements appear not only in the structure of Euripides' agon speeches but also in their content. Speakers in his agones use a variety of rhetorical devices and methods of argument, some of which are comparatively

---

[33] Cf. Navarre 1900: 277–326; Martin 1974: 147–66.
[34] See below, p. 97.
[35] Cf. Ant. 1. 31; Lys. 1. 47–50, 3. 46–8, 13. 92–7, 19. 64. Points of view: Tietze 1933: 69–74; Graf 1950: 160; Finley 1967: ch. 1; Macleod 1983: 55 f.
[36] Assuming that *El.* 1097–9 and *Or.* 602–4 are spurious. *IA* 373–5 is also doubtful (see Johansen 1959: 36).

close to natural self-expression while others are more artificial and seem specifically to evoke current practices in the lawcourts.

The argument from probability was almost a hallmark of rhetorical sophistication, and one of the features which marked the Sicilian rhetoric as something new and different. The argument is common in the extant forensic speeches of Antiphon and Lysias, and there are virtuoso displays of it in the first of Antiphon's *Tetralogies* and in Gorgias' *Palamedes*. In Euripides, it occurs at *Hi.* 962–70, 1007–15; *An.* 192–206; *Hec.* 1195–207; and *Tro.* 976–82 in the agones of extant plays. Probably earlier than any of these is the fragmentary *Cretes*, where the word εἰκός actually appears twice.[37] In all these cases, the argument from probability is used to analyse possible motives, and it tends to appear when a character is trying to make the best of a weak case.[38] Hippolytus, Andromache, and Hecuba in *Hecuba* are all actually in the right, but all are in situations where it is difficult for them to establish their case. In view of the distinctively contemporary flavour of the argument from probability, it is not surprising that occurrences in Sophocles (e.g. *Ant.* 284–9, *OT* 587–602) are fairly unostentatious. Even in Euripides, it is used only in speeches which are otherwise marked by unusual rhetorical sophistication and where there is a specific point in the speaker using every available means of persuasion.

Other rhetorical devices are less easy to assess. The examples of the argument from probability mentioned above are all also examples of hypophora. In this figure, the speaker poses a problem or question; various alternative solutions are suggested, standardly in the form of further rhetorical questions; each solution is then rejected, often by means of another rhetorical question. The sequence of questions is regularly introduced by πότερον, and both answers and subsequent questions tend to be introduced by ἀλλά.[39] Hypophora is very common in Euripides, with other notable examples at *Alc.* 1049–61 and *Med.* 502–8,[40] and there are some striking instances in Sophocles at *Aj.* 457–70, *OT* 1375–86, and *El.* 534–47. Hypophora is used so widely in tragedy, and by such a wide variety of characters, that it seems to be a fully assimilated feature of the high tragic style. A consideration of possible courses of action such as

[37] *Cretes* fr. 82. 11, 19 Austin. [38] Cf. Solmsen 1975: ch. 1.
[39] Cf. Kells 1967: 183 n. 2 and note on S. *El.* 534–45; Edwards 1985 on Ant. 5. 58. For the term 'hypophora', see Hermogenes, *Inv.* 3. 5 (Spengel ii. 207); Volkmann 1885: 47. Latin *subiectio*: Quintilian 9. 2. 15; [Cic.] *Rh. Her.* 4. 33. Cf. Carey 1989 on Lys. 31. 24–33.
[40] Cf. also *An.* 344–51; *Hec.* 258–64; *Su.* 543–8; *El.* 373–9; *HF* 295–9, 1281–90; *Pho.* 1615–21; *IA* 1185–93.

S. *Aj.* 457–70 has its roots in Homer,[41] and it could be denied that it is under rhetorical influence of any immediately contemporary kind.

Nevertheless, there is an element of rhetorical artificiality in hypophora, and Denniston observes that it occurs in Plato only in the *Apology*: 'naturally, where you have a live person to talk to, there is less need for a dummy'.[42] There are formalized examples in the earliest extant orators: Antiphon 5. 57–9 and in his *Apology*; Andocides 1. 148, 3. 13–15; Lysias 10. 23. The most elaborate of all extant examples is to be found at G. *Pal.* 6–21. Sophocles and Euripides offer examples of hypophora, already with formulaic elements, which are earlier than any in extant oratory, but our evidence does not allow us to settle the question of influence and we can do no more than point to the parallel.

We do, however, have some knowledge of the philosophical background to the rhetorical use of hypophora. The examples so far discussed can be described, in philosophical terms, as disjunctive or dilemma arguments. This type of argument, used in philosophical contexts by the Eleatics, was used for rhetorical purposes by Gorgias. His use of it is described as follows by G. E. R. Lloyd: 'to refute a thesis, he first subdivides it into a number of subordinate theses one of which must be true if the thesis itself is to be true, and then demolishes each of these subordinate theses in turn'.[43] Gorgias uses this argument in the (at least ostensibly) philosophical work *On What Is Not*, and also in the rhetorical exercises on mythological subjects, *Helen* and *Palamedes*. These are, of course, less formal, and Lloyd comments 'in neither speech are the alternatives such as to be formally mutually exclusive and exhaustive',[44] and this is even more applicable to the Euripidean examples. It is clear, however, that there is a complex background to Euripides' use of hypophora, and that this figure does itself always provide the context for his use of the even more overtly rhetorical argument from probability.

Sophistication in argument generally lay in the ability to manipulate hypothetical situations, rather than confining oneself to direct evidence for what actually happened. This was true of the argument from probability, and more generally of hypophora, and is also true of προκατάληψις, a figure in which the speaker answers an imagined objection.[45] This device occurs

---

[41] See Fenik in B. C. Fenik (ed.), *Homer: Tradition and Invention* (Leiden, 1978).
[42] Denniston 1954: 11.   [43] G. E. R. Lloyd 1979: 82.
[44] Ibid. 83; cf. p. 80 nn. 104, 105 for examples of disjunctive or dilemma arguments in Antiphon and Lysias.
[45] Cf. [Ar.] *Rh. Al.* 1432ᵇ11 ff.; Volkmann 1885: 139, 279; Fraenkel 1957: 54 f.; Johansen 1959: 99 n. 148; Martin 1974: 277. Distinguish προκατάληψις, which deals with

regularly in Euripides, especially in the agon, and is clearly related to hypophora. The sophistication of the device lies in the fact that the speaker is not answering an objection which the opponent has actually made, but is imagining a hypothetical objection which he might make. The need and opportunity to do this generally arise only in long and formal speeches when the opponent has no chance to interrupt. The imagined objection is regularly introduced by τάχα, ἴσως, *forte*, or the like (as in 'perhaps you will object . . .').[46] In Athenian court cases, the speaker would doubtless not have had to exercise too much imagination, since preliminary arbitration would have revealed the main lines of his opponent's argument.[47] This figure is used widely in Euripides, and is sometimes significant as being part of the armoury of a skilled speaker (e.g. *Tro.* 938, 951). More often, however, προκατάληψις seems to have been absorbed into Euripides' argumentative and rhetorical style, and to be used in a more natural and less obviously calculated fashion (e.g. *Hi.* 962; *An.* 929; *Su.* 184, 537; *Ion* 629; *Pho.* 561; *Or.* 665; *Ba.* 204).[48]

A more elaborate method of argument which appears regularly in Euripides' agones is the *reductio ad absurdum*, of which there are examples at *Alc.* 699–702; *An.* 215–19, 662–7; *Su.* 537–41, 542–8; *El.* 1041–5; *Tro.* 983–6; *Pho.* 541–7; *Or.* 508–11, 566–71. This type of argument is common in the philosophers, especially the Eleatics, and was also found useful by the early orators (e.g. Lys. 3. 29–34; 6. 4–5; 10. 13; 12. 88; 24. 8, 12; 30. 32).[49] Lysias has a characteristic way of developing this argument, with the absurdity emphasized by some such phrase as οὐκ οὖν δεινόν, εἰ . . . Euripides does not use this particular phrase, and another difference is that several of the absurdities in Euripides are elaborated in a somewhat baroque fashion, whereas Lysias' style is more sober. The only notable parallel between Euripides and Lysias in their use of the *reductio ad absurdum* is between Orestes' evocation of the absurdity of wives being allowed to get away with killing their husbands (*Or.* 566–71) and Euphiletus' drawing-out of the consequences of adulterers not being punished (Lys. 1. 36).

---

imagined objections from an opponent who is present, from the not especially rhetorical process of imagining what a third person (not present) might say (e.g. H. *Il.* 6. 459; A. *Eum.* 756; S. *Aj.* 504).

[46] Examples in orators: Ant. 4β3; Lys. 6. 13, 35; 10. 6; 12. 50; 13. 52, 70; 20. 17; 22. 11; G. *Pal.* 23; Pl. *Ap.* 20c4; Dem. 19. 237.

[47] Cf. A. P. Dorjahn, 'Anticipation of Arguments in Athenian Courts', *TAPA* 66 (1935), 274–95.

[48] *Held.* 169 is another possible example, but the text is corrupt. *Su.* 184 is the earliest, and only Euripidean, example of the characteristic 'perhaps'.

[49] Cf. Bateman 1962: 161–8; G. E. R. Lloyd 1979: 66–79.

Euripides does, however, have a distinctive style of his own in his use of this type of argument. Four examples of it in the agones of his extant plays conclude with one-and-a-half lines, introduced by εἶτα, which drive home the absurdity of the suggestion (*Alc.* 701 f.; *An.* 218 f., 666 f., *El.* 1044 f.).[50] It is perfectly possible that this stylistic feature was peculiar to Euripides but, nevertheless, one cannot but suspect that the regular occurrence in agonistic speeches of formulaic elements of this kind is due to some rhetorical influence and reflects the style of the contemporary courts.

Another variety of the argument from probability that is common in Euripides' agones is the hypothetical syllogism. In this type of argument, the speaker postulates a condition which would substantiate his opponent's position. He then points out that the condition was not fulfilled, so that his opponent's position collapses. Lysias' use of this argument has been well analysed by J. J. Bateman, who points to the formulaic phraseology in which it is expressed.[51] Lysias typically uses the form 'if . . . then . . .; but in fact . . .', for example at 3. 22–3: 'he should, if this were true . . . but he did nothing of the sort . . . this is proof that he is lying'. Antiphon also uses this type of argument (e.g. 5. 52), but it is interesting that he never uses the standard Lysian formula. Euripides, however, makes frequent use of the hypothetical syllogism, and he expresses it in phraseology very similar to that of Lysias. This is almost a test case for his use of rhetoric in the agon, since his earliest extant example of the hypothetical syllogism precedes its appearance in Lysias by some thirty years.

The earliest extant examples of Euripides' use of the hypothetical syllogism are in *Medea*, where there is no ostentatious formality about it, and where, viewed in isolation, the argument might seem to be no more than a natural piece of self-expression. At *Med.* 488–91, Medea accuses Jason: 'you betrayed me, and took a new wife, although we had children; if you were still childless, it would be pardonable for you to desire another wife'. This argument comes at a structurally ambiguous point of Medea's speech, between a lucid section of narration and a passage of emotional invective. Rather more formal is *Med.* 585–7:

> ἐν γὰρ ἐκτενεῖ σ' ἔπος.
> χρῆν σ', εἴπερ ἦσθα μὴ κακός, πείσαντά με
> γαμεῖν γάμον τόνδ', ἀλλὰ μὴ σιγῇ φίλων.

---

[50] *El.* 1041–5 is also the only example in Euripides of a type of hypothetical argument, common in Antiphon, which Solmsen named 'hypothetische Rollentausch oder Umkehrung' (Solmsen 1931: 10). Cf. Lys. 3. 38, 7. 36–7; Edwards 1985 on Ant. 5. 38.

[51] Bateman 1962: 168–70. Examples of the hypothetical syllogism cited by Bateman include Lys. 1. 31, 40–2; 3. 31; 13. 22, 36, 88–90; 24. 11; 25. 5; 30. 17.

Medea's argument does not have an explicit conclusion, and does not really need one in the context, but it is close to the Lysian pattern, and especially resembles Lys. 12. 32–3 (χρῆν δέ σε ... εἴπερ ἦσθα χρηστός ... νῦν δέ ...).

The most explicit and elaborate example of this argument in Euripides is at *Hec.* 1217–23, where it comes immediately after an argument from probability and in a speech which is overtly rhetorical in other respects also. Hecuba says to Polymestor: 'you should, if you were a friend to the Greeks, have given the gold to them in their need; but you do not give it to them even now, but keep it in your palace (χρῆν σ', εἴπερ ἦσθα ... σὺ δ' οὐδὲ νῦν πω ...)'. Compare Lys. 22. 11–12 (ἐχρῆν ... εἴπερ ... νῦν δ' ...), although the passage from *Hecuba* has the further refinement of an *a fortiori* argument in the conclusion. Euripides seems to have evoked the lawcourts most immediately in the agones of his plays of the 420s, where there seems to be a specific point in the fact that Hippolytus, Andromache, and Hecuba are innocent defendants who make use of the most sophisticated arguments to defend themselves.[52] Hecuba's speech in *Hecuba* is the most extreme example of this. The style of Euripides' later plays is, if anything, even more rhetorical, but the evocation of the courtroom in later agones is less specific. Rhetorical influences are so pervasive in the later plays, and they are so thoroughly assimilated, that their presence in the agon becomes less remarkable.

The agon in *Electra* is thus highly rhetorical, and contains no fewer than three hypothetical syllogisms, but the outlines of the form are less obvious than they are in *Hecuba*. At *El.* 1024–9, Clytaemestra argues that Agamemnon's sacrifice of Iphigenia might have been pardonable if it had been in a good cause, but in fact the only purpose of the expedition was to recover the promiscuous Helen (κεἰ μέν ... συγγνώστ' ἂν ἦν ... νῦν δ' ...). Compare Lys. 12. 28–9 (εἰ μέν ... ἴσως ἂν ... συγγνώμην εἴχετε). *El.* 1030–4 and 1086–93 are oblique and subtle examples of this type of argument, in which Euripides obscures the outlines of the form by omitting the instantly recognizable formulaic phraseology. This method of argument has been absorbed into his style, and he has no further need to advertise the rhetorical skill of his characters. This is clear in the final example in his extant plays, *Or.* 496–504, where there is no more than a hint of the formulaic phraseology (χρῆν ... νῦν δ' ...).[53]

Euripides thus makes sophisticated use of artificial proofs in his agones, and natural proofs are also common. Frequent appeals are made to witnesses,

---

[52] See Ostwald 1986: 237 f. on the impact of the sophists in the 420s.
[53] Cf. also fr. 451, from *Cresphontes* (before 424).

for example at *Hi.* 972, 977, 1022, 1075, 1076; *Med.* 476 f.; *Hcld.* 219; *Tro.* 955; *Pho.* 491; *Or.* 532 f.; *IA* 365.[54] Oaths are especially important in *Hippolytus* (960, 1026, 1037, 1055, 1063), but see also *Med.* 492–5. Tyndareus' claim to have been defending the law (*Or.* 523) can be compared to various appeals to the jury in the orators (e.g. Ant. 1. 3; Lys. 10. 32).

Technical legal vocabulary, ubiquitous in Aeschylus' *Oresteia*, is not especially common in Euripides. Some of the more striking examples are ἀναφέρειν (*Or.* 597), ἀξιόχρεως (*Or.* 597), ἐχέγγυος (*An.* 192), παρρησία (*El.* 1049), μηνυτής (*Hi.* 1051), μηνύειν (*Hi.* 1077). The agon in *Hippolytus* is, in fact, especially rich in legal vocabulary: ἁλίσκεσθαι (913, 959, cf. *An.* 191),[55] ἐξελέγχειν (930, 944), ἀγωνίζεσθαι (1023), ἄκριτος (1056). Less specifically technical are κατηγορεῖν (1058) and αἰτία (961, 1036, 1067). Euripides is not normally so interested in evoking the courts so precisely, and the perversion of proper legal forms is a specific theme of the agon in *Hippolytus*. Stylistic features such as antitheses and rhetorical questions often appear in rhetorical contexts in Euripides, and are common to him and the orators, but cannot be regarded as having specifically forensic associations.[56]

RHETORICAL SELF-CONSCIOUSNESS

The impact of contemporary rhetoric on Euripides' agon speeches shows itself most clearly in their self-consciousness. This self-consciousness manifests itself in formal statements of the subject of the speech, concern for τάξις, enumeration of points, explicit references to the act of speaking itself, and point-by-point refutation of the opponent. This kind of thing is not, on the whole, to be found in speeches that are, or purport to be, natural pieces of self-expression.[57] Many of these features appear in a much exaggerated form in Gorgias, but he did not originate them.[58] Furthermore,

---

[54] Cf. Ar. *Rh.* 1375^{b}26 ff.; Page 1938 on *Med.* 476; Duchemin 1968: 198 f.

[55] *Hi.* 912 f. are deleted, perhaps rightly, by Barrett 1964, and ἐλεῖν should probably not be read at either *Hi.* 1002 or 1024.

[56] Cf. Lechner 1874: 18 f.; Norden 1898: i. 28 f., 75 f.; Graf 1950: 146–64; Duchemin 1968: 192–7, 212–16; Finley 1967: ch. 2; Solmsen 1975: ch. 1.

[57] See, e.g., Ant. 5. 1–7 for self-consciousness about the act of making a speech, concern for τάξις pointed by such expressions as πρῶτον μέν (5. 9) and ἔπειτα δέ (5. 11), and detailed refutation of the opponent (5. 13). Cf. Lys. 1. 4–5, 7. 5, 12. 1–3; Graf 1950: 150, 158 f.; Finley 1967: 12; Bond 1981 on *HF* 172.

[58] On Agathon's speech in Pl. *Sym.* (written in a Gorgianic style) see Dover 1968: 90–2; Dover 1980: 123 f.

this self-reflexive quality shows that rhetorical artifice in Euripides' agones is not just a result of the poet himself being influenced by contemporary trends in rhetoric, but is also a matter of the characters themselves being represented as skilled speakers.[59]

Some agones are considerably more explicit in their use of rhetoric than others. The agon in *Medea* is much more so than that in *Alcestis*, and the contrast between these two agones has suggested to some scholars that rhetoric made its decisive impact on Euripides between 438 and 431.[60] This deduction is extremely hazardous, not least because Euripides continued to write agon speeches that are not especially explicit in their use of rhetoric. There is, for example, a sharp contrast in the agon of *Hippolytus* between Theseus' speech, which is impassioned and shows little rhetorical influence, and the elaborately rhetorical speech of Hippolytus. Another example of an agon in which one speech is much more explicitly rhetorical than the other is that in *Hecuba*; Polymestor's speech is mostly narrative, while Hecuba's reply is one of Euripides' most formally rhetorical speeches. After an elaborate proem, which she explicitly identifies as such (1195), she replies to Polymestor's speech in detail, introducing the various sections with πρὸς τόνδε δ' εἶμι (1196), ἐπεὶ δίδαξον (1208), and ἄκουσον (1217). She concludes with a formal appeal to the judge (1232–7).[61]

The agon in *Supplices* is self-conscious in a rather different way. It is treated as a kind of game, with several references to the verbal contest (403, 409 f., 426–8, 456, 465 f., 476–8, 566–70), as well as frequent use, in a didactic manner, of such expressions as πρῶτον μέν (403, 430, 489, 517). The most self-conscious of all Euripides' agones is that in *Troades*, where Helen's speech has an elaborate proem and a very careful concern for τάξις (919, 920, 923, 931, 938 f., 945, 951), while Hecuba answers point-by-point (969 f., 983, 998, 1010) and concludes with a self-referential appeal to Menelaus (1029).

CONCLUSION

The investigation of Euripides' relationship to contemporary rhetoric is inevitably hampered by the almost complete lack of forensic speeches

---

[59] Cf. Lechner 1874: 14 f.; Goebel 1983: 280.
[60] Norden 1898: i. 76 n. 2; Goebel 1983: 275–89.
[61] See Graf 1950: 79 n. 1 for εἶμι in references by a speaker to his progress from point to point, see *An.* 627, *Or.* 550. Rhetorical use of διδάσκω is common in Antiphon and Lysias, and occurs also at S. *El.* 534, 585. Imperative of ἀκούω marking transitions: *Hec.* 1137, *Su.* 428, *Tro.* 923, *Or.* 565.

delivered during his career. Some conclusions can, nevertheless, be drawn. The structure of the speeches in his agones shows rhetorical influence most clearly in the proem, where he usually uses the forensic commonplaces in a dramatic and purposeful manner. He rarely uses the four-part structure, and never in any straightforward way, and tends to adopt a distinctive division of a speech into a series of self-contained arguments or points. Rhetorical influence does, however, seem to show itself in the speakers' self-consciousness about structure and about the whole process of making a speech.

The methods of argument employed in Euripides' agones also seem to reflect rhetorical theory and practice to some extent. There can never be a clear-cut distinction, either in Euripides or in the orators themselves, between natural modes of self-expression and sophisticated rhetoric, but some types of argument seem to be more rhetorical than others. The argument from probability was generally recognized to be advanced, and Euripides uses both this argument and others which seem to be related to it. There can be little doubt in some cases that he was influenced by contemporary rhetoric, and even that the forensic assocations of these arguments are significant in the context of the play. The atmosphere of the courtroom seems to be evoked most specifically in Euripides' plays of the 420s, but we are in no position to say when rhetorical influence first made itself felt on him.

The significance of this rhetorical influence on Euripides' agones varies from play to play, although it always contributes to the clarity of his style and the formality of his structures. In his earlier extant plays, rhetorical sophistication tends to have some significance for character, in that the speakers are actually being portrayed as skilled orators, although this is never the main reason for the presence of rhetorical elements. In later plays, rhetorical influence is more pervasive, and all characters alike are equipped with the rhetorical expertise which they need in order to express themselves.

3

Early Agones: *Alcestis, Medea, Hippolytus, Andromache*

THE agon in Euripides has been discussed so far in this book largely in terms of features which the agones in different plays have in common. It is now time to investigate more closely the relationship of the various agones to the individual plays of which they are parts. Four comparatively early agones can conveniently be treated together from this point of view: those in *Alcestis*, *Medea*, and *Hippolytus*, and the agon between Hermione and Andromache in *Andromache*. These scenes all involve two persons rather than the three usually involved in later agones, and the opponents in all four cases are closely related to each other. In *Alcestis*, a son prosecutes his father and concludes by rejecting him, while in *Hippolytus* father prosecutes son and concludes by sending him to his death. In *Medea*, a wife confronts her faithless husband, while in *Andromache* a wife attacks her husband's concubine. There are parallels in the dramatic contexts of the agones in *Alcestis* and *Medea* as well as an interesting contrast of style, while there are many points of similarity between the agones of *Hippolytus* and *Andromache* as an innocent defendant uses rhetorical expertise in the futile attempt to convince an irrational opponent.[1]

ALCESTIS

The agon in *Alcestis* shows few signs of rhetorical influence, and contrasts interestingly in this respect with the other three agones in which the problem arises of how far rhetorical speeches can express character. The agon here is introduced naturally, without the formality of Euripides' later agones, as Admetus reacts with an angry outburst to Pheres' expressions of sympathy (629–72). Pheres' words are, in fact, conventional enough, with his praise of Alcestis (615) resembling the chorus' (442, 742) and his

[1] Cf. Strohm 1957: 3–16.

farewell to her (626 f.) resembling theirs (436, 743 f.), but such language is inappropriate in his mouth. Admetus' speech already reveals the structural principles which Euripides was to follow in most of the speeches in his agones, in that it comprises a series of more or less self-contained arguments or points which combine to form a cumulative whole.[2]

Admetus begins by contrasting the grief which his father should have expressed earlier with his unwanted offerings and laments now (629–35). This proem may not be overtly rhetorical, but it does have rhetorical parallels in the type of aggressive proem in which the first speaker tries to undermine his opponent's right to speak.[3] Medea, for example, begins her speech in the agon of *Medea* by rejecting Jason's very presence ($\mathring{\eta}\lambda\vartheta\epsilon\varsigma$ *Alc.* 629, *Med.* 467). The rhetorical device is more obvious in Medea's speech, but seems also to be present in an embryonic and natural form in Admetus'.

The next section of Admetus' speech contains two interlaced ideas, that Alcestis is his real father and mother, and that his parents did not have much time left to live anyway (636–50). There is no need to look for elements of the rhetorical *narratio* here. Admetus does indeed make some factual statements (e.g. 642–7), but in order to make argumentative points rather than to inform Pheres of facts of which he is, in any case, well aware.

In the third section of his speech (653–68), Admetus begins by pointing out that Pheres was prosperous (653 f.), and goes on to describe the three aspects of this prosperity. He was a king in his prime; he had a son to inherit; and his son treated him well. He did not, however, repay his son for this good treatment ($\tau\hat{\omega}\nu\delta\epsilon$ 660), and Admetus will therefore ($\tau o\iota\gamma\acute{\alpha}\varrho$ 662) not perform the usual filial duties. There are factual statements in this section (e.g. 653–7) but, again, they do not constitute anything resembling a rhetorical *narratio*. Whatever else one may say about this section of Admetus' speech, it contains a lucid argument which proceeds in an orderly way to its conclusion. There is a subtle $\pi\varrho o\kappa\alpha\tau\acute{\alpha}\lambda\eta\psi\iota\varsigma$ when Admetus begins a rejection of a point which Pheres might make by saying $o\mathring{\upsilon}\ \mu\mathring{\eta}\nu\ \dot{\epsilon}\varrho\epsilon\hat{\iota}\varsigma$ (658).[4] This figure is often introduced by $\dot{\epsilon}\varrho\epsilon\hat{\iota}\varsigma$, and there is no way of deciding whether Admetus' words are a sophisticated variation of an established rhetorical device or a natural piece of self-expression which has yet to harden into a formula. Admetus' speech has a gnomic conclusion, as is usual in a two-person agon.

[2] Cf. Solmsen 1975: 25 f., who perhaps breaks the speech down a little too much.
[3] Cf. above, p. 26.
[4] Cf. above, pp. 30 f.

Pheres' speech is similarly constructed, answering Admetus' points in reverse order before launching a counter-attack. He begins with a proem which establishes his right to speak (675–80). This type of defensive proem is sometimes necessary when the first speaker has tried to undermine his opponent's right even to speak (compare Diodotus' opening at Thuc. 3. 42 f.). Pheres complains that Admetus has treated him like a slave, and points out that he is a free Thessalian and will answer back. There are certainly echoes of Athenian public speaking here, especially as Pheres does not make the more obvious complaint that Admetus has failed to show the respect proper to a father.[5] Pheres' defensive proem also has an aggressive component, as defensive proems often do, and he attempts to undermine Admetus' speech by describing his words as νεανίας (679).[6] Such an attempt to dismiss one's adversary's speech as an immature and ill-judged outburst is common in rhetoric and has parallels elsewhere in Euripides (*An.* 184, 192; *Ba.* 274).

The two central sections of Pheres' speech answer the two central sections of Admetus' speech in reverse order, with 681–90 answering 653–68, and 691–3 answering 636–50. Pheres concludes by pointing out that Admetus, having refused to die himself, cannot then (εἶτα 696, 701) criticize him for not doing so (694–705).

The structure of both speeches is typical of Euripides and both have a clear and logical argument, with Pheres' speech offering a point-by-point rebuttal of Admetus'. There are traces of what were, at least later, rhetorical devices, although they are not ostentatious. The agon ends with angry stichomythia of the usual kind, followed by the exits of both participants and the end of the act.

The structure of the agon may be lucid enough, but its meaning and function are much more open to doubt. Interpretations of it reflect the radically different views which have been taken of the play as a whole, and in particular of the character of Admetus.[7] Scholars who argue that his acceptance of Alcestis' sacrifice should be condemned, and that criticisms of his behaviour are implicit in the earlier part of the play, regard the Pheres scene as the explicit attack on him which we have been waiting for.[8] Other scholars argue that the question of whether Admetus ought to have accepted the sacrifice is not raised in the play, or even that he was actually

---

[5] Cf. Stevens 1971 on *An.* 186.   [6] Cf. Collard 1975*b* on *Su.* 580.
[7] See M. Lloyd 1985: 119 f.
[8] Von Fritz 1962: 307; Knox 1979: 335; Conacher 1988: 39 f.

right to accept it, and that Pheres is too disreputable a character for his criticisms to be taken seriously.⁹

These differences of opinion seem to reflect the fact that everything that Admetus does during the play is both obviously correct and totally inappropriate. His lamentation for Alcestis, for example, is in some ways paradoxical, and it is taken to the point where it seems to make her sacrifice futile. He would, however, be intolerable if he cheerfully availed himself of the life which she had died to give him. Similarly, when Heracles arrives, it is both unacceptable for Admetus to offer him hospitality, as the chorus points out (551 f.), and quite rational for him to do so, as he points out himself (553–60).

This same tension between the correctness and the inappropriateness of everything that Admetus does is also to be found in the agon. On the one hand, Admetus' criticism of his parents is in itself reasonable enough. Their advanced age was manifestly a reason why one of them should have volunteered to die in his place, and this is stated or implied in several passages. It is implied by Apollo (γεραιάν 16)[10] and by Heracles (ὡραῖος 516), and is stated in strong terms by the chorus (466–70). Most impressively of all, Admetus' parents are condemned by Alcestis (290–7), and Admetus echoes this condemnation in his own speech (648–50).[11] Pheres himself seems to accept that he will die δυσκλεής (725 f.), and he is indeed portrayed in a most unattractive light in the agon, where he seems aggressively shameless and his defence is only effective *ad hominem*. Euripides might have made him a much more sympathetic figure, and given him quite strong arguments that he had no actual obligation to die for Admetus, whatever the moral pressure on him to do so.[12]

Pheres thus deserves all the criticisms that he receives from Admetus, but it is also completely inappropriate that Admetus should make these criticisms. Pheres points out vigorously enough in the concluding section of his speech that Admetus is not in a position to criticize other people for being afraid of death (694–705). Furthermore, it is a very bad thing in itself that Admetus should hate his parents in this way, as he himself later realizes (958 f.), and his complete rejection of them is an extreme step.[13]

---

⁹ Dale 1954: pp. xxii–xxix; A. Lesky, 'Der angeklagte Admet', *Maske und Kothurn*, 10 (1964), 203–16 (= Lesky 1966: 281–94); Burnett 1971: ch. 2; Dyson 1988.
[10] On line 16 (del. Dindorf), see Conacher 1988, ad loc.
[11] Cf. Rohdich 1968: 34; Lesky 1966: 281 f.
[12] Dyson 1988: 19 n. 11 provides Pheres with a stronger defence than he is actually given in the play.   [13] Cf. Conacher 1988 on *Alc.* 734–8.

Euripides has organized his material in such a way that the play represents, not Admetus' acceptance of the sacrifice, but the problems which face him once he has accepted it.[14] His acceptance of the sacrifice may well be regarded as a highly discreditable action; it is criticized by Pheres (694–8, 730–3) and Admetus himself envisages similar criticism from his enemies (954–61). No defence is put forward, either by Admetus himself or by anyone else in the play. On the other hand, the very fact that he never defends himself is one of several factors which combine to push the question of his acceptance of the sacrifice into the background. The agon is, in fact, the very point in a Euripidean play where one would expect to find a full discussion of a question of this kind, if it was indeed of central importance. Compare the agon in *Medea*, where Medea attacks Jason for his desertion of her. The agon in *Alcestis*, however, is first and foremost a debate about Pheres' refusal to sacrifice himself, and it deals only incidentally with Admetus' acceptance of Alcestis' sacrifice. Admetus, as prosecutor, speaks first, and the structure of the scene gives him little scope to answer Pheres' passing jibes about his own cowardice and selfishness. The question of Pheres' guilt is not in itself very important, but the discussion of it in the agon of *Alcestis* fits into a sequence of scenes which show the exquisite tension between the correctness and the inappropriateness of everything that Admetus does.

MEDEA

There are some structural similarities between the agones in *Alcestis* and *Medea*.[15] In both, the principal character (Admetus, Medea) is on stage at the beginning of the scene; a secondary character (Pheres, Jason) arrives and makes a short and provocative speech; this leads to an angry speech from the main character, to which the other replies; both scenes then conclude with a passage of angry dialogue. In both plays it is too late for the agon to have any practical effect, since, in *Alcestis*, Alcestis has already died, while, in *Medea*, Jason has already deserted Medea and married someone else.

The overall structure of the agon in *Medea* may resemble that of the agon in *Alcestis*, but it differs in that both participants are clearly well versed in rhetorical technique. Medea's speech is an interesting combination of sophisticated rhetoric and passionate invective, and this combination of

---

[14] For fuller discussion, see M. Lloyd 1985.   [15] Cf. ibid. 131 n. 36.

styles is especially evident in its proem (465–74). She begins by insulting Jason, but goes on immediately to comment self-reflexively on her own action in doing so (465 f.).[16] She then rejects Jason's very presence, as Admetus had done that of Pheres, but proceeds to indulge in a rather pedantic discussion of the correct word for the quality of mind which prompted him to come (467–72). She concludes her proem with remarks on the purpose of her speech, and the self-consciousness of these remarks shows clear signs of rhetorical influence.

Medea's proem encapsulates the conflict within her between reason and emotion, which is a central theme of the play. Her emotional side manifests itself here in her outburst of hatred, while the self-consciously rhetorical elements of her proem reflect her attempts to control herself and to make a lucid and rational speech. Her use of rhetoric is thus significant in terms of character, and in the context of this particular speech what it signifies is the more controlled side of her divided personality. This division has been apparent earlier in the play in the unmediated juxtaposition of her impassioned offstage anapaests with her formal and orderly opening speech (214 ff.). The cool and analytical style of this speech is in some ways typical of the Euripidean *rhesis*, but has a specific meaning in the present context.[17]

Medea's speech in the agon is one of the few in Euripides to have anything approximating to a rhetorical *narratio* (475–87), and her comparative calmness in this section is marked by her explicit concern for τάξις at the beginning (475). After this narration, she seems to be moving on, in the approved rhetorical manner, to a section of discussion, and she begins this section with a hypothetical syllogism of a kind which has many rhetorical parallels (488–91).[18] At this point, however, the orderly rhetorical structure breaks down, and she launches into an emotional outburst (492–8). It is unusual in Euripides' agones for the outlines of the four-part structure to be as clear as they are in this speech, and he seems to evoke the rigid rhetorical structure precisely in order to highlight Medea's departure from it. After this outburst, Medea regains control with a self-reflexive headline of a typically rhetorical kind (499–501), before her speech comes to an impassioned climax (502–15). Rhetorical formality is re-established with her gnomic conclusion (516–19).

Jason's speech also uses rhetoric in a way that reflects his character, but the effect of his rhetorical self-consciousness is quite different from that

---

[16] Cf. Pelliccia 1987: 43–6.
[17] See Conacher 1981: 11–15 for a useful discussion of the different effect of *Med.* 214 ff. and *Hi.* 373 ff. despite their superficial similarity of manner (on which, see Gould 1978: 55–7).
[18] See above, pp. 32 f.

of Medea's. The structure of his speech is more typical of the Euripidean agon, with proem and epilogue framing three separate and independent arguments (526–31, 532–46, 547–68). Jason's speech is a highly self-conscious performance, as he comments regularly on his own speaking (522–5, 529 f., 532, 535) and shows elaborate concern for τάξις (536, 545 f., 548–50). In this speech, in contrast to Medea's, the use of rhetoric implies the insincerity of the speaker, and Jason's speech is indeed the outstanding example in Euripides of rhetoric being used to promote the weaker case. Both the chorus (576–8) and Medea (579–83) comment that he is using clever speaking to defend unjust behaviour. It is mainly the context which makes clear that this is the significance of Jason's use of rhetoric, but the proem of his speech is also revealing in this respect. He begins by stating the need for him to be a clever speaker, and, while there are parallels for this gambit, it is much more common for speakers to claim that simple truthfulness is enough.

Medea and Jason are both highly articulate, and one effect of this articulacy is that important issues do not go by default because no one in the play can express them properly. Their use of sophisticated rhetoric also has implications for their characters, suggesting in both cases some degree of intellectual control. In the case of Jason, this aspect of his character is not balanced by any appropriate emotional response or moral judgement, and his speech seems correspondingly shallow and insincere. Within Medea, on the other hand, the conflict between reason and passion is one of the central themes of the play.

HIPPOLYTUS

The agon in *Hippolytus*, unlike those in *Alcestis* and *Medea*, is part of a larger structure and does not occupy a complete act. It is thus incorporated more thoroughly into the action than they are, more thoroughly, indeed, than many of Euripides' later agones. Hippolytus' entrance at line 902 has been preceded by over a hundred lines of mounting emotional tension as Phaedra's body is discovered, Theseus arrives unawares and laments her death, and then discovers her letter denouncing Hippolytus. Theseus' curse (887–90) has the effect of making the whole agon futile since nothing that Hippolytus says could now save him, and the play thus resembles *Alcestis* and *Medea* where the agones also come too late to have any substantial effect.

The difference in *Hippolytus* is that Euripides could easily have delayed the curse until after the agon and thus greatly enhanced the urgency and relevance of the scene. He seems positively to have avoided this apparently more natural and dramatic arrangement, and the structure which he actually adopted is very revealing of his principles in incorporating the agon into the action of a play. Two false explanations must first be dealt with. Barrett argues that Euripides did not want to repeat the sequence of events in the first *Hippolytus* where Theseus gave Hippolytus a hearing before cursing him.[19] This would not, however, be an especially convincing motive, even if we were sure of the arrangement in the earlier play, and Barrett's explanation fails to give a positive account of what Euripides is doing in the extant play. A more plausible explanation is that Euripides is emphasizing the futility of the whole debate by making it clear that Hippolytus would be doomed even if he could persuade Theseus of his innocence.[20] The objection to this view is that Euripides, far from emphasizing that the curse has made the agon futile, suppresses all thoughts of it for the rest of the scene. Theseus has no sooner pronounced it than he expresses doubt about whether it will be fulfilled, and he then seems to forget about it altogether. He actually rejects the death penalty as an adequate punishment of what Hippolytus has done (1045–9), and so much emphasis is placed on the question of exile that it is very surprising when the curse resurfaces in the messenger speech.

Euripides has thus gone to some lengths to detach the agon from the obvious relevance and excitement which it might have had if Hippolytus' life had depended upon it. Equally, however, he eschews the ironic effects which might have flowed from stressing the futility of the whole scene. The agon comes at a critical juncture of the play, but it is not tied down even to the possibility of any substantial influence on the action. Its significance is not as the words of Theseus and Hippolytus at this particular moment, and the important thing about it is neither its influence on the action nor its failure to influence the action. The function of the agon in *Hippolytus* is, rather, to represent through the medium of a formal debate the whole conflict between Theseus and Hippolytus. The agon cannot, therefore, be allowed even the possibility of playing a causal role in the development of that conflict. The debate cannot save Hippolytus, not because Theseus happens already to have cursed him, but because of the fundamental lack of contact between the two men.

Euripides introduces the agon in a subtle manner which brings out this lack of contact. Theseus refuses to reply to Hippolytus' inquiries about

---

[19] Barrett 1964: 40–2 and note on lines 887–9. Cf. Schwinge 1968: 43 n. 17. R. M. Newton, '*Hippolytus* and the Dating of *Oedipus Tyrannus*', *GRBS* 21 (1980), 5–21, at 7–10 argues that there was no agon in the first *Hippolytus*.   [20] e.g. Strohm 1957:10 f.

what is wrong, despite the latter's explicit requests for him to do so (902–15). He responds instead with three pieces of abstract moralizing which are manifestly directed at Hippolytus, although they do not explicitly acknowledge his presence (916–20, 925–31, 936–42). Theseus' style of moralizing may seem typically Euripidean, but it has significance for his character in the present context. Hippolytus' response (923 f.) to the first piece of moralizing shows that he regards Theseus' manner of speaking as eccentric and inappropriate, and he realizes only gradually that he himself is being attacked. Theseus does in fact feel too much loathing for Hippolytus to address him directly, just as Hippolytus himself had earlier attacked Phaedra and the Nurse (616 ff.).[21] Theseus' moralizing is significant for its content as well as for its style; the questions of the teachability of virtue and of the difficulty of discerning who is really just are obviously relevant to the wider themes of the play, as well as powerfully ironic in this context.[22]

Theseus' third piece of moralizing (936–42) turns out to be the beginning of a long speech, as he finally, and with climactic effect, applies his generalizations to Hippolytus. Gould comments on the 'jury-directed tone' of this speech, citing σκέψασθε (943), while Knox states that Theseus 'speaks to the audience as often as he does to his son'.[23] Both these statements are exaggerated. The agon in *Hippolytus* has more forensic language than most agones in Euripides, and σκέψασθε is indeed often used rhetorically by the orators, but imperatives of this kind are also common in passages in tragedy where there is no question of any jury.[24] The imperative σκέψασθε here is addressed, as are Theseus' generalizations, to the world at large rather than to the audience or to any imagined jury. It is not, in fact, clear that the agon has yet established itself or that there is any question of juries, although there is certainly a forensic flavour to ἐξελέγχεται . . . ἐμφανῶς (944 f.).

The next section of Theseus' speech (946–57) is devoted to general abuse of Hippolytus' character, mocking his moral pretensions and religious eccentricity. This section expresses an ambiguity which is central to the meaning of the play. It seems, on the one hand, that Theseus is revealing

---

[21] Cf. Barrett 1964 on *Hi.* 616 ff.; Conacher 1972: 206 f.; Mastronarde 1979: 78. These scholars are more convincing than Gould 1978: 57 f., who denies character significance to 'the exchange of general statements on the order of things'.

[22] Cf. Winnington-Ingram 1958: 183 f.; Segal 1970: 289 f.; Conacher 1972: 207.

[23] Gould 1978: 57; Knox 1979: 222.

[24] Cf. Willink 1986 on *Or.* 128–9; Bain 1987: 4. Parallels in orators: Ant. 1. 21, 5. 40; Lys. 1. 37, 39, 43; 3. 24; 6. 21; 10. 11; G. *Pal.* 13.

a long-standing resentment of Hippolytus' behaviour which predisposed him to believe Phaedra's charge. This is suggested by his readiness to believe that Hippolytus is guilty, the vivid detail of his criticisms of his son's religious beliefs, and his use of the inclusive τοὺς τοιούτους (955). A psychological interpretation of Theseus' resentment can be pressed further. Segal, for example, argues that 'it is partly his own temperament, lustful and passionate, which makes him incapable of believing Hippolytus innocent'.[25] His belief that young men are liable to having their senses disordered by lust (966–70) does not apply to Hippolytus, while fitting his own behaviour all too well. A further complication is that Hippolytus himself is the product of one of his illicit amours.

On the other hand, however, it could be argued that Phaedra's denunciation of Hippolytus, backed up by her suicide, is enough by itself to convince Theseus, and that it is only his belief in the charge that provokes a bitterness about his son's way of life that he did not previously feel. The ambiguity is carefully judged, and Theseus resembles other characters in the play in being placed in a situation where a reasonable response is difficult to distinguish from an unbalanced overreaction. Hippolytus' denunciation of women is another example of this.[26]

Theseus then anticipates three possible lines of defence which he thinks that Hippolytus might adopt (958–70). This is the only section of his speech in which Theseus makes any attempt at rational analysis, and this is reflected by his use of the rhetorical device of προκατάληψις. His arguments are in themselves plausible enough, but the intervention of Aphrodite means that arguments from probability are necessarily misleading.[27] Theseus begins by suggesting that Hippolytus will argue that Phaedra's death has saved him, and his reply to this is that no oaths or arguments that Hippolytus might produce could be more convincing than Phaedra's corpse (958–61). Theseus appeals to a witness, in the approved forensic manner, but this dumb witness is deceptive, and it is Hippolytus' oaths and arguments which have truth on their side.[28] Theseus goes on to deny that Phaedra would have been motivated by hostility to Hippolytus on account of his illegitimacy (962–5). His reasoning has some plausibility since, although Phaedra did indeed resent Hippolytus' illegitimacy, her suicide cannot be understood without reference to Aphrodite (725–31). The third imagined

---

[25] Segal 1986: 202.   [26] Cf. Kovacs 1987: 62.
[27] On the fallibility of rational thought in Euripides, see Dodds 1960 on *Ba.* 430–3; Rohdich 1968; Mastronarde 1986.
[28] Dumb witnesses: 418, 972, 976–80, 1074–7. Cf. Segal 1970: 288–91; Goff 1990: 19 f., 25.

line of defence which Theseus rejects is that sexual irresponsibility is more likely to be a female fault than a male one (966–70). This is the kind of belief which characterizes Hippolytus in the play, and Theseus is quite right to reject it, but it remains true that Hippolytus is innocent and that it is Phaedra who has actually been affected by Aphrodite.

Theseus is about to continue with his arguments, but he loses patience even with his fairly brief attempt at reasoning (971 f.). This recalls the conflict in Medea's speech between attempts at self-control, reflected in more formal rhetoric, and a more natural and emotional style of utterance. It has gradually become clear that this is the first speech of an agon, and Theseus here uses one of the key words that signals an agon (ἀμιλλῶμαι 971). He has already established Hippolytus' guilt to his own satisfaction by means of artificial proofs in the form of misleading arguments from probability. Now he appeals to a clinching natural proof, the dead witness who is explicit in her evidence. He proceeds immediately to sentence Hippolytus to exile (973–80). The perversion of legal processes could not be more manifest.

Hippolytus' defence speech evokes the lawcourts to a greater extent than any other speech in Euripides. He shows full command of formal rhetoric and of the various methods of proof.[29] In contrast to Theseus, who misused forensic procedures and came to the wrong conclusion, Hippolytus makes the best possible case for himself. The tragic aspect of his situation is not only that this does him no good, but that it actually alienates Theseus still more. This is not to say that Hippolytus should not have used rhetoric at all, or that he should, for example, have tried tactful persuasion. He is doomed anyway, since Theseus has already cursed him, and the function of the agon is not to play a causal part in Hippolytus' alienation from his father, but to represent that alienation in a particular way. Hippolytus is capable of emotional outbursts, as in his tirade against women (616 ff.), but it is highly appropriate to his character that he should make a rational and controlled speech in response to Theseus' impassioned attack on him.

Hippolytus begins with a formal proem, which serves to establish that an agon is in progress and which uses rhetorical formulae in a significant way (983–91). He contrasts fine words with the truth, points out that he is not accustomed to public speaking, and recognizes that he must nevertheless defend himself. The various elements of this opening are commonplace in the orators, and the significance of Hippolytus' use of them has been much discussed. Barrett writes of his 'peculiar priggishness'

[29] Cf. F. Solmsen, *AJP* 88 (1967), 88 f.

and of his 'contempt for his audience', and similar views have been widely held.[30] Gould dissents from this kind of interpretation, comparing the style to that of Antiphon's *Tetralogies*, and arguing that 'personality is as little relevant here as in interpreting the linguistic strategies of barristers'.[31]

It is significant in itself that Hippolytus uses rhetorical formulae, and the way in which he uses them is also interesting. For example, the commonplace that the speaker is unaccustomed to public speaking tends to be used by the orators in a rather deferential manner. Hippolytus, by contrast, uses highly coloured language to express his contempt for the mob (ὄχλος 986, 989), and says that one needs to be κομψός and φαῦλος to address it convincingly. He implies that his actual audience is a mob of this kind, and implicitly contrasts it with the σοφοί whom he prefers to address. A virtuous defendant was not to express himself in so antagonistic a manner again until the Socrates of Plato's *Apology*.[32] However many people are actually on the stage at this point, Hippolytus is really only addressing his father.[33] Theseus may have some of the qualities of a raging crowd, but the real relevance of this opening lies in the expression it gives to Hippolytus' attitudes. Speakers of actual forensic speeches sometimes criticize juries, but never express such comprehensive contempt for the circumstances of the trial.[34] Another point is that this particular proem formula is used nowhere else in Euripides. It seems to be especially appropriate to Hippolytus, who is presented in the play as being aristocratic, withdrawn from politics, and preferring the company of the ὀλίγοι.[35]

In the next section of Hippolytus' speech (991–1006), rhetoric is again used in a revealing way. He replies to Theseus' attack on his character (946–57) by trying to establish that he is σώφρων. The rhetorical tone is stressed by his explicit matching of point for point, and it is indeed common for a defendant to present his character in the best possible light in order to demonstrate that he could not possibly have committed the alleged crime.[36] Arguments of this kind would normally be reinforced by more specific points, but Hippolytus' oath prevents him from dealing with the details of the case and he is compelled to remain at a

[30] Barrett 1964 on *Hi.* 986–7. Cf. Grube 1941: 188 f.; Winnington-Ingram 1958: 184 n. 2; Conacher 1981: 15.
[31] Gould 1978: 57. Cf. Heath 1987: 131 f. [32] Cf. North 1988: 127 f.
[33] On the size of Hippolytus' audience, see Barrett 1964, note on line 884 and p. 435; O. Taplin, *Greek Tragedy in Action* (London, 1978), 189 n. 7.
[34] Cf. Dover 1974: 23–5; Macleod 1983: 92.
[35] Cf. Knox 1979: 220; J. Blomqvist, 'Human and Divine Action in Euripides' *Hippolytus*, *Hermes*, 110 (1982), 398–414, at 414; Michelini 1987: 307 f., 314.
[36] Cf. Ar. *Rh.* 1356ª4–13; G. *Pal.* 28–32; Usher 1965.

general level.³⁷ He does, however, go beyond the rhetorical need to show that he was too virtuous to commit the alleged crime, and actually claims pre-eminence in σωφροσύνη (993–5). He repeats this claim later (1100, 1365), and, whatever view one takes of such assertions, they are in accordance with Hippolytus' general attitude in the play.³⁸ Euripides thus adapts rhetorical procedures to the character of the speaker. An ironic twist is that, while Hippolytus has no alternative to this type of argument, it is likely to infuriate Theseus still further (compare 949 f.).

Hippolytus goes on to argue that he could have had no possible reason to dishonour Phaedra (1007–20).³⁹ His rhetorical sophistication is evident in his self-conscious comments on the progress of the argument and in his use of arguments from probability. His use of hypophora echoes Theseus' use of this figure.

He begins this section by implying that Phaedra was not outstandingly beautiful, goes on to argue that he would have been foolish to hope to take over Theseus' house by taking an heiress as his wife, and finally denies that tyranny is attractive to the sensible man.⁴⁰ It is clear enough why Hippolytus rejects the first and third motives here, but it is not so obvious why he considers the second suggested motive to be self-evidently absurd. It could be because Phaedra was not technically ἐπίκληρος at all, and that the point is that marriage to her would have carried no rights to Theseus' property.⁴¹ This would certainly be true in Athenian law, but there is no reason why Hippolytus' position should be assessed strictly in terms of Athenian law even if he does use language which evokes its terminology. In the heroic age, there were heroines such as Penelope, Clytaemestra, and Jocasta who were closely enough attached to the throne for it to be reasonable to say that one could become king by marrying them. Barrett could be right that Hippolytus' use of the word ἔγκληρον (1011) implies some such situation, but in that case it might have been reasonable for

---

³⁷ Vickers 1973: 292 is better on this than Winnington-Ingram 1958: 187. Cf. Macleod 1983: 103–13 on the Plataean Debate in Thucydides.

³⁸ Kovacs 1987: 24 f. is favourable. Hyperbole is a stock rhetorical device (cf. *Alc.* 642, *Hcld.* 151, *Or.* 493; Carey 1989 on *Lys.* 14. 7), but speakers normally use it to criticize their opponents rather than to praise themselves. The whole subject of σωφροσύνη in *Hippolytus* is well discussed by C. Gill, 'The Articulation of the Self in Euripides' *Hippolytus*', in Powell 1990: 76–107.

³⁹ Phaedra acused Hippolytus of rape (885 f.), but this is not made explicit at any point in the scene between Theseus and Hippolytus, where language is used which could refer either to seduction or to rape (944, 1008, 1044, 1073). Cf. Kovacs 1982: 46 n. 44.

⁴⁰ On the rejection of tyranny, see D. C. Young, *Three Odes of Pindar* (Mnem. Suppl. 9, Leiden, 1968), 9–19; West 1987a on *Or.* 1155–6.

⁴¹ Thus Kells 1967.

Hippolytus to hope to gain the throne by marrying Phaedra.[42] The absurdity would then lie in the fact that Theseus was still alive.[43]

Difficulties have been detected in the overall structure of Hippolytus' argument in this section, and various deletions have been proposed, but these problems can be resolved if we recognize here what G. H. Goebel has termed the 'couldn't/wouldn't' argument.[44] In this type of argument, the speaker proves both that he could not have committed the alleged crime, and that he would not have done so even if he had been able. Hippolytus thus rejects the imaginary charge of making an attempt on the throne by arguing that wealth was unattainable and tyranny undesirable (but by implication also unattainable).

Gould denies that there is any particular psychological significance in Hippolytus' use of rhetoric, comparing Pasiphae's speech in *Cretes* where the argument from possible motives is also used in defence against a charge of sexual incontinence.[45] There is no denying that these two passages are, looked at in isolation, very similar in style. This logical and analytical approach, redolent of the lawcourts, is common in Euripides' agones, and there are obviously limits to the inferences which can be drawn from it about the character of the speaker. Nevertheless, superficially similar rhetorical strategies can differ greatly in significance according to the difference in their contexts. In the passage from *Cretes*, Pasiphae cannot deny that she committed the offence of which she is being accused and the circumstances are grotesque. In *Hippolytus*, on the other hand, Hippolytus is definitely innocent, and the tragic point is that these feeble arguments are the only ones that he can use. His behaviour in the agon is also characteristic. Accused of a sexual offence by a hot-tempered man, he reacts with a cool analysis of the possible motives that he might have had. His use of sophisticated rhetoric, and its inability to save him, reflects the pattern of the whole play.

The next section of Hippolytus' speech (1021–31) begins with an ostentatious concern for τάξις that emphasizes his attempt to present a rational case. Theseus had ended his speech with an appeal to the dead witness Phaedra (972), and now Hippolytus, who has no witnesses, can only refer to the evidence that Phaedra would have given had she been alive. Hippolytus is well aware of the proper methods of proof, but normal forensic procedure is no use to him. His last resort is to swear an oath that

---

[42] Cf. Barrett 1964 on *Hi.* 1010–11. [43] Cf. Lloyd-Jones 1965: 170.
[44] Goebel 1989. Suspicion of 1012–15: Barrett 1964 on 1014–15; Kells 1967; Kovacs 1982: 45–7. [45] Gould 1978: 57, citing *Cretes* fr. 82 Austin.

he is innocent,[46] and he concludes his speech with four enigmatic lines hinting at the truth (1032–5).

Theseus' response to Hippolytus' speech shows that his use of rhetoric is significant, and not to be regarded merely as the stock style of the Euripidean agon. He describes him as an ἐπῳδός and a γόης (1038), language which is strikingly reminiscent of Gorgias' description of the orator (*Hel.* 10–14).[47] He also complains about Hippolytus' εὐοργησία (1039), which must refer, if not to Hippolytus' use of rhetoric, then at least to the cool and rational manner of which the use of rhetoric was an aspect. It should be noted that Theseus is not worried by such points as Hippolytus' alleged tactlessness in referring to Phaedra's lack of outstanding beauty. Hippolytus continues to infuriate his father in the angry dialogue, predominantly distichomythia, which concludes the scene.[48] Here, it is not so much his manner as his virtue itself which provokes Theseus (e.g. 1060–3, 1074 f.).

The agon of *Hippolytus* reflects, through the medium of formal debate, the fundamental tragic conflict of the play. The manner in which Hippolytus expresses himself in his debate with Theseus can be seen either as evidence of his remoteness and inability to communicate, or as an example of how rational behaviour is doomed to failure in an irrational situation. This ambiguity is carefully calculated, and is central to the meaning of the play.

ANDROMACHE

The agon between Andromache and Hermione in *Andromache* resembles the agon in *Hippolytus* in that Andromache is an innocent defendant who is attacked in an angry speech and makes use of elaborate rhetoric to defend herself. A further similarity is to be seen in the way in which the agon is integrated into the action. Hippolytus was already doomed by Theseus' curse before the agon in *Hippolytus* even began, but Euripides obscures this fact by allowing the curse to be forgotten during the debate. Andromache's fate is also sealed before the agon begins, because Menelaus and Hermione have been plotting her death from the beginning of the play. But Euripides also,

---

[46] At [Ar.] *Rh. Al.* 1432ᵃ33 ff., oaths are the very last kind of evidence discussed. On oaths in *Hippolytus*, see Segal 1972.
[47] Cf. de Romilly 1975: 3–32; W. Burkert, Γόης: Zum griechischen "Schamanismus"' *Rh. M.* 105 (1962), 36–55, at 40 n. 17; G. E. R. Lloyd 1979: 84, 99.
[48] On Hippolytus keeping his oath (1060–3), see Bain 1977: 29–31; Knox 1979: 220 f.; Erbse 1984: 39. On 1078 f. see Winnington-Ingram 1958: 186 f. (also Lesky's comment in the discussion, 192); Gould 1978: 57 f. On legal vocabulary in *Hippolytus*, see above, p. 34.

as in *Hippolytus*, avoids making a negative point about the futility of the whole debate, and he misleadingly raises the possibility that Hermione might be satisfied with something other than Andromache's death.

Andromache reveals in the prologue that she cannot persuade Hermione of her innocence, and that Hermione wants to kill her (39 f.). Her presence at the altar shows the desperate nature of her position, and Hermione says flatly that it will not save her and that she will die (161 f.). She reiterates the threat of death after Andromache's speech (245, 254 f.). Menelaus' offstage plot to capture Andromache's child is in progress during the agon (68 f., 73, 262–8, 309 f.), and it emerges that the intention is to kill them both (425–32, 806 f.). The agon thus comes in the middle of a plot to kill Andromache and her child, and their deaths are effectively determined before it. It is theoretically possible for the death sentence to be lifted, but the sequence of events strongly suggests that it is in practice too late. Euripides has thus again, as in *Hippolytus*, avoided the more obviously dramatic sequence of events in which the plot only begins after the failure of discussion in the agon, and organized his material in such a way that the agon has no real chance of achieving anything.

On the other hand, Euripides makes nothing of the ironies which this might have yielded, and admits hints that Andromache might yet escape with her life. In the parodos, the chorus advises her to leave the altar and to submit to her masters. This is not necessarily good advice, but it does raise the possibility that some compromise might be possible. Hermione herself envisages the humiliation that Andromache would have to endure if she were saved (163–8). These hints serve the same function as Theseus' doubts about the curse in *Hippolytus*, obscuring the fact that it is already too late for debate to achieve anything.

Hermione's speech, like Theseus' speech in the agon of *Hippolytus*, expresses her character and attitudes in a comparatively natural way. The proem, however, is exceptionally subtle (147–53). It is only with the final word (ἐλευθεροστομεῖν) of this long and ornate sentence that its rhetorical purpose becomes clear. Hermione describes her elaborate costume because it is part of her dowry; the richness of this dowry establishes the prestige of her father and her own independence within marriage.[49] She can thus express opinions of which her husband might not necessarily approve, such as resentment of his concubine. Her right to free speech is partly due to her Spartan origin (151), and we may compare Pheres' insistence that he

---

[49] Cf. R. Seaford, 'The Structural Problems of Marriage in Euripides', in Powell 1990: 151–76, esp. 167–70. For this theme in New Comedy, see Hunter 1985: 90–2.

is a free Thessalian (*Alc.* 677 f.). Hermione not only establishes her own right to speak, but also attempts to deny this right to Andromache. The continuation of her speech (σὺ δ' οὖσα δούλη 155) expresses a contrast between her own freedom and importance and Andromache's subservient status.[50] She thus not only warns Andromache against alienating the affections of her husband, but also tries to subvert her right to reply. Rhetorical techniques are embedded in the texture of a highly individual speech.

The rest of Hermione's speech is in an unsophisticated style which reflects the low intellectual quality of its content. This is one aspect of the contrast in this scene between Andromache, the noble barbarian, and Hermione, the barbarous Spartan.[51] Hermione's generalizations about barbarians are of doubtful value in themselves, and are preposterous as criticisms of Andromache, who has no choice whatever about her position in Neoptolemus' household.

Andromache's speech, by contrast, shows signs of rhetorical sophistication. Her proem (184–91) tries to overcome the disadvantages of her own status as a slave (τὸ δουλεύειν 186) and suggests that she understands the rhetorical purpose of Hermione's proem. She fears that her status will mean that even victory in the debate will harm her, but asserts (like Hippolytus) that she must nevertheless defend herself. Hermione does not, in the event, take at all kindly to what Andromache says (234 f., 245), and Euripides has selected a type of proem that is particularly appropriate to her situation.

In the next section of her speech (192–204), Andromache analyses the possible motives that she might have had for trying to supplant Hermione. This analysis, reminiscent of Hippolytus' speech, is highly rhetorical in its appeal to probability and its use of hypophora. Goebel has given a useful account of Andromache's argument here, as she first shows that she could not supplant Hermione (194–8), and then that she would not have wanted to even if she could (199–204). Goebel points out that Euripides blurs the outlines of this rhetorical form by using θέλω in the first part (where the emphasis is, however, on the participial phrase), and by using an argument in the second part which is *per se* about possibility.[52]

Andromache's use of rhetoric resembles Hippolytus' in showing the difficulty which faces a character in making a convincing rational defence

---

[50] μέν (147) is thus picked up by δέ (155). Line 154 is an interpolation.
[51] Cf. Hall 1989: 161, 188, 212–14. On parallels between Hermione and Andromache, see H. Golder, 'The Mute Andromache', *TAPA* 103 (1983), 123–33, at 126 n. 13.
[52] Goebel 1989: 32–5.

when she is in the power of someone who has irrational suspicions of her. She differs from Hippolytus, however, in not being a character for whom the use of rhetoric is obviously appropriate. Theseus drew explicit attention to Hippolytus' cool rhetoric, while Hermione here is riled only by Andromache's moralizing and argumentativeness, and does not comment on her rhetoric as such (234 f.). Euripides is perhaps moving towards the style of his later plays, in which formal rhetoric tends to be used without particular significance for character. The parallel with *Hippolytus* might, however, suggest that there is more to it than this. Greeks did not regard barbarians as proficient in the art of persuasion, and tended to think that they preferred to use magic, poison, or violence.[53] This is certainly the attitude that Hermione has towards Andromache. Since there is in this play a notable reversal of the traditional roles of Greek and barbarian, it could be that Andromache shows her intellectual and moral superiority partly by her command of sophisticated techniques of persuasion.

Andromache does not, unlike Jason or Hippolytus, maintain a rhetorical tone throughout, and the second half of her speech (205–31) is in a more natural style. This section, with its own headline (205 f.), consists of advice to Hermione on how a wife should behave and is only implicitly an answer to her charge. Since this part of Andromache's speech contains neither argument nor explicit response to Hermione, the formality of the beginning of her speech is perhaps also necessary to establish that an agon is in progress. Andromache's intellectual and moral superiority is clear in the stichomythia that follows, as she clearly wins every exchange.

The four scenes discussed in this chapter show how Euripides detaches the agon from the immediate action. In *Alcestis* and *Medea* it is already too late for the agon to have any effect, while in *Hippolytus* and *Andromache* Euripides positively avoids what seems like a more natural arrangement of events in which the agon might have some chance of having an effect. All four scenes represent a crucial conflict in the play without being in themselves decisive contributions to the way in which the conflict develops in terms of the action. These agones are closely integrated with the themes of the plays, and cannot be dismissed as excrescences or showpieces. Even when the speeches show the influence of advanced rhetoric, this seems to be significant for character, although this kind of psychological appropriateness became less important for Euripides in his later plays.

[53] Cf. Hall 1989: 200, citing Buxton 1982: 58 f., 64, 161–3.

4

Electra

THE agon in *Electra* resembles the scenes discussed in the previous chapter in that it involves two persons, who are closely related to each other. The resemblance to *Hippolytus* is especially striking, where the agon also comes towards the end of the play, is part of a larger structure rather than occupying a complete act, and involves a character arriving unawares into a situation in which he has already been condemned to death.[1] The *Electra* agon differs, however, in both the balance and the complexity of the arguments on each side. Of Euripides' earlier agones, only that in *Alcestis* presents a problem about which side is in the right, at least on the narrower issues of the debate. The agon in *Electra* resembles those in *Troades* and *Orestes* in being finely balanced, with good arguments on both sides. Perhaps as a result of this, the arguments in these three scenes are detailed and complex, although another factor could be that all three scenes deal with much-discussed problems.

The agon in *Electra* also differs from the earlier scenes in its use of sophisticated rhetoric. Especially in *Medea* and *Hippolytus*, this was related to the character of the speaker, at least in broad terms. This is not the case in either speech of the agon in *Electra*. Both Electra and Clytaemestra are expert speakers and, while rhetorical elements (e.g. in proems) are used with some regard for character, there is no significance in the use of rhetoric as such. Both characters are given the necessary rhetorical skills to do justice to the issues. The evidence suggests that this development in Euripides' use of rhetoric took place in the late 420s (assuming *c*.422–416 as the date of *Electra*), but it would be rash to be too confident about this.[2]

The agon in *Electra* comes towards the end of the play, and is part of a complex structure in which the revenge on Aegisthus and Clytaemestra is accomplished (747–1146). The revenge sequence is really spread over two acts, divided by a strophic choral ode (860–79), but this formal division

---

[1] See Strohm 1957: 10–16.
[2] Date of *Electra*: Zuntz 1955: 69–71; Cropp 1988: pp. 1–li.

is very light,[3] and the real dramatic division comes at line 962 when Clytaemestra is seen approaching. This section of the play is thus divided into two equal parts, the first dealing with Aegisthus and the second with Clytaemestra. Each half has two major speeches, one of which shows the victim in a comparatively sympathetic light (the messenger speech and Clytaemestra's defence speech), while the other is a ferocious attack by Electra which stresses the victim's sexual misdemeanours.

Recognition and plot occupied the previous act (487–698), and Strohm observes that the order of the plot elements is the opposite of what appears in Sophocles. Sophocles has the sequence agon, messenger speech, recognition-and-intrigue, while Euripides has recognition-and-intrigue, messenger speech, agon.[4] It should, however, be observed that Euripides subordinates both the messenger speech and the agon to the revenge action, while in Sophocles they are essentially independent. The agon in Sophocles is part of a sequence in which the isolation and heroic obstinacy of Electra are stressed,[5] while Euripides has a quasi-judicial agon immediately before Clytaemestra's death.

These structural parallels between the sections of the play dealing with Aegisthus and Clytaemestra reflect similarities in the way the two characters are depicted. It has often been remarked that they appear in a much more sympathetic light than Electra's account of them has led us to expect. A. W. Schlegel regarded this more sympathetic treatment as 'a gratuitous torture of our feelings', a sign of Euripides' incompetence that he aroused irrelevant and distracting emotions.[6] Others have thought that the validity of the revenge itself is called into question because Aegisthus and Clytaemestra seem not only more amiable but also more ordinary and vulnerable. The murder of Aegisthus takes place at a religious ceremony of a rather mundane kind, in a peaceful rustic setting, to which Aegisthus has invited Orestes in a warm and unsuspecting manner. The murder itself, carried out in a particularly unpleasant way, is described with vivid realism. 'The realism has its effect, creating a sickening alienation from revenge. The roles are reversed, but so are our sympathies.'[7] More specifically, scholars have commented on the different ways in which Aegisthus is portrayed. Goldhill writes: 'Electra describes Aegisthus as a drunken abuser of her father's grave (326 ff.), a tyrant and bully. The messenger speech presents him as a respectably generous host, properly

---

[3] Cf. Cropp 1988 on El. 860–79.   [4] Cf. Strohm 1957: 12.
[5] On the agon in Sophocles' Electra, see Winnington-Ingram 1980: 219–23; G. J. Swart, 'Dramatic Function of the ἀγών Scene in the Electra of Sophocles', AClass 22 (1984), 23–9; Stinton 1986: 76–8 (=1990: 467–70).
[6] Schlegel 1909: 133. Cf. Wilamowitz 1883: 219, 222.   [7] Vickers 1973: 561.

sacrificing to the Nymphs.'⁸ Some scholars have seen this as a contradiction, and argued that Electra's view of Aegisthus and Clytaemestra is simply refuted by the more sympathetic way in which they are portrayed in some parts of the play.⁹ Goldhill himself sees this as one example of the way in which *Electra* offers 'a variety of ways of viewing people and actions—a plurality of *logoi*',¹⁰ and he associates this with the way in which Euripides juxtaposes conflicting illusions of reality and 'does not allow the audience to develop a single, coherent level of reality'.¹¹

It is not, however, clear that there is any actual conflict or contradiction between the various accounts of Aegisthus in the play. It is perfectly possible for the same individual to be both a drunken bully and adulterer and an affable and generous host, and the most that one can say is that these various aspects of Aegisthus' character are not reconciled explicitly. It remains open how, if at all, such a reconciliation should be effected.

The problem remains of the more sympathetic portrayal of Aegisthus in the messenger speech itself. It is difficult to sustain the view that the justification of the revenge is questioned, since such good qualities as Aegisthus displays are of comparatively minor importance when set against the enormity of his past crimes. Furthermore, it is nowhere suggested in the play, even by Castor, that Aegisthus' death was not just. The messenger himself regards it as a manifestation of divine justice (764), as do Electra (771) and the chorus (877), and his delight is shared by Aegisthus' own servants (854 f.) and by the chorus (859–65, 874–9).¹² The murder remains ugly and disturbing, and Euripides' point could be that murder, even when entirely justified, can take place in attractive surroundings and ordinary contexts, and that the perpetrators of evil deeds do not have to be villainous all the time. This realism serves partly as preparation for the much more problematic murder of Clytaemestra.

A very different impression of Aegisthus is given by the long and elaborate speech which Electra makes over his body (907–56).¹³ After a formal introduction (907–13), she deals briefly with the murder of Agamemnon (914–17) before moving on to an attack on Aegisthus' character which concentrates on sexual insults. This speech continues the indirect presentation of Aegisthus in this play, in which he does not appear while alive, and it corresponds to the abuse of him at the end of Aeschylus' *Agamemnon* and the taunting of him before his death in Sophocles' *Electra*.

---

⁸ Goldhill 1986: 253. ⁹ e.g. Arnott 1981: esp. 183 f.
¹⁰ Goldhill 1986: 253.   ¹¹ Ibid. 252.   ¹² Cf. M. Lloyd 1986: 15 f.
¹³ His body, not just his head: see P. D. Kovacs, 'Where is Aegisthus' Head?', *CP* 82 (1987), 139–41.

It is characteristic of Euripides to embody all this in a set speech. Much of what Electra says is consistent with Aegisthus' personality elsewhere in the myth, and her portrayal of him generally reflects the behaviour that the Greeks expected of tyrants.[14] The speech does, however, tell us almost as much about Electra herself, and reflects some of her characteristic preoccupations.[15] This contributes to the lack of resolution in the picture of Aegisthus which the play presents. This speech also corresponds to Electra's speech in the agon with Clytaemestra. In both there is reference to Agamemnon's status as general of the Greeks (916 f., 1081 f.), to the unprovoked wrong done to Orestes and to Electra herself (914 f., 1086 f.), and a variety of sexual insults.[16] This underlines the parallelism of structure between the two revenge actions, although the second poses much greater moral problems than the first.

Aegisthus is no sooner disposed of (961) than Clytaemestra appears. The ensuing dialogue between Electra and Orestes (962–87) is the kind of extended announcement used on several occasions in tragedy for arrivals of particular emotional significance.[17] This dialogue partly corresponds to the dialogue between Orestes and Clytaemestra at A. *Cho.* 892–930, dealing as it does with his hesitation and the overcoming of it by reference to the need for revenge and the demands of Apollo. There is, however, a notable difference in Euripides' treatment. The short and powerful dialogue in *Choephori* deals not only with Orestes' hesitation but with the whole question of Clytaemestra's guilt, and it is clear that her fate depends upon it. Euripides divides this material into two sections, the dialogue between Orestes and Electra and the agon between Electra and Clytaemestra.

Thus, in the dialogue, the anguished question τί δῆτα δρῶμεν; (*El.* 967) recalls A. *Cho.* 899; ἔθρεψε (*El.* 969) recalls ἔθρεψα (A. *Cho.* 908); the paradox that Clytaemestra must suffer τὸ μὴ χρεών (A. *Cho.* 930) is taken up, much less confidently, by Orestes at *El.* 973; the equal impiety of not avenging Agamemnon (A. *Cho.* 924 f.) is considered at *El.* 975–8, while the fact that Clytaemestra will perish by the same guile with which she killed Agamemnon (A. *Cho.* 888) is mentioned by Electra at *El.* 983 f. Euripides' Electra does not mention the command of Apollo immediately after Orestes' initial doubt, as Pylades does so impressively in Aeschylus, but it is referred to often enough in what follows (*El.* 971–3, 979–81, 986 f.).[18] There are, however, differences between Euripides and

---

[14] Cf. Cropp 1988 on *El.* 907–56.   [15] Cf. M. Lloyd 1986: 16 f.
[16] Cf. Strohm 1957: 14; F. Stoessl, 'Die *Elektra* des Euripides', *Rh. M.* 99 (1956), 47–92, at 71.   [17] Cf. Taplin 1977: 198–200, 297–9.
[18] Cf. Aélion 1983: i. 122.

Aeschylus in the way in which these points are made. Orestes advances the objections which in Aeschylus are put forward by Clytaemestra, while Electra takes the part of Orestes in Aeschylus. The scene in Euripides takes the form of a conflict between his hesitation and Electra's ferocious insistence on revenge. The doubts of Euripides' Orestes are more pronounced, while Aeschylus' Orestes does not waver in his determination after Pylades' intervention and replies confidently to Clytaemestra's pleas.

Euripides does, however, save up some elements of the dialogue in *Choephori* for the agon between Electra and Clytaemestra. These notably include references to Aegisthus (A. *Cho.* 894 f., 904–7), absent from the dialogue between Orestes and Electra except for the textually dubious line 984, but prominent in the agon. The question of Clytaemestra's ill-treatment of Orestes and Electra (A. *Cho.* 913–17) also comes up in the agon (*El.* 1086–93), and in both passages there is the implication that she took Aegisthus in exchange for her children. Reference to Agamemnon's infidelities (A. *Cho.* 918–21) is also confined to the agon in *Electra* (1030–40). Euripides thus separates general discussion of Clytaemestra's character, especially with regard to sexual matters, from Orestes' hesitations about killing her. The former is dealt with in the agon, the latter in the dialogue between Orestes and Electra before she arrives. Aeschylus combines both in the one dialogue between Orestes and Clytaemestra.

The effect of Euripides' organization of his material is to detach the agon from any practical consequences, since Orestes has already decided to kill Clytaemestra before she arrives. In theory, either he or Electra could change their minds in the course of the agon, but in dramatic terms the decision is taken when Orestes leaves the stage, and it cannot be reversed.[19] This detachment of the agon even from the possibility of practical effect is reminiscent of the agones in *Hippolytus* and *Andromache*.[20] In *Electra*, also, it seems that it would have been more obviously dramatic for Euripides to have tied the agon more closely into the action, and Aeschylus provides a model of how this could have been done. Euripides' adaptation of Aeschylus makes clearer than ever his determination to separate the agon from any process of decision. In *Hippolytus* and *Andromache* it seemed that the agon was being used to portray a conflict rather than to be itself a causal element in the development of that conflict. This is also true of *Electra*, but there is in addition a more specific point. From Orestes' point of view,

---

[19] Vickers 1973: 562 is thus wrong when he writes 'this is another of those Euripidean debates on the outcome of which a life depends'. Preferable is Strohm 1957: 14 f.
[20] See above, Ch. 3.

there are only two important facts: that Clytaemestra has killed Agamemnon, and so must die herself; and that she is his mother, so that it is wrong for him to kill her. This crucial dilemma (cf. *El.* 1169–71, 1185–9, 1244, *Or.* 538 f.) would be blurred, even trivialized, by being associated with detailed discussion of Clytaemestra's precise responsibility and motivation. It is nevertheless essential that some account be given of Clytaemestra's case and of the objections to it and Euripides reserves this for the agon, at a point after Orestes' decision has been taken. The question of Clytaemestra's precise degree of guilt is thus kept separate from Orestes' decision to kill her. Such problems did not face Aeschylus so acutely because the whole question of Clytaemestra's deed, and the possible justifications for it and objections to it, has already been aired at some length earlier in the trilogy.[21]

Clytaemestra's entrance is striking, not only because of the extended announcement which prepares for it, but also because it is on a chariot and because she is greeted in fulsome terms by the chorus (988–97). Taplin argues convincingly that chariot entries, while they were used routinely for royal personages in the pre-*skene* theatre and regularly in the fourth century for spectacular effect, occur only twice in extant Euripides (and never in Sophocles).[22] In the present case, Clytaemestra 'brings the corrupt riches of the palace to the yeoman's cot',[23] while Andromache's arrival on a chariot at *Tro.* 568–76 has a strongly pathetic effect. There is also, in fact, a pathetic effect in the present case, and this effect is heightened by the allusion to the arrival of Agamemnon in Aeschylus' *Agamemnon*. Clytaemestra's glory is all too hollow, and she herself says that it is a poor substitute for her lost daughter (1000–3).

Similar points can be made about choral greetings, which also tend to occur in honorific contexts and in situations of high pathos.[24] The present case, also, seems to come into both categories. A further point is that the greeting here is unusually fulsome, especially in its comparison of Clytaemestra to the gods (994), which is sarcastically echoed by Electra (1006). The only parallel for this degree of flattery, apart from the spurious greetings at *IA* 590–606 and *Rh.* 379–87, is A. *Pe.* 150–8 where there

---

[21] F. Solmsen, 'Zur Gestaltung des Intrigenmotivs in den Tragödien des Sophokles und Euripides', *Phil.* 87 (1932), 1–17, at 5, argues that, in Euripides' intrigue plays (including *Electra*), the stress is on personal motives and that discussions of justice tend to be isolated in agones.

[22] Taplin 1977: 75–9. [23] Ibid. 76.

[24] Cf. ibid. 74 f. The association of Clytaemestra with the Dioscuri (990–3) looks back to 312 f., 746 and forward to the *deus ex machina*, but also serves to point the difference between the gods and the suffering and guilty humans (see Cropp 1988 on *El.* 1233–7).

seems to be some characterization of oriental subservience. The choral greetings at A. *Ag.* 783–809 and E. *Or.* 348–55 are considerably more cautious, and they are both addressed to conquerors returning after many years. Contrast S. *OT* 31–4 for a more usual Greek attitude to the status of kings as compared to that of gods (at A. *Cho.* 59 f. it is prosperity itself, not prosperous people, that is compared to a god). The chorus' greeting is powerfully ironic, and it is perhaps also trying to draw down divine φθόνος on Clytaemestra. It is unsympathetic to her (1051–4), and Clytaemestra herself seems to be doing something similar to Agamemnon in Aeschylus' *Agamemnon*.[25]

The opening dialogue (998–1010) continues to evoke this blend of luxury and pathos, as Clytaemestra mentions both the spoils of Troy and the loss of Iphigenia for which this luxury is some kind of compensation. Electra's mock deference, as she compares herself to the Trojan slaves, raises the question of her resentment of her mother's prosperity, but also serves to provoke Clytaemestra to an elaborate self-defence. The debate is introduced naturally and without delay.[26]

Clytaemestra's speech begins with a two-line introduction (1011–12) in which she replies to Electra's complaint that she is an exile, a prisoner, and an orphan by saying that this is all Agamemnon's fault. These two lines arise naturally from the dialogue, but also serve as a headline to the speech. There is a corresponding two-line summary at the end (1049 f.).

Clytaemestra completes her proem by mentioning the disadvantages under which she labours, a stock rhetorical technique (1013–17).[27] 'When ill repute possesses a woman her words are unwelcome, but people should listen to what she has to say before forming an opinion of her.'[28] This rhetorical concern for reputation is also in keeping with Clytaemestra's character. Her concern for public opinion has already been mentioned in the play (30, 643), and it contrasts with her truculence in Aeschylus (e.g. *Ag.* 1401–6). Even this rather formal agon reflects character to some extent, and the argument from prejudice also has a tragic point in that the case is indeed prejudged.

[25] Cf. Fraenkel 1950 on A. *Ag.* 904; Sheppard, cited by Denniston 1939 on *El.* 988–97. See also M. J. O'Brien, 'Tantalus in Euripides' *Orestes*', *Rh. M.* 131 (1988), 30–45, at 38 n. 18, on 'greetings laced with inordinate praise and followed by a reversal of fortune'.

[26] Electra as a slave: cf. A. *Cho.* 135; S. *El.* 814, 1192.

[27] See above, pp. 26 f.

[28] This is Seidler's interpretation. Cf. Cropp 1982: 52–4, and the note in his commentary (1988) on 1013–17, although he slightly favours Matthiae's interpretation 'there is some harshness in the talk about her'. Cropp rightly rejects Diggle's κακῶς (1015).

Clytaemestra begins the main body of her speech by arguing that it was not part of the terms on which Tyndareus gave her to Agamemnon that he should kill her or her children (1018–23).[29] Nevertheless, he took Iphigenia to Aulis, and sacrificed her there. Revenge for the murder of Iphigenia is Clytaemestra's best argument (cf. A. *Ag.* 1412–21, 1523–9, 1551–9; S. *El.* 530–3), but she still needs to show that it was an offence by Agamemnon against her. Iphigenia was also his child, and the legal situation is obscure. Sophocles' Clytaemestra (*El.* 530–3) expands on the idea in Aeschylus (*Ag.* 1417 f.) that the mother has greater affection for the child, and even a greater stake in it, because of her pain in producing it. Euripides' Clytaemestra takes a rather different line, appealing to an imaginary contract between Agamemnon and Tyndareus in order to show that *she* was wronged (ἠδικημένη 1030) and that *her* child was killed (παῖδα τὴν ἐμήν 1020, cf. 1029). The wife typically appeals to her father as the guarantor of her rights when they are threatened by her husband (compare the part played by Menelaus in *Andromache*). Clytaemestra associates herself with her children in this 'contract' in order to reinforce the idea that murdering them is an offence against her, just as much as if she herself had been killed. Denniston is worried by the implication of 1020–2 that Agamemnon took Iphigenia with him from Argos, but the exaggeration is of little significance after such a lapse of time. The problem would only be important if Clytaemestra were supposed to be making 'a wild charge, which we are not meant to take seriously'.[30] This section of Clytaemestra's speech is thus a self-contained, and rather subtle, argument. Elements of narrative (e.g. 1020–3) add to the argumentative force by suggesting, through their vividness, the sheer horror of what Agamemnon did.

Clytaemestra also deals with Iphigenia in the next section of her speech (1024–9), and argues that the sacrifice of her might have been justifiable if it had been for some good cause like saving the city (which justifies a sacrifice in *Erechtheus*) or the rest of the family (as in *Heraclidae*). But Agamemnon killed her only in order to retrieve Helen.[31] This is a powerful argument, directly balancing the innocent Iphigenia against the guilty Helen.

This section has a rather ambiguous relationship to S. *El.* 563–76, where Electra argues that Agamemnon had to kill Iphigenia if the expedition was

---

[29] On ὥστε (1019), see Denniston ad loc.
[30] Denniston 1939 on *El.* 1020–2. Jouan 1966: 264 n. 6 classes this with other misrepresentations by Euripidean pleaders.
[31] See above, p. 33 for the type of argument here. πολλῶν μίαν ὕπερ reverses a common type of expression: see Fraenkel 1950 on A. *Ag.* 1455; Lesky 1966: 151 n. 15.

to proceed or even for the troops to be able to go home. The whole question of the relationship between the two Electra plays has been much debated, and this section shows with especial clarity the kind of problems that can arise in this area.[32] On the one hand, it could be pointed out that Euripides' Clytaemestra argues that the recovery of Helen did not justify the sacrifice of Iphigenia, by way of rebuttal of the argument of Sophocles' Electra that the expedition could not proceed without the sacrifice. On the other hand, the Sophoclean Electra argues not only that the army could not proceed to Troy without the sacrifice but also that it could not even return home (S. *El.* 573 f.). Furthermore, Clytaemestra argues in both plays that the sacrifice was performed for Menelaus' sake, but it is only in Sophocles that Electra explicitly denies this (S. *El.* 576). Euripides' Electra does not, in fact, offer any justification for the sacrifice whatever, and it could be argued that Sophocles is making good an omission in Euripides. The whole question is clearly incapable of resolution.

The next section of Clytaemestra's speech (1030–40) has been wrongly suspected because it seems to interrupt the exposition of her grievances about Iphigenia.[33] The subtlety of Clytaemestra's argument does, in fact, lie in her refusal to settle unequivocally on one reason for killing Agamemnon. In the previous section of her speech, she has said nothing so straightforward as that she killed him in revenge for Iphigenia. All she said was that what he did would have been pardonable if it had been in a better cause (1026). She then promptly denies that she would have killed him for this reason, and moves on to his bringing back Cassandra. But Agamemnon's infidelity is no excuse for murder, so Clytaemestra uses it only to justify her own adultery with Aegisthus. The problem here is that 'this specious excuse (echoing A. *Cho.* 918–20) is inapplicable to Clytaemestra's own case; her adultery with Aegisthus preceded Agamemnon's return'.[34] That is why she avoids saying in so many words that she imitated Agamemnon's infidelity, and keeps her language in 1035–40 studiedly vague. The conclusion of this section can be taken in two ways (1039 f.). On the one hand, it could mean that women should not be blamed for adultery when they are only imitating their husbands,

---

[32] Wilamowitz 1883, arguing that Euripides wrote first, was criticized by Vahlen 1891, who was in turn criticized by Pohlenz 1954: ii. 131–3. See also Matthiesen 1964: 87 f.; Vögler 1967: 179–86; H. Lloyd-Jones, review of Vögler 1967, *CR* 19 (1969), 36–8; Winnington-Ingram 1980: 231; Cropp 1988 on *El.* 998–1096.

[33] See Cropp on *El.* 1011–50 for a good account of Clytaemestra's strategy, defending the transmitted order of the lines.

[34] Cropp on *El.* 1036–8. There are obscurities in Clytaemestra's speech about the chronology of her relationship with Aegisthus. Cf. Denniston 1939: pp. xvi f.; Erbse 1984: 171.

which would justify her adultery with Aegisthus. On the other hand, Clytaemestra could be arguing that, since women are blamed for adultery, men should be blamed too and that she may thus have had some reason for killing Agamemnon. The first interpretation is perhaps more obvious, but the second brings the argument of this section full circle and gives neat ring composition with 1030 f. The ambiguity is part of Clytaemestra's rhetorical strategy, as she presents a moving target to her opponent.[35]

The argument about Cassandra does not come up in Sophocles, but it has good precedent in Aeschylus (e.g. *Ag.* 1260–3, 1440–7), and Cassandra claims responsibility for the death of Agamemnon elsewhere in Euripides (*Tro.* 356–60, 404 f., 461). Clytaemestra's argument gains force from the implicit contrast between the daughter who was taken away and the concubine who was brought back. She plays up Agamemnon's outrage by describing Cassandra contemptuously (1032, cf. A. *Ag.* 1440–7), by using the strong verb ἐπεισέφρηκε (1033),[36] and by stressing that Agamemnon wanted to keep them both in the same house (1034). At S. *Tr.* 543–6, Deianira contrasts the tolerable existence of an outside mistress with the intolerable prospect of cohabitation, although Hermione is not treated very sympathetically on account of this problem (E. *An.* 213–28).[37]

Clytaemestra then returns to the subject of Iphigenia with a brilliantly recherché *reductio ad absurdum*, which happens also to be the only example in Euripides of the hypothetical role-reversal (1041–5).[38] She asks whether, if Menelaus had been abducted, she should have killed Orestes in order to get him back: that is, whether she should have killed Agamemnon's son to save her sister's husband as Agamemnon killed her daughter to retrieve his brother's wife. Cropp well translates the conclusion of this argument: 'then was it wrong for him to die for killing my child, though right for me to be punished by him?' The lines make sense as they stand, but Cropp's conjecture τἀκείνου (with Denniston's θανεῖν) is certainly attractive.[39] This is an argument that Agamemnon was rightly

---

[35] On μῶρον (1035), see Barrett 1964 on *Hi.* 642–4 and, for self-criticism by women in drama, Hunter 1985: 83 f. On different attitudes to adultery by men and women, see A. *Cho.* 919–21 (and Garvie 1986 ad loc.); S. Pomeroy, *Goddesses, Whores, Wives, and Slaves: Women in Classical Antiquity* (New York, 1975), 86 f.

[36] Cf. Barrett 1964 on *Hi.* 866–7.

[37] Obsession with adultery in this agon: O'Brien 1964: 31; M. Kubo, 'The Norm of Myth: Euripides' *Electra*', *HSCP* 71 (1966), 15–31, at 24–9; Conacher 1967: 208; F. I. Zeitlin, 'The Argive Festival of Hera and Euripides' *Electra*', *TAPA* 101 (1970), 645–69, at 666–8; Donzelli 1978: 168–78; Cropp 1988: p. xxxvii.

[38] See above, p. 32.

[39] Cropp 1982: 51 f., differing from J. Diggle, 'Notes on the *Electra* of Euripides', *ICS* 2 (1977), 110–24, at 121 f.

killed, since it would have been so obviously right for Clytaemestra to be killed in the hypothetical situation.

This section of Clytaemestra's speech is comparable to S. *El.* 534–45, where she asks the perhaps more obvious question why Menelaus could not have sacrificed one of his own children. Some scholars have argued that Euripides makes use of a rather strained argument here in order to avoid what they see as the more natural line of argument adopted in Sophocles.[40] Arguments on this topic must, however, have been frequently rehearsed in both literary and educational contexts, and it need not be Sophocles' version that Euripides is avoiding. The argument of Euripides' Clytaemestra is not open to the obvious retort to the Sophoclean version, that Artemis demanded one of Agamemnon's children and not one of Menelaus'.

Clytaemestra's next point is that she had to turn to one of Agamemnon's enemies, since obviously none of his friends would help her (1046–8).[41] At S. *El.* 591–4, Electra denies that it would be right to marry enemies for the sake of a daughter, and the question again arises of the relationship between the two agones. In the present case, either passage could be seen as answering the other, and the matter is further complicated by the fact that many other treatments of this theme must be lost. The comparison of these two passages does, however, serve to illustrate the kind of points that can be in the background of a given argument.

Clytaemestra's speech ends with a two-line conclusion (1049–50), which balances the first two lines of the speech, sums up the theme that Agamemnon died justly, and invites Electra to reply.

The material between the two main speeches is unusually elaborate (1051–9). Normally there are two or three lines from the chorus, and the only other exception to this is *Su.* 513–16, where Adrastus bursts in and is silenced by Theseus. The vehemence of the chorus' condemnation of Clytaemestra is not in itself surprising (cf. *Tro.* 966–8, 1033–5),[42] and it offers one of the stock paradoxes that constantly recur in this story (cf. 1244, *IT* 559, *Or.* 194). Their reduction of the problem to a matter of correct wifely behaviour is, however, an inadequate response to the situation. Electra's elaborate verification of her right to free speech recalls S. *El.* 552–7, 626–9, but this comparison makes her caution seem all the

---

[40] Vahlen 1891: 358 f.; Denniston 1939 on *El.* 1030–48.

[41] On the political sense of φίλος in *Electra*, see D. Konstan, '*Philia* in Euripides' *Electra*', *Phil.* 129 (1985), 176–85.

[42] Cf. Dover 1983: 42 (= 1987:87 f.), criticizing Adkins 1960: 185. Cf. S. *El.* 558–60 (spoken by Electra).

odder. Sophocles' Electra is under the power of a Clytaemestra whose tolerance of free speech is far from inexhaustible, while Euripides' Clytaemestra is not only in a far weaker position, but has freely offered Electra permission to speak. Electra's question at 1058 seems especially gratuitous, and it is clear that she is relishing the irony of the situation.

Electra' speech begins with an insult (1061), which she describes as the beginning of her *prooimion*. Denniston thinks that the *prooimion* is the sketch of Clytaemestra's character which lasts until line 1085, but he is rightly criticized by Diggle, who is suspicious of a rhetorical disposition in which the *prooimion* occupies two-thirds of the speech. Diggle thus suggests παρρησίας (1060), although he leaves it in the *apparatus* of his text.[43] Collard thinks that ἀρχή . . . προοιμίου is a 'regular tautology',[44] and Cropp accordingly translates 'this is my start consisting of an introduction'. None of Collard's parallels supports this. *Med.* 475, *HF* 538, and *Pho.* 1336 are all of the form 'begin a *logos* with a *prooimion*' or 'begin at the beginning'. *Tro.* 712 does indeed have 'begin a *prooimion*', but, since Andromache interrupts Talthybius after three lines, neither she nor we are in any position to say that he has completed his *prooimion*. There is thus no reason to translate 'make a beginning consisting of a *prooimion*'.

Euripides' rhetorical strategy can, however, easily be paralleled. He often has proems which consist wholly or mainly of insults, sometimes in the form of an initial exclamation expanded by a γάρ clause (e.g. *Med.* 465–74, *Hi.* 936–45). In the present case, therefore, the concise insult in line 1061 is the beginning of a proem which extends until 1068. This proem not only contains the insulting comparison with Helen, but also the actual charge (1066–8) which serves as the headline to the speech. The rest of the speech is introduced by ἥτις (1069), and with this may be compared *An.* 592 and *Or.* 494, where ὅστις connects an insulting proem with the main body of the speech. These passages are examples of the more general use of ὅστις to introduce a proof (e.g. *Alc.* 620, *Su.* 220, *Or.* 573).[45]

Electra makes the common comparison between Clytaemestra and Helen as two sisters who are beautiful but bad, and the idea of their shaming Castor occurs several times in Euripides (*Tro.* 132 f.; *Hel.* 137–42, 720 f.). In the paradoxical versions of her fate in *Helen* and *Orestes*, Helen will actually

---

[43] Denniston 1939 on *El.* 1060; J. Diggle, 'Marginalia Euripidea', *PCPS*, NS 15 (1969), 30–59, at 53–5. Cropp 1988 on *El.* 1060 compares A. *Ag.* 810–28, where the φροίμιον occupies nearly half the speech, but the term there does not have the rhetorical connotations which it has at *El.* 1060.

[44] C. Collard, reviewing Diggle's OCT, *CR* 34 (1984), 13.

[45] Cf. Johansen 1959: 126 n. 80.

be joined with the Dioscuri in enjoying divine honours,[46] and she will be vindicated by them at the end of *Electra* (1280–3). Electra's comparison of Clytaemestra and Helen is thus, in a sense, proved wrong, although Castor does not pursue the implications of Helen's innocence for the rest of the play in any detail.[47]

Electra then expands on the accusation in her proem that the murder of Iphigenia was merely an excuse (1067), and argues that Clytaemestra had been adorning herself even before that, something that no respectable woman would do (1069–75). The question whether Clytaemestra's motive was revenge or adultery is much discussed in treatments of this myth,[48] and Electra's argument that adultery was the real motive cannot merely be put down to her obsession with sexual matters, although such factors may make the argument more appropriate in her mouth.[49]

Electra here differs from her Sophoclean counterpart in making no attempt to defend Agamemnon and concentrating her argument on attacking Clytaemestra. Otherwise, the two speeches cover basically the same ground, arguing that the murder of Iphigenia was not Clytaemestra's real motive, criticizing Aegisthus, discussing Clytaemestra's persecution of her children, and turning the *lex talionis* against her. The determination of Euripides' Electra to attack Clytaemestra rather than defend Agamemnon could be seen as due to her vindictiveness, but it is perhaps also her best line of argument. Euripides' secular reading of Agamemnon's dilemma, which is to be seen most clearly in *Iphigenia in Aulis*, makes it difficult to defend the murder of Iphigenia now that there is no longer the imperious divine command which is so prominent in Aeschylus. Electra is thus on firmer ground in trying to argue that Clytaemestra's motive was really adultery. The factual question of whether Clytaemestra really did behave in the manner alleged by Electra is left wholly unresolved. Clytaemestra does not contest Electra's accusations in the ensuing dialogue (1102–22), but she seems by then to have lost interest in arguments of this kind.

Electra continues her attack on Clytaemestra's character by arguing that she was pleased when the Trojans did well in the war, hoping that Agamemnon would not return (1076–85). This is another unverifiable assertion (compare *Tro.* 1002–9 for a rather similar accusation levelled at Helen). Electra goes on to argue that virtue would have been easy for

---

[46] Cf. Cropp 1988 on *El.* 1064.   [47] Cf. Erbse 1984: 172 n. 11.

[48] On Pindar *Pythian* 11. 22–4, see Garvie 1986: pp. xxiv f.; E. Robbins, 'Pindar's *Oresteia* and the Tragedians', in Conacher 1986: 1–11.

[49] On Electra's obsessions, see above n. 37, and also Wilamowitz 1883: 230; Arnott 1981: 184; Michelini 1987: 220; Winnington-Ingram 1980: 231.

Clytaemestra because Agamemnon was so distinguished, and would have been greatly renowned because of the contrast with Helen.[50] This concludes Electra's attack on the character of her mother, which parallels her speech over the body of Aegisthus and is perhaps elaborated in order to distract attention from the murder of Iphigenia.

The next section of Electra's speech (1086–93), which is generally parallel to S. *El.* 584–605, argues that the murder of Iphigenia (to which line 1086 is a fleeting and evasive reference) does not justify Clytaemestra's exclusion of her children, and her use of their inheritance to buy a husband.[51] If she were really so concerned with retributive justice for her children, then Aegisthus should have been exiled in return for the exile of Orestes, and killed in return for the fate of Electra herself, since she has suffered at his hands twice the death that Iphigenia suffered from Agamemnon (cf. 247, 914). Clytaemestra thus has no interest in justice for her children, alive or dead, but is only interested in Aegisthus.

Electra concludes (1093–6) by arguing that according to the *lex talionis* which Clytaemestra herself has invoked she should be killed by her children to avenge Agamemnon. A similar argument appears at S. *El.* 580–3, although there it is expressed more hesitantly. It is possible that in Sophocles the implications of this argument for Electra and Orestes themselves should not be considered,[52] but it is difficult to believe that they should not be considered here. The argument comes with great prominence at the end of Electra's speech, and she knows that Clytaemestra's death is imminent. The fallacy lies in Electra's use of the first person (ἀποκτενῶ 1094) but there is, of course, no one else who could take revenge. Line 1096 makes a powerful climax to Electra's speech, echoing the end of Clytaemestra's, and lines 1097–9 were thus rightly deleted by Hartung.[53] There is no need, however, for the additional deletion of 1100 f.[54] All agon speeches in Euripides are followed by a choral comment, and the comment here, while not especially profound, is consistent with the chorus' earlier reduction of the situation to marriage problems (1051–4). It remains possible that a different choral comment has been displaced. Their tone here is neutral, while earlier it was hostile

---

[50] Clytaemestra's hypocrisy at A. *Ag.* 874–6, 887–91 may have influenced Electra's attack here. The appeal to authority (1082, cf. *Alc.* 683 f., *Or.* 512) is a rhetorical device: see Carey 1989 on Lys. 1. 2.

[51] Cf. A. *Cho.* 132 f., 916 f.; Aélion 1983: i. 122 n. 56.

[52] Cf. Heath 1987: 136 f.

[53] Cf. Fraenkel 1946: 85 f. The lines are defended by Donzelli 1978: 175; de Romilly 1983.

[54] See Willink 1986 on *Or.* 602–4, 605–6.

to Clytaemestra, but this is not a real problem (compare *Med.* 520 f. and 575—7).

The agon concludes with a dialogue (1102—22), which differs from what is usual in the agon in that Clytaemestra becomes more conciliatory.[55] Normally, the hostility on both sides is increased, and there is violent antagonism in the corresponding section of the agon in Sophocles' *Electra*. There is then a subtle transition into a section (1123—40) which is not part of the agon, but is an example of a common type of scene, 'the mocking and luring of a doomed victim'.[56] There is, as often in such scenes, much use of irony, and it is interesting that in the corresponding scenes in Aeschylus and Sophocles it is Aegisthus who is the victim.

Many scholars have been impressed by the gentler side of Clytaemestra which reveals itself especially in this section.[57] She begins by refusing to be provoked by Electra's attack (1102—5), and then goes on to express regret for what she did (1105 f., 1109 f.). All this is in sharp contrast to Sophocles' ferocious Clytaemestra (e.g. S. *El.* 549—51), and also to the powerful figure in Aeschylus, although the latter does have a complex attitude towards the end of *Agamemnon*. The redeeming features of Euripides' Clytaemestra have sometimes been exaggerated. She may have saved Electra's life, but the Farmer is quick to disparage her motives (27—30), and lines 656—8 show only that Electra thinks that she will come to shed crocodile tears over her low-born grandchild. Even here, she seems rather impatient with Electra (e.g. 1128). Nevertheless, her attempts at conciliation are striking at a point in the agon when hostility is normally exacerbated, and her expression of fear (1114) and her concern for public opinion make her seem a human and vulnerable figure.[58] These more attractive features of Clytaemestra seem to be parallel to the amiable side of Aegisthus which was revealed shortly before his death.

The agon in *Electra* is in some ways similar to that in *Hippolytus*. Both take place after the death of the defendant has effectively been determined, but in neither is there any emphasis on the fact that the agon is therefore futile. The agon is not significant as the words of the characters at a particular moment, but as a portrayal, through the medium of formal debate, of a central conflict in the play.

---

[55] Cf. Schwinge 1968: 47—50. Weil's transposition of 1107 f. is well defended by Cropp ad loc.

[56] Cropp 1988 on *El.* 1102—46. Cf. Matthiesen 1964: 161—3.

[57] e.g. Wilamowitz 1883: 222 f.; Denniston 1939: p. xxx; O'Brien 1964: 21 f.; O. Zwierlein, reviewing Steidle 1968, *GGA* 222 (1970), 202; Lloyd-Jones 1971: 154. *Contra* Steidle 1968: 66; Aélion 1983: ii. 303—11.

[58] Steidle 1968: 66, and Aélion 1983: ii. 306 f., go too far in seeing Clytaemestra's more conciliatory tone as prompted only by Electra's death threat.

The agon in *Electra* is, however, more complex than that in *Hippolytus*, both in its dramatic context and in its content. In *Electra*, Clytaemestra has two opponents, not just one, and these two characters have different attitudes and motivations. The material of the dialogue between Orestes and Clytaemestra in Aeschylus' *Choephori* is divided by Euripides into two parts. Orestes' basic dilemma is treated in his dialogue with Electra as Clytaemestra enters, where it is clear that the deed is problematic because Clytaemestra is his mother and not because she displays this or that redeeming feature.[59] The agon, on the other hand, shows the conflict between Electra and Clytaemestra, and deals at greater length with the details of Clytaemestra's guilt. This material is not directly related to Orestes' dilemma, but does, in a sense, reflect it. For the first time in Euripides' extant agones there is a fine balance between the arguments of the two characters. Both are equipped with the rhetorical skills which they need to make their cases, and both make good points. This not only gives substance to the question of Clytaemestra's guilt, but also, through the impossibility of deciding which character is in the right, reflects the central dilemma of the play.

[59] Cf. Heath 1987: 60 n. 41 (overstated in some respects).

5

Political Debates: *Heraclidae, Supplices, Phoenissae*

THE agones in *Heraclidae*, *Supplices*, and *Phoenissae* form a distinct group, with more features in common with each other than with any of Euripides' other agones. In the first place, there is no obscurity about the relation of the agon to the action in any of these three plays. Demophon, Theseus, and Eteocles are confronted with strongly worded demands which are backed up by the threat of force; their rejection of these demands leads directly to armed conflict. The failure of debate to achieve reconciliation is itself an important theme in these three plays, since there is still the possibility of agreement when the agones begin. Elsewhere in Euripides, the agon tends to be detached even from the possibility of influencing the action.

Secondly, the formal structure of the agon in each of these three plays is in complete harmony with its subject matter. Formal arbitrations are being portrayed, and it is thus quite natural that the participants should make balancing rhetorical speeches. The formality of the agon is less plausible in naturalistic terms in such plays as *Electra*, where it is not especially likely that either character would make a set speech.

Thirdly, while most agones in Euripides are broadly related to the form of the trial, the agones in *Heraclidae*, *Supplices*, and *Phoenissae* are essentially deliberative. They are discussions about the proper course of action to be followed, rather than forensic debates about a specific crime.[1] This distinction should not, however, be pressed too hard, because consideration of the justice of past actions looms large in all three scenes. There are references to δίκη in *Heraclidae* at lines 138, 142 f., 179, 187, 190, 194, and 252–4. Similarly in *Supplices*, where Theseus stresses δίκη and νόμος (526, 530, 541, 563 f.), and in *Phoenissae*, where Polynices claims δίκη (490–3), Eteocles admits ἀδικία (524 f.), and Jocasta deals generally with the issues of justice and fairness (e.g. 532, 548 f.).

---

[1] On the contrast between forensic and deliberative speeches, see Ar. *Rh.* 1358^{b}13–17.

The parallels between Demophon, Theseus, and Eteocles serve also to bring out the differences between them. Demophon is plainly right to reject the demand of the Argive herald to give up the suppliants. Theseus is also right to insist on the burial of the corpses, but less obviously so, because he is obliged to interfere rather than merely to resist a demand. These two Athenian kings exemplify the pious response of Athens to supplication, and her support of the weak against tyrannical wrongdoers.[2] Eteocles' reaction resembles theirs in several ways, but the conflict in *Phoenissae* is more troubling and ambiguous, and his resistance of the demands of Polynices is more difficult to justify.[3]

HERACLIDAE

The agon in *Heraclidae* is the most straightforward in Euripides, clear-cut in its issues and regular in its form. There is no doubt which side is right, and Demophon assesses the issues correctly and makes the right decision. He is the model judge, listening to both sides and making a decision based on impeccable principles of rationality and justice.[4] Only Agamemnon in *Hecuba* approaches this standard, but his commitment to justice has not been at all consistent. Menelaus is an inadequate and indecisive judge in both *Troades* and *Orestes*, while Jocasta in *Phoenissae* makes an elaborate judgement but has no power to enforce it.

The agon in *Heraclidae* is also perfectly regular in form. It comes at the beginning of the first episode and expounds the basic conflict of the play. The formal structure is explicit. Demophon invites the Herald to speak (132 f.), and the latter announces in advance the purpose of his speech (135). The balance of speeches is emphasized by the chorus (179 f.) and by Iolaus (181–3), and agonistic terminology is applied to the proceedings. The speeches are of similar length, and Demophon's judgement speech is followed by stichomythia of an entirely regular kind. The balance and regularity of this structure is in itself significant, demonstrating as it does the fairness and impartiality of Athenian justice. The simplicity of this agon means that Euripides can rapidly expound the essential issues of the play,

[2] Cf. Zuntz 1955; Conacher 1967: 109.
[3] Cf. F. I. Zeitlin, 'Thebes: Theater of Self and Society in Athenian Drama', in J. P. Euben (ed.), *Greek Tragedy and Political Theory* (Berkeley/Los Angeles, 1986), 101–41, for the idea that Thebes 'provides the negative model to Athens's manifest image of itself with regard to its notions of the proper management of city, society, and self' (p. 102).
[4] Fitton 1961: 451 f. contrasts the more complex situation in *Supplices*.

and he does, in fact, manage to cover the basic ground of Aeschylus' *Supplices* by line 287.[5] This initial clarity becomes gradually more clouded as the play goes on, first with the need for human sacrifice, and then with the morally and structurally complex near-agon with Eurystheus at the end of the play. The pattern is somewhat similar to that in *Medea*, where a shift in sympathies is also expressed in the contrast between a one-sided agon and a more troubling near-agon at the end of the play.

The combination of an agon with supplication at an altar is common in tragedy.[6] Iolaus' prologue speech makes clear that the present situation has been repeated many times in the past (17–25). Athens is the last city to be approached by the suppliants (31, 151), which intensifies the crisis as well as glorifying Athens.[7]

The agon in *Heraclidae*, in some respects more rigidly formal than the agones in other early plays such as *Hippolytus* and *Andromache*, is in another way more naturalistic, since it is actually portraying a formal debate in which the participants might be expected to make set speeches. An impersonal tone is imparted by the involvement of the Herald, since heralds are primarily vehicles for arguments rather than individuals whose personal motives and characteristics command any interest in themselves. The Herald's speech here is thus governed primarily by the requirements of rhetoric. It has a clear rhetorical structure, and can be related to ancient rhetorical theory and practice.

Aristotle distinguished three types of oratory: forensic, deliberative, and epideictic.[8] The present speech clearly comes into the deliberative category. The deliberative speech deals with what is going to be done, and its τέλος is τὸ συμφέρον, while the forensic speech deals with what has been done, and its τέλος is τὸ δίκαιον.[9] Aristotle's terminology is useful for the analysis of actual speeches, although different characteristics cannot be apportioned quite so neatly to the three types, and *Rhetorica ad Alexandrum* admits a wider range of factors which are relevant in a deliberative speech, including justice and expediency.[10] Speakers in

---

[5] Cf. Burian 1977: 4.   [6] Cf. Strohm 1957: 17–32; Taplin 1977: 192 f.
[7] The patriotic commonplaces are conveniently summarized by Heath 1987: 65.
[8] Ar. *Rh*. 1358ᵃ36 ff. Cf. Kennedy 1963: 85–7, 117 f.
[9] On the τελικὰ κεφάλαια, see Radermacher 1951: C 62; Macleod 1983: 55 f.
[10] [Ar.] *Rh. Al.* 1421ᵇ20–33. Cf. 1424ᵇ27–1425ᵃ8 for a more specific discussion of speeches for or against alliances. G. Kennedy, 'Focusing of Arguments in Greek Deliberative Oratory', *TAPA* 90 (1959), 131–8, at 134 f. comments on the deliberative aspect of the Herald's speech in *Hcld.*, but he is wrong to say that the Herald concentrates entirely on expediency, and perhaps exaggerates the tendency of Greek oratory in the 5th century to focus on a single type of argument (cf. Kennedy 1963: 183). Cf. M. Heath, *Historia*, 39 (1990), 397–9.

Thucydides sometimes emphasize one factor to the exclusion of others: in the Corcyrean debate, for example, the Corcyreans' stress on expediency is more persuasive than the Corinthians' stress on justice (1. 32–43). In the Mytilenian debate, Diodotus' stress on expediency is also successful (3. 42–8). Ideally, however, the orator will try to show that the course of action which he recommends combines expediency with justice; examples of this in Thucydides are the Mytilenian speech at Olympia (3. 9–14) and the speech of Hermocrates at Camarina (6. 76–80).

The Herald in *Heraclidae* insists both on the justice of his cause and on the expediency for the Athenians of giving up the suppliants to Argos. After a short proem (134–7), the Herald asserts the justice and lawfulness of his case (137–43). His argument is that the suppliants have been condemned to death in Argos, and that the Argives have the right (δίκαιοι 142) to try their own people. After this fairly brief account of the justice of his case, the Herald moves on to a longer discussion of expediency (144–61). The first part of this section stresses that no other city has taken in the suppliants, and that it would be foolishness to do so. The second part explains why it would be foolish, contrasting the profits of surrendering the suppliants with the problems of taking them in (τί κερδανεῖς; 154. Cf. *Su.* 473 ff. for the contrast). The Herald contrasts the folly of interference (147, 150, 152) which is in fact just with the cleverness of self-interested action.[11]

In the next section of his speech (162–8), the Herald combines the concepts of justice and expediency when he rhetorically contrasts the claims of the suppliants with more obviously compelling reasons to fight. He also raises the important question of Demophon's accountability to his people. Demophon does, in fact, take personal responsibility here, in contrast to Theseus in *Supplices* who consults the people in advance. Later, however, Demophon explains that, while it is acceptable for him to involve the Athenians in a war on behalf of suppliants, there are some things that he could not ask them to do (410–24). The Herald's final argument stresses that any possible repayment by the children would be remote and uncertain (169–74). This argument about time recalls discussion of physical remoteness in speeches about alliances in Thucydides (e.g. 1. 36. 1; 3. 13. 5).[12] The conclusion of the speech combines the ideas of justice and expediency, exploiting the ambiguity of ἀμείνονας and κακίονας (174–8).

[11] On ἀβούλως (152), see Zuntz 1955: 34 n. 8; and, on this perversion of terms for intelligence, see Thuc. 3. 82. 4–5, 7; Macleod 1983: 126–31.
[12] Cf. [Ar.] *Rh. Al.* 1425ᵃ1-6; Macleod 1983: 88.

The proem to Iolaus' speech (181–3) serves not only to draw attention to the balance of speeches which is a feature of the Euripidean agon, but also makes it clear that the opportunity for speeches on both sides is characteristic of Athenian democracy.[13] The formality of the agon here is in itself significant. In the next section of his speech (184–91), Iolaus repudiates the section of the Herald's speech in which he appealed to justice and claimed Argive jurisdiction over the suppliants (137–43). Iolaus puts forward a legal argument against this, and appeals to justice himself (δικαίως 187, δικαιοῦτε 190). It is interesting that Demophon does not, in the event, decide in Iolaus' favour because he agrees with him on this narrower question of law and justice. Iolaus holds his own in this particular exchange with the Herald but, even if he had not done so, it seems that Demophon would have decided in his favour. Demophon accepts the suppliants primarily because they are suppliants, and not because of his views on the more technical details of their case (cf. 250–4). This point is not pressed here, but elaborate distinctions will be made in *Supplices* between the various reasons which might be relevant to Theseus' decision to help the suppliants.

The next section of Iolaus' speech is distinguished by his turning from Demophon to address the Herald directly (189–204).[14] This part of his speech answers the second main section of the Herald's speech (144–61), in which he pointed out that no other city had dared to confront the might of Argos on behalf of the suppliants, and criticized them for expecting Athens alone to be so foolish as to pity them. Iolaus' response to this is explicitly to distinguish Athens from other cities, and to argue that it would be a shameful loss of freedom for Athens to yield to Argos through fear. This is one of the three considerations which influences Demophon, and he echoes Iolaus' terminology in his judgement speech (242–6). The most important consideration for Demophon is one which Iolaus only touches on in his speech (196, 221, 224), the respect due to suppliants (cf. 238 f.). The third consideration (240 f.) is based on what Iolaus says in the next two sections of his speech, in which he stresses first the blood relationship between Demophon and the Heraclidae (205–12) and then the obligation of Theseus to Heracles (213–22).[15] This part of Iolaus' speech is, in a sense, an answer to the latter part of the Herald's speech in which he challenged Demophon to consider the reasons that he could give for

---

[13] On the Euripidean mannerism introduced by Wilamowitz's γάρ (181), see Pelliccia 1987: 43–5.

[14] See below, p. 98.

[15] On kinship as a secondary motive, see Mastronarde 1986: 209 n. 10. On the χάρις theme, see Zuntz 1955: 81–3; Conacher 1967: ch. 6.

helping the Heraclidae (162–74). His decision will be based on obligation rather than on profit, so the victory goes to τὸ δίκαιον rather than to τὸ συμφέρον. Iolaus concludes with an impassioned peroration (223–31).

Demophon's speech is a model of rationality and fairness, made without any of the anguish of Pelasgus in Aeschylus' *Supplices*. Problems only arise later in the play. The stichomythia which concludes the agon is very plain in style, and the end of the scene is clearly marked by the exit of the Herald and the choral anapaests.[16]

This agon has its counterpart in the near-agon at the end of the play where, as in *Medea*, a previously powerful and unsympathetic figure appears broken and defeated in the hands of a vengeful and unforgiving woman.[17] There is a similar effect in *Hecuba*, where there is a full agon at the end, although the reversal of sympathies is less marked. In both *Medea* and *Heraclidae* the woman disdains a full speech (*Med.* 1351–3, *Hcld.* 951 f.), and in both there are echoes of the earlier scene in the later (ὦ μῖσος *Hcld.* 52, 941, *Med.* 1323; ὦ παγκάκιστε *Med.* 465). The dialogue between Alcmene and the Servant recalls the stichomythia between the Herald and Demophon in the opposition of Greek law to vindictive claims purporting to be just (254–61, 961–74, cf. 1009–13). After Eurystheus has delivered what is essentially a full agonistic defence speech, the play concludes, as do *Medea* and *Hecuba*, with a human being performing the function of a *deus ex machina*.[18]

SUPPLICES

Theseus in *Supplices* faces a far less straightforward decision about whether to accept a supplication than did Demophon in *Heraclidae*. Rather than being threatened with invasion by an obvious villain, he is being asked to undertake an aggressive war in order to recover the bodies of men who died on a highly questionable expedition.

The agon with the Theban Herald does not take place until the second episode, and the earlier part of the play shows the development of the attitudes which Theseus expresses in that debate. This kind of development

---

[16] Cf. Ritchie 1964: 230; Schwinge 1968: 39 f. On the postponement of the tragic crisis, see Burian 1977: 8 n. 17.

[17] There are implausible defences of Alcmene by A. P. Burnett, 'Tribe and City, Custom and Decree in *Children of Heracles*', *CP* 71 (1976), 4–26, at 22–6, and Erbse 1984: 126–9. Contrast the more sensible views of Zuntz 1955: 35–8 and Burian 1977: 15–21.

[18] Cf. Knox 1979: 304 f.

is found in Euripides only here, and is very subtly portrayed. His agones normally portray a clash of long-held views, and certainly of views which had developed before the beginning of the play. In *Supplices*, on the other hand, Theseus begins by taking a harsh and critical attitude towards Adrastus, and only relents under the influence of his mother Aethra. The correct response is one which combines Theseus' initial awareness of the folly of the Seven with Aethra's pity for the mothers of the dead warriors and her piety towards the gods. Theseus' speech in the agon shows that he has now realized that he must help the suppliant women even though their sons died in a bad cause.

Aethra's presence in Athens is a novelty in the myth,[19] and Euripides uses her to express the instinctive pity which is one aspect of the correct response to the suppliant women. This pity is evident in her prologue speech, where her attitude is summed up in the key terms οἰκτίρουσα (34) and σέβουσα (36). She is moved by the contrast between her own actual and hoped-for prosperity and the suffering of the suppliants, and this contrast between suffering and prosperity is an important theme in the play (3, 5, 124, 166, 176–9, 225, 269 f., 328–31, 463 f., 728–30, 734 ff.). The Thebans show ὕβρις in prosperity, whereas one should in fact recognize the dependence of human prosperity on the gods. Aethra is aware of the suffering of the women (11, 13, etc.), and describes the expedition only as δυστυχεστάτην (22). Her piety is clear as she begins with a prayer, refers to an oracle piously accepted (7), and comments on the impiety of the non-burial (19).

The prologue thus adumbrates some of the questions of which Theseus will have to take account, and the first episode shows the formation of the attitudes which he will express in the agon. This episode has a symmetrical structure, contrasting the unsuccessful plea of Adrastus with the successful plea of Aethra. Theseus shows some initial signs of pity (96, 104) and recognizes that the corpses should be buried (123), but he cannot see what this has to do with him (108, 127), and he also establishes that the expedition set out in defiance of the gods (155–61).

Adrastus' speech (163–92) is a plea for pity (168) which does not depend on any claim about the justice of the original expedition.[20] Theseus replies as a δικαστής (253) in an intellectual and unsympathetic manner.[21] His

---

[19] Cf. Collard 1975b: 5 n. 11.

[20] On the importance of pity (*Su.* 168, 179, 194, 280 f.), see Macleod 1983: 74 f., 96, 112 f., 121 f.

[21] On the rhetorical device of beginning with reference to one's own previously stated opinions (*Su.* 195 f.), see Macleod 1983: 92.

abstract and apparently irrelevant response recalls his manner at *Hi.* 916 ff., and the way in which he speaks makes a character point in both cases. In the present case, Mastronarde has convincingly associated him with Jocasta in *Phoenissae* and Tiresias in *Bacchae* as an 'optimistic rationalist' who believes that 'the world is orderly and comprehensible and that there are elements in that order which have been fashioned for the good of man'.[22] Theseus thus argues that things are basically good, so that it needs positive folly to fall into misfortune, and that this is especially so because uncertain decisions can be aided by augury. Risky behaviour would be justified only if things were generally bad, and if one had no divine assistance in making decisions. Theseus thinks that there are clear-cut distinctions between the prosperous and the wretched, and between the just and the unjust, and his analysis of the three classes (238–45) again shows his propensity for confident theorizing and clear distinctions.[23] The abstract and discursive tone precisely suits Theseus' detachment and high-mindedness, but his fine-sounding sentiments are, in fact, inadequate as a response in the present case, and he takes a very different line later.[24]

Mastronarde points out that his attitude here is taken up by the Herald in the agon, in which Theseus himself has a more generous attitude that takes account of the instability of human fortune.[25] This is not to say that Theseus' immediate response to Adrastus' plea is entirely wrong. His condemnation of the expedition of the Seven is appropriate enough, and something more is certainly needed than Aethra's undifferentiated pity. His mistake is to allow his justified criticism of Adrastus to lead to the conclusion that he has no obligation to ensure that the corpses are buried (compare the response of the chorus at 250 f.). The correct response which Theseus eventually adopts combines his own strongly defined sense of right and wrong with Aethra's awareness of the uncertainty of human life. Her speech (297–331) makes it clear why Theseus should accept the supplication despite his belief that the expedition was wrong. She refers to the gods (301 f., cf. *Hcld.* 238 f.), to the laws of Greece (306–13), to shame (314–20, cf. *Hcld.* 242–6),[26] and to the naturally enterprising spirit of Athens.[27] This last point is important, since Athens is being asked to interfere and not merely, as in other suppliant plays, to defend people who are being attacked.

---

[22] Mastronarde 1986: 202.   [23] Cf. ibid. 203.
[24] Cf. Strohm 1957: 22 f. For a useful discussion of the structure of *Su.* 219–37, see Johansen 1959: 38–42.
[25] Mastronarde 1986: 204.   [26] Cf. Dover 1974: 226–9.
[27] On the connotations of the contrast between πόνος and ἡσυχία, see Gomme 1956 on Thuc. 1. 70. 8; Ehrenberg 1947; Collard 1975b on *Su.* 324–5, 577; Bond 1981 on *HF* 266.

Theseus is persuaded by Aethra's arguments, and his speech (334–64) echoes her concern for what people will say (314, 343) and her reference to πόνος (319, 342, cf. 373 f., 394). The other reason which he gives for accepting the supplication is respect for his mother (344, 359–64), and he makes only the most fleeting reference to the question of the justice of the cause which he is undertaking (341). He does, however, show in the agon that he has taken in others of Aethra's arguments, referring to Panhellenic law at 526 (cf. 311), instability at 549–57 (cf. 331), and to εὐκλεία and πόνος at 573–7 (cf. 315, 317). Theseus' speech also shows the importance of persuasion. He himself is persuaded by Aethra (334–6), he will in turn persuade the people of Athens (355), and his first approach to the Thebans will be by means of persuasion (347). His attempt to persuade the Thebans is, in effect, the agon. Theseus' willingness to change his mind in response to persuasion not only helps to distinguish the various issues that are involved in his acceptance of the supplication, but also illustrates one of the main qualities of democracy.[28]

Theseus is in the process of formulating a moderate and polite request to Creon when the Theban Herald bursts in (381–94, cf. 668–74). The agon thus develops as a response by Theseus to the demands of the Herald and not, as would be more natural, the other way round. The impression of Athenian aggression and interference is thus further mitigated. The scene has a unique structure in that Theseus and the Herald have two distinct debates, the first on the relative merits of tyranny and democracy, and the second on the immediate issue of the burial. The democracy debate is subordinate, both in length and in relevance, and corresponds structurally to the preliminary skirmishing that takes place before the main speeches in most agones. The second agon in *Andromache* (547–746) also has two pairs of speeches, in this case on the same subject and with the main speeches coming first, so that the subordinate pair of speeches corresponds to the angry dialogue that normally concludes an agon. The structure of the agon in *Supplices* is clearly marked (457, 465 f.), as if Euripides were being careful to signpost the way through this rather unusual scene.

This scene has a more abstract tone than most agones in Euripides, partly because of the participation of a herald, and partly because Theseus has a propensity for abstract theorizing. The formality of the agon is natural here, as it was in *Heraclidae*, since a diplomatic exchange of this kind will naturally take place through conflicting formal speeches.[29] Theseus takes part in the agon himself, and does not merely arbitrate as Demophon did

---

[28] Cf. Zuntz 1955: 7–9.   [29] Contrast Collard 1975b: 27 f.

in *Heraclidae*, in order to keep the guilty Adrastus at a distance and to make it clear that the issue of burial is separate from the question of the justice of the original expedition.

The democracy debate is the most extreme example in Euripides of the agon as abstract debate, apparently detached from the issues of the play.[30] Theseus himself comments on the irrelevance of this discussion, and he blames the detour on the garrulousness of the Herald (426–8, 456–62, cf. 567). Whatever Euripides' own taste for abstract debate, the indulgence in it here is explicitly treated as a feature of the characters in the play. The Herald is criticized for digressing, and Theseus himself has already revealed a tendency to engage in political theorizing. The democracy debate is not, however, introduced for the purpose of characterizing the participants. The relevance of the issues themselves is difficult to dispute, and Euripides characterizes Theseus and the Herald just enough to lessen the improbability of their engaging in a full discussion of these issues at this particular moment. The relevance of this debate lies in the fact that *Supplices* uses the narrower issue of burial to illustrate the contrast between a tyrannical wrongdoer and a pious democracy which interferes to do right. This particular act of interference was central to the Athenian democratic myth, and its significance can be understood only in the context of a more general discussion of democracy.[31]

The democracy debate develops in a fairly natural way, with speeches of 4, 6, 17, and 37 lines and no choral distich between the speeches. One effect of this is to avoid giving the impression that any of these are the main speeches of the agon, and Theseus is careful to mark this as a digression (426–8, 456–62). His short introductory speech (403–8) contains several significant terms from what must have been a lively contemporary debate on the virtues and vices of democracy: δῆμος ἀνάσσει (406, cf. 352 f., 442), ruling ἐν μέρει (406, cf. *Pho.* 478, 486), πλεῖστον and ἴσον (408, cf. *Pho.* 538–40).[32] The image of the tyrant was typically used in discussions of this kind to highlight the positive features of democracy, even though tyranny was not actually a danger in Athens after the Persian Wars.[33]

The Herald's speech (409–25) stresses the self-consciously competitive aspect of the agon, and this looks forward, as in *Phoenissae*, to the armed conflict. He answers Theseus point by point, replacing the stock democratic

---

[30] Cf. Schlegel 1909: 140; Duchemin 1968: 132–5; Conacher 1981: 23–5; Heath 1987: 134.
[31] Cf. Zuntz 1955: 8; Collard 1975b: 207–9.
[32] Cf. Finley 1967: 21–8; Collard 1975b: 212; Loraux 1986: ch. 4.
[33] Cf. V. J. Rosivach, *QUCC*, NS 30 (1988), 43–57; Brock 1989: 160 f.

vocabulary with tyrannical equivalents: ὄχλος (411) for δῆμος (406), πονηρός (424) for πένης (408), and ἀμείνων (423) for πλοῦτος (407).[34] The problem of the demagogue swaying the assembly for private gain (413) has already been recognized as a problem by Theseus (236 f.), and was a feature of contemporary Athens.[35] The glib demagogue, mentioned by the Herald (412–16), appears again at *Or.* 903, and often in Thucydides, Aristophanes, and Plato, and διαβολαῖς (415) evokes Cleon.[36] Advice against τάχυς (419) is respectable enough (cf. *Pho.* 452 f.). The problem of part-time politicians (417–22) is recognized in Pericles' Funeral Speech and in Plato's *Protagoras*.[37] The Herald's speech describes many features of the real Athens, reflected also in the Argos of the play (see, e.g., 232–45), although Athenian democracy in the play is seen in an ideal light.[38]

Theseus' speech in reply consists mainly of an attack on tyranny, which has its own headline, connected with what follows by ὅπου,[39] and self-referential conclusion (456). Theseus begins (426–8) and ends (457–62) with criticism of the Herald's verbosity, which justifies the digression and also has a rhetorical function of its own.[40] Theseus does not answer the Herald's specific criticisms of democracy but gives a general defence of it, using tyranny as a foil. In the agon of *Orestes*, Orestes similarly ignores the specific points made by Tyndareus and advances an argument on his own terms. Stock ideas and words recur, which were already sketched in his first reply to the Herald: the importance of νόμος, ἰσότης both in the assembly and in the lawcourts,[41] and the contrasting attitudes to young citizens of tyrants and democracies.

The transition from the democracy debate is very clearly marked (456–66), and the Herald begins his main speech by demanding the expulsion of Adrastus, forbidding Athenian interference in burying the corpses, and offering the choice between peace and war (467–75). The agon is organized so that the Herald makes the demands, and thus speaks first, and this has the effect of mitigating what might have seemed to be Athenian aggression and interference. The Herald goes on to warn against the irrational emotions which blind people to reason (476–85). This is

---

[34] Cf. W. D. Smith, 'Expressive Form in Euripides' *Suppliants*', *HSCP* 71 (1966), 151–70, at 169 n. 17.   [35] Cf. Willink 1986 on *Or.* 902–16.
[36] Cf. Finley 1967: 23, 29.   [37] Cf. Loraux 1986: 183 f.
[38] Cf. Fitton 1961: 433; R. B. Gamble, 'Euripides' *Suppliant Women*: Decision and Ambivalence', *Hermes*, 98 (1970), 385–405, at 399 f.; M. H. Shaw, 'The ἦθος of Theseus in *The Suppliant Women*', *Hermes*, 110 (1982), 3–19.
[39] See above, p. 66.   [40] See above, p. 26.
[41] See Collard 1975b: 226. Note that ἴσος means 'equal' at 434, 'fair' at 432, 441. On 432, see M. Lloyd, 'A Note on Menander, *Epitrepontes* 348', *ZPE* 67 (1987), 11 f.

sensible advice, recalling Theseus' admonition of Adrastus (232–45), as indeed is much of the Herald's speech.[42] This section of the Herald's speech shows the relevance of the democracy debate, in that he regards the democrat as prone to θυμός because of a belief in freedom (477 sarcastically recalls 405). He also thinks that the democratic assembly is especially likely to engage in aggressive warfare because of ἐλπίς (note the references to voting at 481 and 484). These criticisms are highly applicable to the Athens of Euripides' own day, although the decision to fight in the play is in fact taken sensibly and correctly. The whole debate is much more subtle than the agon in *Heraclidae* because of this awareness of the potential failings of democracy.[43] The Herald goes on to discuss the advantages of peace over war (486–93), worthy sentiments which also echo Theseus' condemnation of aggressive war in his speech to Adrastus (229–37). The crucial point, however, is that Theseus only condemns war that is unjust and against the will of the gods. He does not advocate the ἡσυχία and avoidance of πόνοι to which Adrastus later seems to be converted (949–54). The Herald's superficially plausible argument tries to obscure the fact that there is sometimes need for an aggressive just war. He goes on to argue that the Seven were villains who were justly punished by the gods (494–505). This echoes, again, Theseus' speech to Adrastus, which came to the conclusion (246–9) that Adrastus' injustice and folly meant that his supplication should be rejected. The chorus rightly observes that the Seven may have deserved to die, but should not be left unburied (511 f.). Creon's opening speech in Sophocles' *Antigone* also uses basically admirable sentiments to arrive at the unacceptable conclusion of non-burial. The Herald ends his speech with an elaborate gnomic conclusion (506–10), in which highly respectable ideas are combined with emotive words for inactivity (ἥσυχος, προμηθία).[44]

The choral distich which standardly separates speeches in the Euripidean agon is followed by a surprising intervention by Adrastus, quickly silenced by Theseus (513–16). This serves to clarify still further the reasons why it is right for Theseus to get involved. He is not taking the side of Adrastus as such, but is concerned with justice and religious propriety, and his intervention is distinguished from Adrastus' enmity towards Thebes (cf. 523, 589–93). He makes a point-by-point reply (cf. 517), which begins

[42] Cf. Fitton 1961: 433 f.
[43] Loraux 1986: 206, 216 f. observes that the Herald expresses criticisms of democracy which are implicit in funeral speeches.
[44] Cf. C. W. Willink, 'The Goddess ΕΥΛΑΒΕΙΑ and Pseudo-Euripides in Euripides' *Phoenissae*', *PCPS*, NS 36 (1990), 182–201.

by responding to the Herald's peremptory tone, signalled by such terms as ἀπαυδῶ (467). (Compare Demophon's reaction at *Hcld.* 286 f. to a similar attempt at bullying). Theseus' response here shows also that he has taken in Aethra's remarks about the criticisms for cowardice to which he will be exposed if he does not intervene (314 ff.). In the next section of his speech (522–7), Theseus denies that he is a warmonger and distinguishes his preservation of Panhellenic law from the aggressive war waged by Adrastus. This not only answers the Herald's warning against making war (476–93), but also shows that he has accepted Aethra's injunction to defend Panhellenic law (311–13). He answers the Herald's attack on the Seven (494–505) by pointing out that they have already been justly punished, and that non-burial does not harm Argos but offends against the gods and the laws (528–41; cf. S. *Aj.* 1343 f.). He reinforces this point with a *reductio ad absurdum* (542–8). His reflections on the mutability of life (549–57) show, again, that he has learnt from Aethra (331, cf. 1 ff.),[45] and his conclusion shows his concern for law and for the gods (558–63).

Theseus' speech is a convincing refutation, looking forward to his victory in battle (for which agonistic terminology is used at lines 637, 665, 706, and 754). He is unique in Euripides in that the attitudes which he expresses in the agon are shown developing in the earlier part of the play. One effect of this is to show his amenability to persuasion, a crucial democratic virtue. Secondly, the correct attitude at which he eventually arrives can be contrasted with incorrect or incomplete responses expressed earlier by himself, by Adrastus, and by Aethra. Adrastus appealed purely for pity, and reacted impatiently to Theseus' moralistic response (253–62). Aethra felt pity for the suppliants, but also introduced the idea of the laws and the gods. Theseus took in her points, as was argued above, but his speech in the agon goes well beyond anything that she said. He achieves a sense of perspective which combines an awareness of the guilt of the Seven (528–30) with a full understanding of the various reasons why they should be buried.

PHOENISSAE

Phoenissae resembles *Heraclidae*, *Supplices*, and other suppliant plays in that a crisis is portrayed, the theatening character appears, an agon takes place which serves only to exacerbate the situation, and armed conflict is needed to provide a solution. In Aeschylus' *Septem*, on the other hand, the brothers

---

[45] Cf. Mastronarde 1986: 204.

do not meet before their duel, although there is a precedent in Stesichorus for an attempt at arbitration between the brothers by their mother.[46] In Stesichorus, however, the meeting takes place before Polynices goes into exile, and it is characteristic of Euripides, whether or not it is an innovation, to have the meeting only after the quarrel has reached a point at which it is unlikely to be settled by discussion.

It is predictable that there will be an agon between the brothers from the moment when Jocasta says in the prologue that Polynices is coming into Thebes under a truce (81–3, cf. 97 f., 170 f.).[47] The agon is indeed the first climax of the play, but it is delayed for 350 lines and the effect of this intervening material is on the whole to favour Polynices. Jocasta has already made it clear that Eteocles is completely in the wrong in having breached their agreement (69–76), and this impression is reinforced by the Paedagogus (154 f.) and by the chorus (258–60). The idea of the voluntary exile is present already at *Su.* 151, 931, and it is not clear how far Euripides is innovating in adopting this tragic version in which the brothers make a vain attempt to avoid the effects of the curse.[48] He has, at any rate, adopted a version of the myth which is very favourable to Polynices.[49] Some scholars have argued that this does no more than to achieve a balance of sympathies between the brothers, since Eteocles has a natural advantage in defending the city.[50] The change of emphasis from Aeschylus should not, in any case, be exaggerated, since Eteocles has a darker side even there while Polynices claims justice (A. *Se.* 637 ff.). In Euripides, Polynices is clearly right in the quarrel itself, and the real problem is whether this justifies his invasion of Thebes.[51]

The teichoscopia presents the Argive army through the eyes of the enthusiastic and impressionable Antigone rather than, as in Aeschylus'

---

[46] On the Lille fragment of Stesichorus, see P. J. Parsons, 'The Lille "Stesichorus"', *ZPE* 26 (1977), 7–36. On the authorship, see M. L. West, 'Stesichorus at Lille', *ZPE* 29 (1978), 1–4.

[47] Mastronarde 1974: 81 writes of 'a gradual gathering of forces' in the first episode, with renewed separation at the end of the play. On the structure of the play, see also Ludwig 1957: 130, who observes that it has a centrepiece dealing with the salvation of Thebes (638–1066), with three important choral odes (on which, see further Arthur 1977). This centrepiece is surrounded by the parallel confrontations of the brothers in the agon and in the duel.

[48] Mueller-Goldingen 1985: 28 n. 48 argues (against Stephanopoulos 1980: 114 f.) that the glancing allusions to voluntary exile in *Supplices* do not imply that it is already an established version. On the myth generally, see Mueller-Goldingen 1985: 14–36; Hutchinson 1985 on A. *Se.* 631–52.

[49] Cf. Mueller-Goldingen 1985: 28.

[50] e.g. de Romilly 1965: 31 f.; Aélion 1983: i. 197–228.

[51] Arthur 1975: ch. 4 makes some interesting criticisms of Polynices, but fails to distinguish between the justice of his claim and the problem of his invasion of Thebes.

Septem, in a context where Eteocles can interpret and control the threat which it presents.[52] She is also, however, aware of the menace of such characters as Parthenopaeus (151–3) and Capaneus (182–92). A similar ambiguity is to be found in the second half of the parodos, where the chorus evokes the threat posed by Polynices but also recognizes that his cause is just (239–60). His entrance is announced at the end of the parodos,[53] where ἀγῶνα (259) refers to the imminent armed conflict but perhaps also hints at the verbal contest which is its counterpart. There is a marked contrast between the nervous Polynices who now enters and the glittering figure described by Antigone (167–9), but his cautious entrance is not necessarily unheroic and he shows no lack of courage in the duel.[54] The agon is further delayed by a lengthy scene between Polynices and Jocasta, which fills in details of the background to his story and arouses sympathy for him as a long-lost son.[55] The long and intellectual stichomythia resembles that before the agon in *Orestes*, and contains hints of the dark side to Polynices (e.g. 411–22), which occur occasionally in the earlier part of the play despite its generally favourable presentation of him.[56]

The speech with which Jocasta introduces the agon (452–68) establishes the significance of its formal tone and structure. She has organized an arbitration (436, 443, 445, 468),[57] in which the brothers might set out their positions in a measured way (the βραδεῖς μῦθοι of 453). The balance of speeches which is characteristic of the agon is thus, as in *Heraclidae* and *Supplices*, a natural feature of the situation being portrayed. Jocasta's explicit introduction (465–8) makes it clear in advance that there will be a balanced pair of speeches, and the scene has an obvious symmetry as she makes a chiastic reply of 58 lines to her sons' opposing speeches of 28 and 27 lines respectively. Jocasta makes it clear that the agon is a trial as well as an arbitration when she invites Polynices as plaintiff to speak first, and hopes that a god will be κριτής as well as διαλλακτής (467 f.).

Jocasta's main term of commendation in this speech is σοφός (453, 460, cf. 86, 394, 530, and her criticism of ἀμαθία at 569 f. and 584), although this reflects more the prevailing intellectualism of Euripides' plays than a distinctive attitude of hers.[58] Her formal introduction not only naturalizes

---

[52] See Goff 1988: 136 for a discussion of Eteocles' loss of status as an interpreter in *Phoenissae*.
[53] See Taplin 1977: 174 on the lyric entrance announcement here.
[54] Cf. Mastronarde 1974: 82; M. Lloyd 1986: 11.
[55] Cf. Mastronarde 1974: 93 f.
[56] On lines 438–42 (del. Leidloff), see Mastronarde 1986: 210 n. 18.
[57] Cf. de Romilly 1965: 28 n. 3.
[58] Cf. Σ *Med.* 665 (Schwartz ii. 177); Winnington-Ingram 1948: 19–21, 162–70; Bond 1981 on *HF* 1254; Willink 1986 on *Or.* 397; Goff 1988: 147 f.

the agon, but also lends significance to the tone and manner of the two brothers. She has encouraged them to forget their grievances and to look one another in the eye, but what they do is to speak in chilly and formal tones, addressing their speeches to her, and referring to each other in the third person with the forensic ὅδε.[59]

Polynices' speech has a clarity of structure which reflects what he sees as the simplicity and justice of his claim.[60] Balancing proem and epilogue frame two central sections which give his account of the situation and his proposal of what should happen.[61] His proem makes the stock rhetorical contrast between the simplicity of the just speech and the sophistries needed by the unjust, and this rhetorical background is emphasized by his use of the term καιρός.[62] His point is that telling the truth is in itself to say what is rhetorically appropriate for the matter in hand, and he does indeed deliver one of the simplest agon speeches in Euripides. This apparent simplicity does, however, conceal the disturbing aspects of what Polynices is doing. He is convincing enough on those aspects of the situation where he is indisputably in the right, but he never faces up to the question whether the justice of his claim can justify the invasion of Thebes. His disingenuousness is revealed in this speech only by what he leaves out, but the complexity of his position is betrayed elsewhere by his use of a variety of linguistic devices of a less straightforward kind, including oxymoron (272, 357, 377, 431, 1446),[63] alliteration (437, 488 f.), artificial contrasts (360, 389, 433 f.), and double meaning (1450). It is open to dispute whether these features of Polynices' speech show his self-awareness[64] or undermine the impression of directness and simplicity given by the proem of his speech in the agon.[65]

Polynices' account of the situation (473–83), agreeing as it does with Jocasta's version in her prologue speech (69–76), is evidently correct.[66] His passion and sincerity is perhaps revealed in the rambling and uncoordinated structure of the sentence which makes up most of this

[59] See Ant. 5. 8, 9, 17; Lys. 3. 44 f., etc. Cf. Rawson 1970: 115 f.; Mastronarde 1974: 99; Craik 1988 on *Pho.* 454.
[60] Cf. Ludwig 1957: 42 f.; Johansen 1959: 138–40.
[61] On the structure of Polynices' speech, see above, p. 24.
[62] On the rhetorical use of καιρός see Radermacher 1951: B VII 24; Kennedy 1963: 66 f.; Macleod 1983: 52.
[63] On oxymora in Euripides, see Kannicht 1969 on *Hel.* 138.
[64] Thus Mastronarde 1974: 82 f.
[65] Thus Arthur 1975: 104 f.; Goff 1988: 142.
[66] A minor difference is that Polynices stresses his own foresight (cf. Arthur 1975: 105). On ἐγὼ δέ (473) marking the transition from the proem to the main body of a speech, see Denniston 1954: 170 f.

section of his speech.[67] The next section (484–93) is not so much a discussion as a plain proposal of what he wants, and it rapidly takes a rather sinister turn. He is prepared to send the army out of the land, which he cannot do at S. *OC* 1418 f., but it is worrying when he then contemplates with apparent equanimity the prospect of sacking his fatherland (488–91). This seems to come as a calculated shock after the moderation of his earlier proposals, and shows up the difficulties of his position. He concludes this section with an appeal to the gods as witnesses, and the whole speech with an epilogue balancing the prologue (ἔνδικα 470, 496; σοφῶν 472, cf. σοφοῖς 495).[68]

Eteocles' speech also has a balancing proem and epilogue, and his proem is a direct answer to Polynices'.[69] This proem, reflecting developments in late fifth-century thought which are charted by Thucydides, denies the objectivity of values altogether. Eteocles thus differs from a villain such as Jason, who lays claim, however implausibly, to the usual epithets of commendation (*Med.* 548–50). He does, in fact, have a point that things are not as simple as Polynices had tried to make out, and, whatever the reason, ἔρις is precisely what we have in the present case (351, 811). 'If the same thing were by nature fine and wise for everyone, there would not be contentious strife for men. But as it is, there is nothing either similar or equal for mortals, except in name; the actuality is not thus.' In other words, we have only terms in common, but these terms do not refer to objective values shared by everyone. There is thus a strong contrast between ἔφυ (499, cf. 469) and ὀνόμασαι (502), and ὅμοιον and ἴσον (501) correspond to ταὐτό (499). This gives appropriate and relevant sense. Ambiguity is, however, occasioned by the use of ἴσον (501). According to the interpretation given above, ἴσον means 'equal' in a fairly neutral sense. This word is, however, also a key value term in this scene, used already by Polynices (487) and prominent in Jocasta's arbitration speech. We could thus, adopting an alternative explanation offered by the scholiast, take ὅμοιον (501) as also implying something like 'fair', so that Eteocles is saying that there is no objective fairness or equality in nature but that these are mere names. In Theseus' speech in the democracy

---

[67] The χρῄζων clause seems to go with both main verbs, and there are two possible punctuations. Mastronarde 1974: 398–401 follows Hermann in taking πάτρος δωμάτων as partitive, and in his Teubner text he prints a colon after ποτε. Pearson, ad loc., followed by Johansen 1959: 139 n. 124, has a colon after τοῦδ᾽, and this is equally plausible.

[68] On φαῦλος as the antithesis of σοφός in Euripides, see Dodds 1960 on *Ba.* 430–3.

[69] Compare the agon in *Iphigenia in Aulis*, where both speeches also begin with a generalization followed by a sharp break. Cf. Johansen 1959: 158.

debate in *Supplices*, ἴσος means 'equal' at line 434 and 'fair' at lines 432 and 441. This interpretation gives Eteocles a crisper denial of the precise value which Polynices had stressed. Eteocles' own language does, in any case, exemplify the very problems about which he is speaking.

The main body of Eteocles' speech begins with the common rhetorical claim not to hide anything (503), and he is indeed fairly candid. The deified personification of Τυραννίς (cf. Εὐλάβεια 782) is a sign of his advanced ideas, and also implies that there are no other gods of comparable importance of which to be afraid.[70] Euripides, as often (compare the agon in *Troades*), does not clarify the relationship between advanced religious ideas expressed in one part of a play and more traditional notions in other parts of it. Eteocles proceeds to live up to the principles enunciated in his proem by redefining moral terms in an idiosyncratic way, describing tyranny as τὸ χρηστόν and giving up τὸ πλέον as ἀνανδρία.

He then speaks of the shame for himself and for Thebes if he were to give up tyranny through fear of Polynices' military force. Eteocles' reasoning recalls that of Demophon in *Heraclidae* and Theseus in *Supplices*, both of whom are also confronted by demands from a threatening character backed by force of arms. His refusal to give up his tyranny, naturally using such words as παρίημι and μεθίημι (508, 514, 519, 523), recalls Demophon's refusal to give up the suppliants (using similar language at *Hcld.* 243 and 266). Eteocles invokes Tyranny as τὴν θεῶν μεγίστην (506), recalling Demophon's appeal in the first instance (τὸ μέγιστον *Hcld.* 238) to Zeus, and Aethra's advice to Theseus to honour πρῶτα μὲν τὰ τῶν θεῶν (*Su.* 301). The possibility of a charge of ἀνανδρία influences both Eteocles (*Pho.* 509) and Theseus (*Su.* 314), and neither they nor Demophon will yield through fear (ὄκνῳ *Hcld.* 245; φόβῳ *Pho.* 514; δείσας *Su.* 316). All three are influenced by αἰσχύνη (*Hcld.* 200, 223, 242; *Su.* 314–19, 343–5; *Pho.* 510), and all three express a preference for peaceful persuasion over violence (*Hcld.* 250–2; *Su.* 346–8; *Pho.* 515–17). Eteocles thus resembles Demophon and Theseus in basing his position on respect for the gods and for what he sees as the supreme values, in feeling shame at the accusations of cowardice that would be prompted by yielding to the threat of force, and in reproaching his adversary for using force rather than persuasion. Eteocles' god, however, is Tyranny, he redefines justice as cowardice (cf. Thuc. 3. 82. 4), and it is only his breach of an agreement that prompts Polynices' threat of force.

Eteocles' speech is not actually inconsistent, but it undoubtedly contains changes of emphasis as he uses a variety of arguments to justify his

---

[70] See Kannicht 1969 on *Hel.* 559–60; Bond 1981 on *HF* 166; Craik 1988 on *Pho.* 506.

retention of tyranny.⁷¹ His denial of objective values in the proem of his speech, recalling the relativism of such thinkers as Protagoras, aims primarily to undermine Polynices' confident appeal to absolute standards of justice.⁷² This proem also serves to introduce his own unorthodox views, implying as it does that different people have different values.⁷³ He himself regards tyranny as the supreme good, and he redefines ἀνανδρία in terms of this.⁷⁴ This section of his speech is consistent with his proem if he is supposed merely to be outlining what is καλόν and σοφόν for him, without claiming any objective validity for it. This is not, admittedly, the impression conveyed by the extremely assertive tone of these lines. The views expressed in them do, indeed, resemble those of Callicles in Plato's *Gorgias*, who argues that it is δίκαιον that τὸν κρείττω τοῦ ἥττονος ἄρχειν καὶ πλέον ἔχειν (cf. *Pho.* 509 f.).⁷⁵ Callicles is certainly not a relativist, and he offers a confident redefinition of value terms. The main difference between Callicles' views and those which Eteocles expresses in this section of his speech is that Eteocles does not make the distinction between νόμος and φύσις.

In the last two lines of his speech (524 f.), Eteocles puts forward a different type of view, asserting that if one has to do injustice one should do so for the sake of tyranny and act justly otherwise. He still regards tyranny as the supreme good, but is less confident now about redefining subordinate values in terms of it. He admits that injustice may be necessary as a means to tyranny, and the defiant tone of the end of his speech rather suggests that he admits that his tyranny itself is unjust.⁷⁶ This would resemble the praise of injustice by Thrasymachus in Plato's *Republic*. Eteocles' use of sophistic arguments to justify tyranny has naturally prompted comparison with the attitude of the Athenians in Thucydides, and especially in the Melian Dialogue (5. 85–111).⁷⁷ There are, however, many differences of detail. The Athenians do not deny that there is an absolute standard of τὸ δίκαιον and τὸ καλόν (e.g. 5. 107), but they argue that these fine-sounding terms have little relevance to the way in which people actually

---

⁷¹ Mastronarde 1974: 101 comments on Eteocles' speech being 'unorganized and emotional (even irrational)', undercutting his brand of σοφία.

⁷² On sophistic relativism, see Guthrie 1971: 164–75; Kerferd 1981: ch. 9.

⁷³ On γάρ (503) introducing an example, see Denniston 1954: 66.

⁷⁴ Cf. Guthrie 1971: 105 n. 1.

⁷⁵ Pl. *G.* 483d5–6. Cf. Dodds 1959: 14 ff.; T. H. Irwin (ed.), *Plato: Gorgias* (Oxford, 1979), on 483b; Ostwald 1986: 307 ff.

⁷⁶ Compare the attitude of Odysseus at S. *Phil.* 82–5. On κάλλιστον (*Pho.* 525), see Adkins 1960: 158–61.

⁷⁷ e.g. Rawson 1970: 123 f.; Finley 1967: 42. On the Melian Dialogue generally, see de Romilly 1951: 250–7; Macleod 1983: ch. 8.

behave (5. 89). They believe that everyone actually follows τὸ συμφέρον (5. 90), one aspect of this being the law of nature that the strong rule the weak (5. 105. 2), and they regard as hypocrites those who claim to be following the dictates of justice when in fact they are only doing what is expedient for themselves (5. 105. 4). These cynical realists would have little regard for Eteocles' excitable use of value terms, and in particular for the influence on him of αἰσχύνη (cf. 5. 101; 111. 3).

Jocasta's arbitration speech (528–85) is far longer than any other speech by a third party in an agon: contrast the shorter speeches of Demophon (Hcld. 236–52), Agamemnon (Hec. 1240–51), and Menelaus (Tro. 1036–41). This is the only agon in Euripides in which the two opposing speeches do not dominate the scene. There are, indeed, elements of the epideixis scene here, in which a character is provoked by some outrageous words or actions to deliver a long and sometimes abstract speech. Euripides thus combines the agon with a related type of scene, just as he does in *Orestes*, where the agon is embedded in a supplication scene.

Jocasta's speech begins with a proem which stresses that wisdom comes from experience (528–30).[78] She then launches into a long section in which she denounces φιλοτιμία and praises ἰσότης (531–48). She replies to Eteocles in his own language of personification, as is shown by her use of τιμᾶν (536, 550), and she uses the key term φιλότιμος at the beginning and end of her address to him (532, 567), just as he began and ended with τυραννίς (506, 523 f.). Her tone is highly rhetorical, with ornate language and many rhetorical questions.[79]

Jocasta's praise of equality is relevant from one point of view, in that she is trying to persuade Eteocles to allow Polynices the equal share of the tyranny which had been agreed. An interesting feature of her argument, however, is that she argues the case for equality from scratch. She makes no reference to the brothers' agreement, which is now the main justification for Polynices' demand for an equal share. If the agreement is disregarded, it is not, in fact, obvious that alternating kingship is implied by Jocasta's doctrine of equality. In the context of an Athenian play of the late fifth century this doctrine can only imply one political system, and that is democracy. Jocasta's speech is, indeed, a defence of democracy against tyranny, which has only superficial relevance to the immediate issue. The question of democracy was relevant in *Heraclidae* and *Supplices*, since those plays did at least deal with Athens, albeit at a period when Athens was

---

[78] On the combination of traditional and modern elements in Jocasta's speech, see Arthur 1975: 113–17; Mastronarde 1986: 204–6.   [79] Cf. Craik 1988 on *Pho.* 528 ff.

theoretically a monarchy. The urgency of this question in the late fifth century is shown by Euripides' introduction of it into the unexpected context of a discussion of the Theban monarchy.

Jocasta supports her recommendation by drawing attention to equality as a cosmic principle. She is trying to get a moral grip on Eteocles by finding a natural defence of equality, and thus answering his denial (499) of a natural basis to morality.[80] The natural and social orders had been associated in various ways from an early period of Greek thought, and the very word δίκη seems originally to have meant 'order of the universe'.[81] This association became more problematic when distinctions began to be made between νόμος and φύσις, but moral and social arguments continued to make use of appeals to the natural order.[82] A cynical appeal to natural laws is made by the Athenians in the Melian Dialogue (Thuc. 5. 105), and Strepsiades uses a natural analogy at Arph. *Clouds* 1290–5 which resembles that in Jocasta's speech in that it concerns πλέον and ἴσον.

The opposition between ἰσότης and πλεονεξία was, indeed, often discussed in these terms. Alcmaeon argued that ἰσονομία leads to health and μοναρχία to illness (fr. 4), while Empedocles insisted on the equality of the elements (fr. 17. 27–9). The Anonymus Iamblichi argued that νόμος, and not πλεονεξία, is natural because human beings naturally need social organization.[83] A more sophisticated approach to this question is to be found in Plato's *Gorgias*, where Callicles derides τὸ ἴσον and puts forward his own law of nature (483c–e), and Socrates then tries to resolve the distinction between νόμος and φύσις in terms of unified principles governing both the social and the natural orders (507c8–508c3). Socrates opposes ἰσότης to πλεονεξία, although he favours geometrical rather than absolute equality.[84]

Jocasta's doctrine of equality does, as was suggested above, inevitably suggest a defence of democracy. τὸ ἴσον, and related terms, are naturally common in such contexts (cf. Hdt. 3. 80. 6; 3. 142. 3; Thuc. 2. 37. 1;

---

[80] The reading νόμιμον (538) brings out the idea of a law of nature which is further developed in Plato's *Gorgias* (cf. Ostwald 1986: 95 ff.), but there is also something to be said for μόνιμον (cf. ἀεί 536, 539).
[81] Cf. Anaximander fr. 1; Heraclitus frr. 94, 114; Parmenides fr. 8. 14. There are arguments from the natural order at S. *Aj.* 669–77, *Ant.* 710–18. See generally Vlastos 1947; H. D. F. Kitto, *Sophocles: Dramatist and Philosopher* (London, 1958).
[82] Cf. Guthrie 1971: 101–34; Ostwald 1986: 260 ff.
[83] DK 89, section 6. This work is of uncertain date, but seems to reflect stock ideas of the late 5th century. Cf. Guthrie 1971: 71–4, 314 f.
[84] Cf. Dodds 1959 on Pl. *G*. 483c5; Guthrie 1971: 148 ff.; Bond 1981 on *HF* 633–6; Brock 1989: 162.

E. Su. 408, 432, 434, 441). The idea of ruling ἐν μέρει, in yearly cycles, was important in democratic theory (e.g. E. Su. 406 f.), and was also stressed by Polynices (Pho. 477 f.).[85] Jocasta echoes this kind of language in her speech (Pho. 541–5).[86] She contrasts equality with Eteocles' pursuit of φιλοτιμία (532) and τὸ πλέον (539, cf. 509).[87] This recalls the contrast in Athenagoras' speech (Thuc. 6. 38 f.) between the ἰσομοιρεῖν of democracy and the πλεονεκτεῖν characteristic of oligarchy.[88]

Eteocles' desire for sole tyranny has thus prompted Jocasta to a rather irrelevant defence of democracy. Her praise of equality is appropriate enough, but her *ab initio* justification of it, ignoring the crucial fact of the brothers' agreement, gives every impression of being more concerned with democracy than with shared tyranny. This impression is reinforced by the next section of her speech (549–57), a general criticism of tyranny of a fairly traditional kind.[89] This section is not appropriate to a speech which is actually proposing a rotating tyranny, but it does fit into the defence of democracy which Jocasta's speech has by now become.[90] These lines are fairly generalized, but Jocasta's disparagement of τὸ πλέον as a mere name (553 f.) seems to use the theories of Eteocles' proem (especially 502) to answer his praise of it (509 f.).[91] Jocasta concludes her address to Eteocles by presenting to him the highly thematic choice between personal ambition and the good of the city (559–67).[92]

Jocasta devotes a much shorter section of her speech to Polynices (568–83). She makes effective use of a kind of dilemma argument, in which she uses rhetorical questions to drive home the intolerable consequences for him both of victory and of defeat. The balance of sympathy hitherto has been greatly in Polynices' favour, and it comes as something of a surprise

---

[85] Cf. Ar. Pol. 1317ᵇ13–20. Thuc. 2. 37. 1 (but the meaning of ἀπὸ μέρους here is disputed: with Loraux 1986: 187 f. contrast J. S. Rusten (ed.), *Thucydides: The Peloponnesian War Book 2* (Cambridge, 1989) 145 f. At Hcld. 182, Iolaus says that the opportunity to speak ἐν μέρει is characteristic of Athens.

[86] Note, however, that Jocasta's τὸν ἐνιαύσιον κύκλον (544) is somewhat different in sense from Polynices' ἐνιαυτοῦ κύκλον (477).

[87] On φιλοτιμία and πλεονεξία, see Ehrenberg 1947: 49 f.; de Romilly 1965: 35–41; Mastronarde 1986: 210 n. 22.

[88] Jocasta's use of democratic language to attack Eteocles' desire for tyranny does not, of course, imply that Polynices is a democrat. Mastronarde 1986: 205 describes him as 'an utterly conventional man in his love of kin and country, and in his acceptance of aristocratic values'.

[89] Cf. above, Ch. 3, n. 40.

[90] Kovacs 1982: 42–5 uses the irrelevance of Jocasta's attack on tyranny as a justification for deleting lines 549–67.

[91] Cf. Fraenkel 1946: 81–9.

[92] Cf. Craik 1988 on Pho. 560. On the contemporary resonances of the word σωτηρία see Ar. Ath. Pol. 29. 2 (with Rhodes).

to find him being criticized so harshly here. Jocasta has given no hint of such an attitude in her earlier conversation with him, and the chiastic structure of the agon has the effect of raising only at the end the objections to his behaviour that had been implicit earlier. These criticisms of Polynices are developed by Eteocles in the stichomythia in trochaic tetrameters which concludes the agon.

This scene represents an interesting development from the agones in *Heraclidae* and *Supplices*. Eteocles resembles Demophon and Theseus in being confronted with strongly worded demands which are backed up by armed force. His rejection of these demands resembles theirs in several respects. The difference, however, is that, while Demophon was right to reject the demand of the Argive herald to give up the suppliants, and Theseus was also right, although less obviously so, to insist on the burial of the corpses, Eteocles is plainly wrong to resist the justified demands of Polynices. Theseus justified his interference in the resonant language of Athenian imperialism, but this admirable πολυπραγμοσύνη has given way to φιλοτιμία and πλεονεξία on the part of Eteocles.[93] The similarities and contrasts between Theseus and Eteocles inevitably suggest an implied criticism of the tyrannical aspects of the Athenian Empire, suitably obscured by having the action located in Thebes.

Jocasta's arbitration speech also combines application to the immediate dramatic situation with veiled political relevance. Her praise of equality is an appropriate response to her sons' dispute, but it can also be read as a defence of democracy which recalls some of Theseus' words in *Supplices*. This affirmation of democratic principles against ambition and civil strife has an obvious relevance to internal Athenian politics around the time of the production of *Phoenissae*. The figure of Theseus in *Supplices* has split into Eteocles, with his obstinate refusal to give way, and Jocasta, the idealistic but tragically impotent defender of democracy.

[93] Cf. Ehrenberg 1947: 49 f.

6

Hecuba and Troades

BOTH *Hecuba* and *Troades* culminate in an agon in which a vindictive and rhetorically expert Hecuba attempts, before a son of Atreus, to demolish the case of a plausible adversary. The two plays generally have much in common. They are set in the period between the defeat of Troy and the departure of the Greek fleet for home, as the Greeks wait for a favourable wind (*Hec.* 900, 1289 f.; *Tro.* 19 f., 456). This period contains fresh suffering for the Trojans, and also gives scope for both retrospect and foreboding. There are also hints, at the end of *Hecuba* and the beginning of *Troades*, of troubles in store for the Greeks. Hecuba is a paradigm of suffering at the beginning of both plays (*Hec.* 55–8, *Tro.* 36–44), and must suffer even more during them. In *Hecuba*, she must face the deaths of her last two children, while in *Troades* she has to endure a series of disasters, each worse than the last, in which every hope and consolation is knocked away.[1] She is on stage, as the embodiment of Trojan suffering, almost throughout the two plays, and her constant presence is an important unifying element.

In both *Hecuba* and *Troades* the agon is the last of a series of confrontations between Hecuba and other characters. She displays an expertise in forensic rhetoric in both scenes, but the significance of this is not the same in each. *Hecuba* resembles others of Euripides' earlier plays, such as *Medea*, *Hippolytus*, and *Andromache*, in that rhetorical sophistication is related to character, at least in broad terms. The whole question of persuasion is also an important theme in the play. *Troades*, on the other hand, resembles Euripides' later plays in that a wide variety of characters have rhetorical skills without this fact having any particular significance for character. Cassandra and Andromache, for example, have already delivered formal speeches in which the abstract issues are far more important than any question of individual characterization. The same is true of the agon, where Hecuba's manner and attitudes are difficult to relate to her behaviour elsewhere in the play. In the agon of *Troades*, as in those of *Electra* and *Orestes*, the participants are

---

[1] Cf. Michelini 1987: 132 f. (on *Hec.*); M. Lloyd 1984: 303 (on *Tro.*).

given the rhetorical skills which are necessary for important themes in the play to be expressed coherently.

HECUBA

Hecuba has two parallel actions of equal length, the first dealing with Polyxena and the second with Polydorus, and the agon comes at the end of the second of these. Persuasion has been an important theme throughout the play,[2] and Hecuba's use of it to gain her ends has already been seen in the two parallel scenes in which she supplicates Odysseus and Agamemnon. It has been argued that Hecuba's character undergoes a change either before or during her supplication of Agamemnon, and our attitude to this question must affect our view of Hecuba's style of argument in the agon.

Hecuba begins her supplication of Agamemnon, after some initial hesitation, in a long passage of stichomythia in which she succeeds in changing his attitude to her from indifference to pity (758–85).[3] In the speech which follows, she makes an appeal, based primarily on νόμος and δίκη, which Agamemnon rejects by turning to go (812 f.).[4] Hecuba then regrets her lack of sophistic training in rhetoric (814–19),[5] before making a final appeal to Agamemnon which exploits his feelings for Cassandra. This approach is evidently successful, since Agamemnon does at least now recognize that Polymestor ought to be punished, although he is unwilling to do anything himself for fear of offending the Greek army. Finally, he acquiesces in Hecuba's proposal to punish Polymestor herself, his final words (903 f.) echoing the conclusion of her supplication speech (845).[6]

Euripides' portrayal of this process of persuasion is subtle and carefully calculated, and there is a clear contrast between the failure of Hecuba's appeal to justice and the success of her exploitation of Agamemnon's relationship with Cassandra. Different attitudes have been taken to what Hecuba does here. Some scholars have argued that Hecuba reveals a deterioration in her character, either by appealing to Agamemnon at all or by her reference to Cassandra. Others have denied that the Cassandra argument is discreditable, or argued that it is at least a legitimate use of

---

[2] Cf. Buxton 1982: 170–86.   [3] Cf. *Or.* 447, and Willink 1986 ad loc.
[4] On Hecuba's view of νόμος see Kovacs 1987: 144 n. 53; M. Heath, ' "Jure principem locum tenet": Euripides' *Hecuba*', *BICS* 34 (1987), 40–68, at 67.
[5] Cf. Michelini 1987: 150 n. 77.
[6] Cf. Tierney 1946 on 903–4; Buxton 1982: 180 f.

a consideration likely to influence Agamemnon.[7] This is the kind of problem, like the question of the justification of Hecuba's revenge, on which agreement is not likely to be reached. Euripides often places his characters in situations in which a normal and appropriate response is hard to distinguish from one which is exaggerated or discreditable. What is important for present purposes is the narrower issue of Hecuba's use of persuasion, and in this respect at least it seems that there is no significant change in her character during the play. The parallels between her supplications of Odysseus and Agamemnon are especially striking here. There are verbal echoes (806 f. recalling 286 f.), and also a visual similarity in the movements away by Odysseus and Agamemnon (342, 812).[8] Hecuba's plea to Odysseus, like her plea to Agamemnon, progresses from the appeal to δίκη to the appeal to χάρις (note 271–3), and the main difference is that Odysseus rejects both pleas while Agamemnon is affected by the appeal to χάρις.

Scholars who argue that Hecuba's moral decline can be charted in a growing devotion to persuasion and to the power of rhetoric have difficulty in dealing with the verbal skill which Hecuba displays in the agon.[9] Euripides organizes the agon so that she is the defendant, not the prosecutor as might be more natural, and she is also clearly in the right. She uses her rhetorical skill to defend herself against attack by an obvious villain, and Euripides has organized the agon in such a way that the punishment of Polymestor does not depend upon it. Her rhetoric in the agon is thus an instrument of justifiable self-defence, and not a significant means of revenge.

Agamemnon agrees on Polymestor's guilt by the end of the supplication scene (850–6, 902–4), and he has already been punished when the agon begins. The immediate outcome of the agon is thus not in itself important, since Hecuba has already taken her revenge, and any retaliation that Polymestor might be allowed to inflict on her would make comparatively little difference to her already desperate plight. Euripides avoids organizing the action in such a way that the punishment of Polymestor depended on the agon, and he thus makes clear that its importance does not reside in the influence that it does or does not have on the actual sequence of events. The agon is significant

---

[7] Hecuba's deterioration: Kirkwood 1947; Conacher 1967: 162 f. For a more favourable view of her, see Kovacs 1987: 78–114.

[8] Cf. Buxton 1982: 183 f., citing Steidle 1968: 49; Macleod 1983: 154.

[9] Neither Kirkwood 1947: 67 n. 13, nor Conacher 1967: 163, has much to say about Hecuba's use of persuasion in the agon.

as a formal demonstration of Polymestor's guilt, although he is actually the prosecutor, and as a re-enactment in verbal terms of his physical destruction.[10]

Agamemnon arrives in response to Polymestor's cries (1109), and pretends not to know who has blinded him. Since he has already agreed that Polymestor is guilty, it is something of a surprise when he introduces a pair of speeches (1129–31). This serves to suggest that Agamemnon has not yet made up his mind, and shows that, as in *Hippolytus*, Euripides avoids making a point of the fact that the agon is prejudged. Agamemnon's formal introduction makes it clear in advance that there is to be an agon, and the formality of the agon here also corresponds to the formality of the trial which is being represented.

Polymestor's speech is not only the prosecution speech in an agon, but also a messenger speech[11] and the iambic exposition of his frenzied dochmiacs.[12] The agonistic element of the speech comes at the beginning, where Polymestor, without a proem,[13] first describes his murder of Polydorus (1132–6) and then tries to justify it (1136–44). Polymestor's speech is not rhetorically sophisticated, but his argument is not altogether without subtlety. He conceals his greed for the gold, suggesting only that he did not want the inconvenience of another Trojan War if Polydorus were to have refounded Troy. The admission of self-interest gives plausibility to this account, and he does not claim explicitly that he acted in the interests of the Greeks until the end of the speech (1175–7). The rest of Polymestor's speech is taken up with straightforward narration, in the style of a messenger speech, of Hecuba's revenge on him (1145–82). The gnomic conclusion (1177–82) is typical of a messenger speech, but unparalleled in an agon speech addressed to a judge.[14]

Hecuba's reply is one of Euripides' most sophisticated pieces of forensic rhetoric. Her proem (1187–94), with its formulaic attack on clever speaking, is paradoxical because it is she rather than Polymestor who is rhetorically expert.[15] In her plea to Agamemnon, Hecuba had regretted her lack of training in sophistic rhetoric (814–19), but now she seems to be in full command of the latest argumentative devices.

---

[10] Contrast A. *Ag.* and E. *El.*, where the victim is defeated verbally before being killed.
[11] Cf. Taplin 1977: 82 n. 2.
[12] The transition from dochmiacs to iambics is eased by Agamemnon's introduction of the debate (1129–31). Cf. Hall 1989: 198.   [13] On λέγοιμ' ἄν, see above, p. 25.
[14] On conclusions of speeches in three-person agones, see above, pp. 27–8. On conclusions of messenger speeches, see Kannicht 1969 on *Hel.* 1617–18.
[15] Cf. Tierney 1946 on *Hec.* 1187 ff.; Buxton 1982: 181.

The next section of Hecuba's speech (1195–8) is a transition from the proem addressed to Agamemnon to the main body of the speech addressed to Polymestor. When an agon takes place before a judge or arbitrator, it is naturally to him that the speeches are addressed. This is the case with Polymestor's speech in *Hecuba*, the Herald's speech in *Heraclidae*, Helen's speech in *Troades*, and both speeches in *Phoenissae*. Rhetorical effect can, however, be derived from turning to address the opponent directly. Hecuba thus addresses the main body of her speech to Polymestor, and only the proem and epilogue to Agamemnon. Similarly, in *Troades* Hecuba addresses most of her speech to her opponent Helen, and only the proem (969 f.) and epilogue (1029–32) to the judge Menelaus.[16] Iolaus (*Hcld.* 189–204) and Tyndareus (*Or.* 526–33) turn more briefly to their opponents in the middle of their speeches, and there is a somewhat similar effect at *Hi.* 946, where Theseus moves from attacking Hippolytus through generalizations and in the third person to addressing him directly.[17]

Hecuba's rhetorical sophistication is shown by her elaborate concern for τάξις, and her first argument is marked by πρῶτον (1199). Hecuba uses a disjunctive argument, based on probability, in order to deny the possibility of φιλία and χάρις between Greek and barbarian. This is not an especially convincing argument, partly because it seems to be undermined by Hecuba's own alliance with Agamemnon,[18] and partly because Polymestor's argument was based primarily on self-interest and only secondarily on any benefit that he might have brought to the Greeks. Her attempt to rebut Polymestor's argument from self-interest (1204 f.) is a mere denial of what he had said (1142–4), and it is left unclear who is right on this particular point. Hecuba uses hypophora to cover up these weaknesses in her case.

The next two sections of Hecuba's speech are much more convincing. Her case is a difficult one to make, because she needs to demonstrate that Polymestor's real motives for killing Polydorus were not the ones which he alleged. She uses a sophisticated type of argument in both sections, the hypothetical syllogism, in order to show that he never had any intention of benefiting the Greeks. She argues first that, if he had really been interested in their welfare, he would either have killed Polydorus or handed him over to them while Troy was still prosperous (1208–16). She goes on to

---

[16] It is possible, however, that *Tro.* 969 f. are addressed to the chorus; and not entirely clear who is being addressed between lines 971 and 981.

[17] Cf. Johansen 1959: 82.

[18] Cf. Buxton 1982: 182. But Hecuba's barbarian status is not necessarily stressed here: see Hall 1989: 212 f.

argue that he ought also to have handed the gold over to the Greeks, but that he has not done so even yet (1217–23). Hecuba is clearly correct about these points, and her command of elaborate rhetorical arguments helps to elucidate the truth rather than to conceal it. She concludes the part of her speech that is addressed to Polymestor with a peroration which resembles *El.* 1080–5 in pointing out that virtuous behaviour would have been both easy and a source of renown. Hecuba concludes with the peroration proper, addressed to Agamemnon (1232–7).

Hecuba's rhetorical skill seems to be significant in the context of a play in which the whole subject of persuasion is so important. Her earlier regrets about the lack of professional training in persuasion (814–19) serve, paradoxically, as a preparation for her expertise in the agon since they do at least show her awareness of what is needed. Hecuba's victory over Polymestor in the agon reflects both her moral superiority and her earlier use of deception and violence to take revenge on him. Her speech is both more convincing and more sophisticated than his, and there is a rather similar contrast in *Andromache* between Hermione's unsophisticated prosecution speech and Andromache's expert defence.

Agamemnon's judgement speech is in itself impeccable, as he makes a lucid assessment of the issues and comes to the right conclusion (1240–51). The wider context of the speech does, however, cast shadows over this model exercise of power. Agamemnon came to recognize Polymestor's guilt only after elaborate attempts at persuasion by Hecuba, and even then he was not prepared to do anything about it himself. His air of calm control is immediately undermined by Polymestor's menacing prophecies, which clearly disturb him (1275–86).[19] The ending of the play resembles that of *Heraclidae*, in which a near-agon is followed by disturbing prophecies from the victim of revenge in the role of *deus ex machina*.

TROADES

Hecuba is also a constant presence in *Troades*, and the play is articulated by the striking entrances of Cassandra, Andromache, and Helen. The three women enter, argue with Hecuba, and depart for their various marriages in Greece.[20] The agon is strongly marked as a separate section by

[19] Cf. Buxton 1982: 183; Strohm 1957: 34.
[20] Cf. Friedrich 1953: 73–5; Strohm 1957: 116 ff.; Steidle 1968: 52–4; Desch 1985/1986: 66 n. 4. On Andromache's departure for Greece as a perverted bridal journey, see R. A. S. Seaford, 'The Tragic Wedding', *JHS* 107 (1987), 106–30, at 130.

Menelaus' second prologue.[21] Helen's own appearance is striking, dressed in her finery (1023) and dragged out by force, and her entrance has been prepared for by a long series of references to her as the cause of Troy's destruction (34 f., 211, 357; 398, 766 ff.).

The agon in *Troades* resembles that in *Electra* in dealing with issues of guilt and innocence that were also treated by other authors. A particular problem in the case of Electra is the relationship of Euripides' play to Sophocles' *Electra*, and it was suggested above that direct influence one way or the other cannot be determined with any probability.[22] There may well have been many other discussions of the guilt of Clytaemestra, the loss of which focuses our attention unduly on the relationship between Sophocles and Euripides. Similar problems arise with regard to the relationship between *Troades* and Gorgias' *Helen*, and it is often alleged, not only that Gorgias has priority, but also that he influenced Euripides.[23] There is no external evidence to settle the question of priority, and the internal arguments carry little conviction.

The most striking and, so far as one can see, original feature of Gorgias' defence of Helen is his attempt to show that she was innocent whatever the cause of her departure for Troy. He argues that there were four possible causes, namely persuasion, love, force, and the gods, and that she would be exculpated whichever of them had operated.[24] Euripides treats the case in less abstract terms, and in *Troades* it is accepted by both Hecuba and Helen that there are circumstances in which Helen would indeed have been guilty. Furthermore, Gorgias focuses on the narrower question of Helen's responsibility, while the agon of *Troades* deals with many other issues.

Nor is there any reason to suppose that Euripides was influenced by Gorgias' treatment of any one of the four causes taken individually. In the agon of *Troades*, the possibility that persuasion might be an excuse is not considered at all, despite its prominence in Gorgias. Euripides' Helen does not propose the power of love as an excuse either, while Hecuba, ignoring Gorgias' arguments, regards the probability of this motive as evidence of Helen's guilt (989–92). Nor does Euripides' Helen argue that she was forcibly abducted, and Hecuba's attribution of this argument to her is thus a mistake (998–1001). Discussion of this possibility did not, in any case,

---

[21] Cf. Schadewaldt 1926: 241.   [22] See above, pp. 62 f. 65.
[23] See Jouan 1966: 185 f.; Guthrie 1971: 192 n. 2; Goldhill 1986: 236–8. There are sensible remarks by D. M. MacDowell (ed. and tr.), *Gorgias: Encomium of Helen* (Bristol, 1982), 12.
[24] On this type of argument, see above, pp. 29 f. Euripides uses it elsewhere, but not to defend Helen.

originate with Gorgias. Helen was abducted by Theseus, and there are passages in the *Iliad* which could be taken to imply that she was also abducted by Paris.[25] The only one of Gorgias' four causes which is actually treated as an excuse in Euripides is the influence of the gods, when Helen points to the part played by Aphrodite. This does, however, appear as a possible excuse as early as H. *Il.* 3. 164, and there is no reason to suppose that Euripides' use of it owes anything to Gorgias.

The differences of emphasis between Euripides and Gorgias are so great that it is difficult to find any direct relationship between their defences of Helen, and the question of priority thus becomes irrelevant. Paradoxical argument was a feature of rhetorical training, and the defence of such characters as Helen and Palamedes was doubtless a stock exercise of which many examples are now lost.[26] The accidents of survival have suggested relationships between works which would have been less obvious at the time of their composition.

Helen speaks first in the agon of *Troades*, although she is the defendant, because, like Clytaemestra in *Electra*, she is so much on the defensive when the scene begins that a further prosecution speech would be superfluous. The order of the speeches is thus irregular in forensic terms, but it has a powerful tragic effect in that Helen must plead for her life against a charge which has not been formally expressed. In this she resembles the Plataeans in Thucydides (3. 53. 2), Gorgias' Palamedes (*Pal.* 4), and Socrates (Pl. *Ap.* 18b1–d7). There is thus a tragic aspect to Helen's rhetorical attempt to remove prejudice at the beginning of her speech (914–17).[27]

Helen's speech shows a very careful concern for rhetorical disposition, and each stage of her argument is clearly marked.[28] In one of Euripides' earlier plays this might have had some significance for character, for example to show Helen's calmness and self-control, but in *Troades* both speakers are rhetorically expert and the main thing is that the conflicting cases should be given the best possible expression.

Helen begins by arguing that she herself was only one link in the causal chain which led to the war, and that others, including Hecuba and the

---

[25] H. *Il.* 2. 354–6 could well be taken to imply physical abduction, however they should correctly be interpreted. Different interpretations are offered by J. T. Kakridis, *Homer Revisited* (Lund, 1971), ch. 1, and J. Griffin, 'The Epic Cycle and the Uniqueness of Homer'. *JHS* 97 (1977), 39–53, at 45. Abduction of Helen by Theseus: L. B. Ghali-Kahil, *Les Enlèvements et le retour d'Hélène* (Paris, 1955), 305–13.

[26] Aristotle refers to demonstrations that Paris was brave and that he was right to take Helen (*Rh.* 1401^{b}20 ff.).

[27] Cf. Macleod 1983: 103 ff. [28] See above, p. 35.

old man, should take their share of the blame.[29] This ἀντικατηγορία is evidently a rhetorical device, but it also makes a serious point.[30] Such problems of responsibility were much discussed in the second half of the fifth century, Antiphon's *Second Tetralogy* being a notable example of this kind of debate.[31] Similar extensions of responsibility to that alleged by Helen are proposed elsewhere in Euripides: Andromache says that Helen killed Achilles (*An.* 248), Peleus says that Menelaus did so (*An.* 614 f.), while Helen regards herself as the murderer of her mother (*Hel.* 280). Hecuba claims responsibility for the actions of Paris (*Hec.* 387 f.), while Orestes blames Tyndareus for those of Clytaemestra (*Or.* 585–7). These arguments are advanced under various degrees of emotional and rhetorical pressure, and some are more convincing than others, but the existence of these parallels suggests that Helen's argument in *Troades* has some substance. Whatever her responsibility for her own actions, it is a serious and valid point that she was not solely responsible for all the suffering in the Trojan War. Euripides seems to have been particularly interested in the long and complex causal chain which led to the Trojan War, and many references are made in his plays to its ἀρχή. At *An.* 274 ff. it is identified as the Judgement of Paris, and a little later the wish is expressed that Hecuba had killed Paris as an infant (*An.* 293 ff.). Regrets about the building of Paris' ships are voiced at *Hec.* 629–37 and *Hel.* 229–39 (cf. H. *Il.* 5. 63).[32]

Helen's second argument is that, given the circumstances of the Judgement, her marriage to Paris was a good thing for Greece (924–37). She claims that Athena offered Paris the military conquest of Greece, while Hera offered him tyranny over Asia and Europe, and argues that it was only because Paris preferred her beauty that Greece avoided subjugation. This argument is rather difficult to assess. There is no direct evidence for a standard version of the story, for which the *Cypria* would no doubt have been the main authority, but Stinton gives a plausible account of what Helen is doing: 'to the gift of Athena, military prowess, is added a detail not in the tradition—conquest of Greece; and Hera's gift of kingship is explicitly extended to Europe.'[33] Helen may be making the details of the goddesses' offers more specific than they were in most versions of the story, but there

---

[29] On the identity of ὁ πρέσβυς (921), see M. Lloyd 1984: 305 n. 12 (= old shepherd); M. Huys, *AC* 54 (1985), 240–53 (= Priam).

[30] Cf. [Ar.] *Rh. Al.* 1442ᵇ7 f.; Volkmann 1885: 77 f.

[31] Cf. Plut. *Per.* 36. 3; Adkins 1960: 102–8, 124–7; Parker 1983: 111.

[32] Cf. Stinton 1965: 14 (= 1990: 27 f.); Solmsen 1975: 66–9. Helen may also be alluding to *Alexandros*, and this would strengthen her case.

[33] Stinton 1965: 36 (= 1990: 44 f.). Cf. Scodel 1980: 101–3; Desch 1985/1986: 84 n. 63; M. Lloyd 1984: 306.

is no reason to suppose that she is actually contradicting the tradition in a way that would make her argument seem obviously false. Hecuba's only response is a questionable argument from probability (971–4), and a Greek audience would not find it difficult to believe that oriental interest in foreign conquest and empire centred on Greece.[34] The conclusion of this section of Helen's argument shows the rhetorical background especially clearly, as she stresses the good that she has done to the judges and the undeserved misfortune that she has suffered herself (935–7).[35]

In the next section of her speech, Helen turns to the question of why she left Sparta for Troy (938–50). She begins by alluding to the deity which accompanied Paris to Sparta (940 f.), but does not immediately draw out the implications of Aphrodite's presence for her own actions. She first launches another attack on Hecuba by alluding to Paris' two names and referring to him as ὁ τῆσδ᾽ ἀλάστωρ (941 f.). The point of this is to stress that Paris was primarily an agent of Hecuba's destruction, and to remind Hecuba of her attempts to avoid the threat which he posed by exposing him (which led to his having two names).[36] Helen then blames Menelaus for going to Crete and leaving her alone to entertain Paris (943 f.). She follows the *Cypria* version here, rather than the version alluded to at *IA* 76 according to which Menelaus had already departed when Paris arrived.[37] He is criticized in somewhat similar terms by Peleus at *An.* 590–5 (where it is not clear which version of the story is being used), although Peleus also has harsh words for Helen's unchastity.

Helen never states explicitly that Aphrodite coerced her, even when she finally gets round to the question of her own responsibility (945). She first asks rhetorically what motive she could have had to abandon her fatherland and her home (946 f.), implying that she must have been compelled. This is an argument from probability about possible motives, of a familiar rhetorical kind, although Helen is only arguing that she was forced to do the deed in question and not, as is more usual in this type of argument, that she did not do it at all. Her argument resembles that of Pasiphae in *Cretes*, who denies that the bull could have attracted her naturally and argues that she must therefore have been a victim of divine influence.

Helen argues next that she could not be expected to resist Aphrodite, since Zeus cannot do so either (948–50). This type of *a fortiori* argument

---

[34] Cf. Hall 1989: 195 f.   [35] Cf. [Ar.] *Rh. Al.* 1444^{b}36–1445^{a}12.
[36] See M. Lloyd, 'Paris/Alexandros in Homer and Euripides', *Mnem.* 42 (1989), 76–9.
[37] Cf. Jouan 1966: 180.

is recommended by Aristotle (*Rh.* 1397^{b}12 f.), but it could be used sophistically, as it is at *Hi.* 451–61 and Arph. *Clouds* 1079–82. Context, however, is important, and in the examples just mentioned the argument is being used to justify bad actions in the future. Helen has reason to believe that Aphrodite did intervene, and she is at least apologizing for what she has done in the past. Theseus makes plausible use of this type of argument in his consolation of Heracles (*HF* 1314–21), and the only way to rebut it was to deny, not always convincingly, that the gods are immoral at all (*HF* 1340–6, *IT* 391; Pl. *Euthyphro* 5d8–6d1).

Helen's argument that she was coerced by Aphrodite is one of the most striking examples of the way in which Euripides confronts detailed and explicit mythology with a human and realistic treatment of events.[38] This is especially notable in late plays such as *Phoenissae* and *Orestes*, where the mythology is more elaborate and the realism more pronounced. In *Orestes*, for example, Orestes, having acted out his role in the myth in the usual way, finds himself being criticized for not behaving like a citizen in a fifth-century *polis*. Helen's defence in *Troades* depends on the literal truth of the myth of the Judgement of Paris, but the style of her speech evokes the courts of late fifth-century Athens. This controlled and intellectual style seems as far as possible removed from the mythical world in which Aphrodite might have coerced her, and this clash between style and content is central to the paradoxical effect of her speech. Helen has much in common with Pasiphae, who uses sophisticated rhetorical arguments to show that she was compelled by the god Poseidon to have sexual intercourse with a bull.

Such arguments from divine compulsion may not have carried much conviction in the Athenian courts, but Helen and Pasiphae are not everyday characters whom one might have met in the streets of fifth-century Athens. They are mythical heroines who exist in a world where the possibility of divine coercion is much more immediate. In Homer there is, in general, an interaction between divine and human motivation which means that divine influence does not count as an excuse.[39] Nevertheless, the possibility that it might be an excuse is never wholly absent, as is shown by Priam's words to Helen at *Il.* 3. 164 f.[40] Helen herself shows no inclination to make excuses (*Il.* 3. 171–80), but the situation does not require self-defence and Aphrodite's coercion is all too evident later

---

[38] Cf. Kamerbeek 1958. Generally: Vernant and Vidal-Naquet 1988: ch. 2.
[39] Cf. Lesky 1958: 129–37; Lloyd-Jones 1971: 150 f.
[40] Cf. Herodotus 1. 45. 2; 6. 135. 3; Solmsen 1975: 136.

(*Il.* 3. 383 ff.). In *Troades*, Helen's reference to the Judgement of Paris, and her description of her marriage to him as θεοπόνητα (953), shows that she is aware that Aphrodite is an anthropomorphic goddess with plans of her own to accomplish which mere mortals cannot be allowed to obstruct. Hecuba does not argue that Helen is guilty whatever the part played by Aphrodite but denies that, as an anthropomorphic goddess, she played any part in Helen's behaviour at all. She implicitly accepts that Helen would be exculpated if her account of the Judgement were correct. Similar excuses to Helen's are advanced by Eurystheus (*Hcld.* 989 f.) and Pasiphae (*Cretes*), both of whom have a plausible case that they were merely the instruments of divine punishment of someone else. Helen's defence in *Troades* contains, within itself, a drastic confrontation of late fifth-century forensic rhetoric and sharply defined mythology, and the paradoxical effect of this should not be weakened by denying the validity of either element.

In the next section of her speech (951—8), Helen admits that she ought to have tried to escape from Troy after the death of Paris, when Aphrodite had no further interest in her remaining in Troy.[41] Her claim that she did indeed try to escape, but was restrained by the guards, will be denied by Hecuba (1010—22), and this is one of those unresolved disputes about matters of fact which occasionally appear in Euripides' agones.[42]

Helen concludes by saying that she does not deserve to be punished with death, because she was married by force and endured a slavery that was bitter to her (961—5). Wilamowitz' deletion of 959 f. must be accepted, and when Helen refers to force she must therefore mean the coercion by Aphrodite mentioned elsewhere in the speech.[43] When Hecuba replies as if physical abduction were meant (998—1001), she is thus misrepresenting what Helen has said. Helen concludes her speech by warning Menelaus of the folly of trying to be superior to the gods.

Hecuba ignores Helen's attempts to spread the blame, but otherwise matches her speech point by point. She begins her speech, without a formal proem, by attacking Helen's version of the Judgement and arguing that Hera and Athena, who had no need to win a beauty contest in order to gain a husband, would not have been so foolish as to make offers to Paris which would have entailed their favourite cities being subjugated to barbarians. The most convincing interpretation of the transmitted text (with αἵ in 975) is that Hecuba does not deny the Judgement altogether, but only that the goddesses would have made offers involving the conquest

---

[41] The rhetorical device here is προκατάληψις: see above, pp. 30 f.
[42] See above, p. 67.   [43] See M. Lloyd 1984: 309.

of Greece by Paris. They may have entered a beauty contest for amusement, but they would not have betrayed their favourite cities.[44] The main objection to this interpretation is that it seems inconsistent with Hecuba's whole attitude to the gods, and in particular with her stance as the goddesses' σύμμαχος (969), to attribute such frivolity to Hera and Athena. Furthermore, it is against the interests of Hecuba's argument to concede that the Judgement took place at all, because any version of the Judgement story implies that Helen might have been coerced by Aphrodite. Hartung's οὐ (975), accepted by Diggle, avoids these problems. It may be surprising that Hecuba should deny such a well-known story as the Judgement of Paris, about which Cassandra seems to have prophesied in *Alexandros*,[45] but her argument requires her to do so, and such a move would be no odder than the denials apparently made by Heracles at *HF* 1341–6.[46]

Hecuba's argument is not convincing on either interpretation, and her use of the argument from probability leads her away from the truth. In all versions of the story, the goddesses took the Judgement very seriously indeed, and the enmity of Hera and Athena to Troy was traditionally due to their failure in it.[47] Hera, at least, took this enmity to the lengths of being prepared to sacrifice any of her favourite cities if only Troy were to be destroyed (H. *Il.* 4. 30 ff.). Hecuba's argument thus depends on an idealistic view of the gods, which is supported neither by the myth nor by what we have already seen of the gods in *Troades*. She resembles such characters as Heracles (*HF* 1341–6) and Ion (*Ion* 429–51), whose high expectations of the gods are shown to be unfounded.

In her next argument, Hecuba tries to refute Helen's claim that Aphrodite accompanied Paris to Sparta (983–97). She argues first that the goddess would not have needed to move from heaven in order to bring Helen, and Amyclae as well, to Troy. She goes on to give a reductive account of Aphrodite, arguing that she is no more than human folly and that Helen was attracted merely by lust and greed. Helen had emphasized the anthropomorphic aspect of Aphrodite, entering a beauty contest and crossing the Aegean to bring her to Troy. Hecuba tries to leave no room for such behaviour, on the one hand treating the goddess in reductive terms,

---

[44] Thus Stinton 1965: 38 n. 1 (= 1990: 46 n. 56). Cf. Desch 1985/1986: 83–5. See M. Lloyd 1984: 311, for a tentative argument that the relative clause could be taken as part of the consequence. [45] Cf. Stinton 1976: 87 n. 36 (= 1990: 250 n. 37).

[46] Thus P. T. Stevens, reviewing Stinton 1965, *CR* 16 (1966), 291.

[47] That this is true even in Homer was pointed out by K. Reinhardt, *Das Parisurteil* (Frankfurt, 1938). Cf. M. Davies, 'The Judgement of Paris and *Iliad* Book XXIV', *JHS* 101 (1981), 56–62.

and on the other giving an exalted picture of a sublime deity who can exercise her power without moving from heaven. Hecuba does, in fact, emphasize the power of Aphrodite even more than Helen had done, and the implication of her argument is that the exalted goddess which she describes would not descend to the antics attributed to her by Helen. Hecuba's Aphrodite recalls Xenophanes' description of God (DK 21 B 26), and in Xenophanes, too, the goodness of God and his absolute power go closely together. The combination of reductivism and idealization which we find in Hecuba's view of Aphrodite recurs in Tiresias' account of Dionysus (*Ba.* 272–313), which also makes use of sophistic word-play.[48]

Hecuba's view of Aphrodite recalls the prayer which she addresses to Zeus earlier in this scene, when it seems that Menelaus will punish Helen (884–8).[49] This prayer is prompted by her pleasure that Helen will be punished, but it seems to go far beyond this immediate dramatic need and to express a distinctive view of Zeus. It is orthodox in form in its concern to find the right name for the deity addressed, Hecuba's vision of the justice of Zeus is traditional, and her account of his silent tread recalls Solon's account of the movement of δίκη.[50] Her view of the nature of Zeus, however, is less orthodox, as she suggests that he might be the αἰθήρ, or the law of nature, or mortal νοῦς.[51] These ideas can be related to fifth-century philosophical speculation, and what they have in common, apart from their modernity, is that they all give a reductive account of Zeus. This looks forward to Hecuba's view of Aphrodite, where her reductive analysis of the goddess is set against Helen's anthropomorphic account.[52]

Hecuba's account of Zeus is not only reductive but also idealistic. She comments on his power and justice (887 f.), just as she later takes an exalted view of Aphrodite. The philosophers whose views Hecuba echoes also combined their reductivism with an exalted vision of the power and goodness of God. Diogenes of Apollonia, for example, thought that 'air is god; it steers, has power over, inheres in, and disposes all things . . . it

---

[48] Cf. P. Roth, 'Teiresias as *Mantis* and Intellectual in Euripides' *Bacchae*', *TAPA* 114 (1984), 59–69; Mastronarde 1986: 206.

[49] Cf. Lee 1976 on *Tro.* 890, and note Hecuba's stress on the justice of Zeus in her prayer (887 f.).

[50] Cf. Schadewaldt 1926: 113–18; Lee 1976 on *Tro.* 884–8; Desch 1985/1986: 91–3.

[51] On these possibilities, see M. Lloyd 1984: 310 nn. 42, 43.

[52] Hecuba does not, however, entirely exclude the anthropomorphic aspects of Zeus and Aphrodite, any more than does Tiresias those of Dionysus in *Bacchae*, but they are played down and frivolity is certainly excluded.

is eternal and immortal'.⁵³ Anaxagoras too, whose views are evoked by Hecuba's mention of νοῦς, seems to have believed in 'not only the ultimate intelligibility, but the ultimate purposefulness and fitness of the whole plan',⁵⁴ and it was this aspect of his theory which interested Plato and Aristotle.⁵⁵

Hecuba's view of the gods in the agon is thus both consistent and distinctive. Her attitudes are those of the 'optimistic rationalist' discussed by Mastronarde, and she has points in common with both Tiresias in *Bacchae* and Theseus in *Supplices*.⁵⁶ Mastronarde remarks that Tiresias 'can combine traditional values with sophisticated theory . . . but the course of events in the play proves that his understanding is not adequate to the harsh realities of Dionysus' power'.⁵⁷ Hecuba's view of Aphrodite is not shown to be inadequate quite as clearly as is Tiresias' view of Dionysus, but her account of the Judgement of Paris is still far from plausible. Mastronarde writes of Theseus in *Supplices* that he believes that 'the course of human failure and misery can be simply analyzed and fault clearly ascribed'.⁵⁸ Hecuba, too, believes in the fundamental goodness of the divine order, and argues that the suffering of Troy can be blamed entirely on Helen. Theseus, however, while in some ways right to criticize Adrastus, later modifies his views and comes to recognize the instability of human life. There is no such development in Hecuba's views in *Troades*, but Helen has made the point strongly that the world is far from perfect and that she herself is not wholly to blame.

Hecuba's view of the gods in the agon is consistent in itself, but is difficult to reconcile with what she says about them elsewhere in the play. There is no hint in the rest of the play of the advanced views which she expresses in the agon, and her words suggest a more conventional and less idealistic attitude (469–71, 1240–5, 1280 f., 1288–90). Some scholars have argued that Hecuba's various utterances can be reconciled in terms of character, and have suggested, for example, that she fluctuates between hope and despair.⁵⁹ This is not impossible, but such a view cannot really do justice to the ways in which her whole approach in the agon is radically different from what it is elsewhere in the play. She does not merely express more

---

⁵³ G. S. Kirk, J. E. Raven, and M. Schofield, *The Presocratic Philosophers*² (Cambridge, 1983), 444. Evidence: DK 64 B 5, 7, 8.   ⁵⁴ Hussey 1972: 139.
⁵⁵ Pl. *Phd.* 97d–99a; Ar. *Met.* 985ᵃ18–21.
⁵⁶ Mastronarde 1986 (but he does not discuss Hecuba in this connection).
⁵⁷ Ibid. 206 f. Cf. Stinton 1976: 83 f. (= 1990: 264).
⁵⁸ Mastronarde 1986: 203. Cf. above, p. 78.
⁵⁹ e.g. Desch 1985/1986: 85. Cf. R. Waterfield, 'Double Standards in Euripides' *Troades*', *Maia*, 34 (1982), 141 f.

optimism in the agon, but displays a rationalism and intellectual power which is not evident in other scenes. This is reflected in the style of her speech, and it was argued above that Hecuba's expertise in forensic rhetoric in the agon cannot be related in terms of character to the style of her utterances elsewhere.[60] Euripides is less interested in the consistency of her character than in using her to express a distinctive view of the world which contrasts in significant ways from that expressed by Helen.

The second half of Hecuba's unusually long speech shows far fewer signs of the philosophical and rhetorical influences that were so striking in the first half. The style of this part of her speech is more natural and more in keeping with her character elsewhere in the play. She begins by denying that Helen could have been abducted by Paris, on the grounds that if she really had been carried off by force she would have raised the βοή and been rescued by her brothers (998–1001).[61] Hecuba's argument here plainly misrepresents Helen's claim that she was married by force (962), which referred to the intervention of Aphrodite.

Hecuba alleges next that Helen always supported the winning side in the war, and was not consistent in her allegiance either to Paris or to Menelaus (1002–9). The truth of this criticism is impossible to determine, but it derives no support from the canonical version of the story in the *Iliad*. Hecuba's argument here is less well focused than the comparable argument of Electra that Clytaemestra was pleased by Trojan success because she did not want Agamemnon to return home (*El.* 1076–9). Hecuba might have argued that Helen favoured the Trojans in the war and used this as evidence of her infidelity to Menelaus. Her complaint that Helen praised Menelaus in order to annoy Paris has some basis in Homer (*Il.* 3. 428–36), but is trivial and distracting in the present context.

In the next section of her speech (1010–22), Hecuba denies Helen's claim that she tried to escape from Troy. She suggests a motive why Helen should have wished to remain in Troy, and it is difficult to weigh this against Helen's appeal to witnesses. In other versions of the story, the question is less why Helen herself did not try to escape than why the Trojans did not return her.[62]

Hecuba's speech resembles the speeches of Medea (*Medea*) and Andromache (in the first agon of *Andromache*) in being elaborately rhetorical at the beginning but becoming looser and more emotional towards the end.

---

[60] See above, pp. 94 f.
[61] On the βοή, see W. Schulze, *Kleine Schriften*² (Göttingen, 1966), 160 ff.
[62] e.g. Herodotus 2. 120.

In the case of Medea's speech, it seemed that this reflected the failure of her attempts to control herself. This kind of development in a speech can, however, also be explained in rhetorical terms, and it is appropriate enough that a speech of this kind should come to an emotional climax. Hecuba thus concludes the section of her speech which is addressed directly to Helen with an outburst of hatred, attacking her for having adorned herself before emerging to meet Menelaus (1022–8). Forensic formality is strongly reasserted in the epilogue, in which she appeals to Menelaus to execute Helen (1029–32).[63]

The agon in *Troades* thus contains many issues on which it is impossible to decide, from comparatively trivial matters of fact to fundamental questions about the gods. This indeterminacy is completed by the obscurity which Euripides introduces into the whole question of the effect of the agon on the action. He tends to avoid integrating his agones into a causally connected sequence of events, so that on the one hand they rarely achieve anything, while on the other hand he shuns the ironic effects that could have been derived from stressing their futility. In *Hippolytus*, for example, Theseus' curse means that the agon comes too late to accomplish anything, but this fact is not emphasized and the curse seems temporarily to be forgotten. Euripides' agones have a wider significance than their effect, or lack of effect, on the immediate action. The agon in *Troades* is thus detached from the fairly unimportant question of whether Helen will, or will not, be punished, and it is interesting to examine how Euripides manages to do this.

The debate between Hecuba and Helen can only have any effect on the action through the impression which it makes on the judge Menelaus. One way in which Euripides detaches the agon from its immediate context is to represent Menelaus as having little or no interest in listening to a debate at all. Normally, it is the judge, if there is one, who introduces the debate (compare Demophon at *Hcld.* 132 f. and Agamemnon at *Hec.* 1129–31), but here Menelaus first rejects Helen's request to be allowed to defend herself (905), and then only grudgingly agrees when Hecuba reinforces her request (911–13). Hecuba's request is, effectively, the formal introduction of the agon (906–10), and it is not only surprising that one of the contestants, rather than the judge, should make this introduction, but also hard to explain in character terms, since Hecuba has no interest in allowing Helen the opportunity to defend herself.[64] The point can

---

[63] On appeals to the jury to set a precedent, see Carey 1989 on Lys. 1. 47. On ἵν' εἰδῇς, see Garvie 1986 on A. *Cho.* 439; Willink 1986 on *Or.* 534–5.

[64] Cf. Grube 1941: 26 f.

only be to detach Menelaus from too close an involvement in the debate. His lack of involvement is equally clear when he comes to make his judgement speech (1036–41). This speech is very short, it shows no sign that he has grasped the complex issues presented to him, and he admits only that Hecuba has confirmed the opinion that he already had. All this is in marked contrast to the balanced responses of Demophon (*Hcld.* 236–52) and Agamemnon (*Hec.* 1240–51).

Menelaus has, in fact, made up his mind what to do with Helen before he enters, and that is to take her to Greece and kill her there. This is made clear in the second half of his entrance speech, where the course of action which he proposes to adopt is explicitly contrasted with two courses of action which he rejects (873–9).[65] He offers no reasons for this rather odd decision, and the introduction of the apparently superfluous and confusing possibility of Helen being killed in Greece seems designed by Euripides to allow the greatest possible scope for leaving her fate uncertain. Menelaus reiterates his decision to kill Helen at every opportunity thereafter (901 f., 905, 1039–41), rejecting her final plea (1046), and emphatically reaffirming his decision with his final words (1055–9). Nothing could be more explicit.[66]

On the other hand, it has often been argued that the scene has features which suggest that Menelaus' resolution is not as strong as it might be. There are two passages, in particular, which raise doubts. Immediately before Helen enters, Hecuba expresses approbation of Menelaus' stated intention to kill her (890); she goes on to warn him against looking on her, lest her charms should affect him (891–4). These lines do no more than raise the possibility that Helen might escape, and this possibility seems immediately to be ruled out when Helen enters and Menelaus looks on her without altering his intention to kill her. Something rather similar happens at the end of the scene, when Hecuba warns Menelaus against sailing to Greece in the same ship as Helen (1049). His fatuous response raises doubts about his seriousness,[67] but Menelaus does actually agree not to sail in the same ship and concludes the scene by reiterating his determination to punish Helen (1053–9).

Hecuba's two warnings can have no other purpose than to suggest that Helen might escape, alluding as they do to the well-established version

---

[65] Emphasis is given by the ascending tricolon, and by the formula 'not A, or B, but C'. This formula is common in answers to questions in Homer: see J. T. Kakridis, *Homeric Researches* (Lund, 1949), ch. 5; S. West on H. *Od.* 2. 30.
[66] Seidensticker 1982: 90 n. 4 rightly criticizes Wilamowitz's idea that Menelaus does not even intend to kill Helen. [67] Cf. Seidensticker 1982: 89–91.

of the story in which Menelaus pardons her.[68] This is not, however, to say that it is clear that Helen will not be punished, and that this makes an ironic point about the injustice of the Greeks and the suffering of the Trojans.[69] Euripides goes to considerable lengths to give weight both to Menelaus' statements that Helen will die and to Hecuba's doubts. The point of this is to leave no secure impression of what is to happen to her, and the whole question of her punishment is further distanced from the agon by the fact that Menelaus has never, at any stage, intended to execute her on the spot, and shows no interest in listening to a debate. The agon, which deals in a profound way with the significance of the Trojan War, is too important to be tied down to the comparatively trivial question of whether Helen will be punished.

The agon in *Troades* has some points in common with that in *Hecuba*, but goes far beyond it in scope. In *Hecuba*, Polymestor is plainly guilty, and Hecuba's refutation of his argument is almost entirely convincing. In *Troades*, on the other hand, Helen's guilt is far less clear-cut and the implications of her alleged crime are more far-reaching. Several matters of dispute are left unresolved, and, with regard to the central issue of the role of the gods, there is not only a conflict between the two speeches, but also tensions and contradictions within them. In Helen's speech, there is the paradox of sophisticated rhetoric being used to advance an argument which relies on a literal belief in myth. Hecuba, on the other hand, adopts a view of the gods, combining idealization with reductivism, which is highly distinctive but not wholly adequate. The presuppositions of the two speeches are completely different, and it is impossible either to decide which is right or to find any middle ground between them.

---

[68] Helen's escape is referred to elsewhere in Euripides at *An.* 627–31 (cf. *Or.* 1287). On the whole question of the relevance in tragedy of aspects of the myth which are not mentioned explicitly, see Stinton 1986 (= 1990: 454–92).

[69] Thus, e.g. Pohlenz 1954: i. 369 f. A further objection to this view is that Menelaus has no obligation to anyone else to punish Helen. The Greeks have given him the choice of what to do with her (873–5), and he regards himself as the person primarily wronged by her (902, 1041).

7

Orestes

THE debate between Orestes and Tyndareus in *Orestes* is the most subtle and complex of all Euripides' agones. Many problems of interpretation are raised by the two main speeches themselves, and questions also arise about the relationship of the debate both to the immediate action and to the overall themes of the play. The earlier part of the play has presented the desperate situation in which Orestes and Electra find themselves, and revealed that Menelaus is their only hope of salvation (52–6). The agon comes in the long second episode (348–806), which contrasts Menelaus' failure to live up to their hopes with the ready help offered by the loyal friend Pylades.

The debate between Orestes and Tyndareus is embedded in a supplication scene in which Orestes asks Menelaus for help.[1] He makes three appeals. The first, in answer to Menelaus' enquiry after him, is very brief (380–4), and is followed by a long and elaborate stichomythia in which he explains his situation (385–447). His second appeal (448–55), which seems at first to be the proem to a much longer speech, is cut short by the arrival of Tyndareus.[2] This short speech adumbrates two themes, the duties of φίλοι and Menelaus' obligations to Agamemnon, which are developed at greater length in the third and final appeal, which Orestes makes after the agon (640–79). The agon thus comes at a crucial moment in Orestes' supplication of Menelaus, but it is typical of Euripides that it has no effect on him. Menelaus pays no attention to the discussion of the matricide, and Euripides further separates the agon from his final response by interposing a speech in which Orestes actually rejects the claim to justice which was so important in the debate with Tyndareus. This speech, his third appeal to Menelaus, merely develops the issues of φιλία and gratitude which had already been sketched before the agon. Menelaus' decision does not depend on a judgement of Orestes' guilt, which in any case he shows no signs of making. Euripides could not have made it clearer that the issues

---

[1] See above, pp. 8 f. Cf. Solmsen 1975: 59 f.
[2] Cf. Strohm 1957: 42; Willink 1986 on *Or.* 448–55.

of the matricide are distinct from the question of whether Menelaus will help. The agon in *Orestes* thus has a somewhat similar relationship to the action as the agon in *Electra*, where the question of whether Orestes should kill Clytaemestra is separated from the detailed discussion of her guilt in the agon.

Menelaus is not influenced by the actual debate, but the structure of the scene does rather suggest that Tyndareus' ferocious threats may have had their effect. Orestes himself certainly believes that Tyndareus' arrival was significant, and he characterizes Menelaus' decision as a preference for his father-in-law over his brother (748–54). Even the effect of Tyndareus' threats, however, is not strongly stressed, as it might have been if Menelaus explicitly changed his mind. He reveals indecision after the agon (632–5), but he had not come to any firm decision even before it, and it is not clear that he ever intended to help Orestes.[3] He has several times expressed his revulsion from the matricide (e.g. 417), and his expressions of sympathy for Orestes (482, 484, 486) are not only ambiguous,[4] but are also designed more to justify speaking to Orestes at all than as indications of an intention to help him. There is thus a rather weak implication that Tyndareus' intervention influenced Menelaus, but the actual arguments in the agon make no impression on him whatever.

Tyndareus' speech begins with a brief proem (491–3), in which line 491 both concludes the stichomythia and introduces the statement of the theme in the next two lines, that Orestes is the most ἀσύνετος of men.[5] Winnington-Ingram gives a convincing defence of Bothe's ἀσοφίας (491), paraphrasing '*Me* stupid? What about *him*?'[6] Tyndareus' proem introduces the agon with unusual explicitness, but the word ἀγών is also used more generally of Orestes' ordeal (878, 1244) and, more specifically, of his trial by the Argive assembly (861). This legal context is frequently alluded to (48 f., 440, 756, 799).[7]

Tyndareus goes on to argue that Orestes should have had recourse to τὸν κοινὸν Ἑλλήνων νόμον (495) and expelled Clytaemestra from the palace (494–506). He explains and justifies this position in the next section of his

[3] Winnington-Ingram 1969: 134 suggests that Menelaus has his eye on the throne (cf. 1058 f., 1660), but there is no hint of this earlier in the play (cf. Willink 1986 on 682–716).
[4] See Willink 1986 on 484.
[5] On 'headline' proems, see above, pp. 25 f.; and, on insulting proems connected with the main body of the speech by ὅστις, see above, p. 66.
[6] R. P. Winnington-Ingram, 'Tragica', *BICS* 16 (1969), 44–54, at 53 f., who also observes that ἀσοφία has a legal flavour, reminiscent of such terms as ἀσέβεια. West 1987b: 285 f., proposes τοῦ σοφοῦ γ' (491), with a question mark after line 492.
[7] See above, pp. 4 f. Willink 1986: p. xlvi discusses agonistic terminology in *Orestes*.

speech (507–17), where he advances the classic argument against vendetta that there is logically no end to the killing.[8] Exile rather than death was thus laid down as the penalty for murder by πατέρες οἱ πάλαι (512). Tyndareus runs together two points which are in theory separable. His main point is that exile is the appropriate penalty for murder, but he also seems to suggest that Orestes should have prosecuted Clytaemestra rather than taken revenge on her himself. This second point does in practice follow from the first since, if the threat of vengeance is ruled out, exile can only be enforced by society at large. There are two main problems with Tyndareus' argument here. The first is whether his whole proposal is anachronistic and absurd; the second is whether, assuming that the idea of prosecution is in principle acceptable, it was ever practicable for Orestes.

Many scholars have argued that Tyndareus' argument is obviously absurd.[9] One objection is on grounds of anachronism, since the trial of Orestes was the first murder trial and the necessary legal machinery therefore did not exist for him to use against Clytaemestra.[10] This objection has little force in itself, partly because there was an alternative version that the first murder trial was of Ares for the killing of Halirrhothius.[11] Secondly, Tyndareus' language is ambiguous enough to be intelligible in the context of the heroic world, for all that his words have strong legal overtones. Line 495 certainly seems to imply that Orestes should have prosecuted Clytaemestra, but can be taken to mean no more than that Orestes should have acted in accordance with common Greek custom or practice.[12] The ambiguity of νόμος allows for some obscurity in what Tyndareus is saying.

There is also some obscurity in Tyndareus' main proposal χρῆν αὐτὸν ἐπιθεῖναι μὲν αἵματος δίκην / ὁσίαν διώκοντ' (500 f.), where the sense seems to be 'he should have imposed a holy penalty for bloodshed, acting as prosecutor'.[13] Three technical legal expressions are present here: δίκη φόνου ('a murder case'), δίκην διώκειν ('to prosecute a case'), and φόνου διώκειν ('to

---

[8] On the *reductio ad absurdum*, see above, pp. 31 f. τόνδε (508) probably refers to Orestes, rather than being indefinite. For absurd personalization in this type of argument, compare *Or.* 659, *Alc.* 690. On the argument against vendetta, see Wedd 1895: p. xxxi (citing Dem. 23. 39); Willink 1986 on 507–11.

[9] e.g. Krieg 1934: 29–32; Grube 1941: 383 f.; Smith 1967: 300 n. 1; Steidle 1968: 105; Aélion 1983: i. 155–7.

[10] Cf. Weil 1879: 675; Winnington-Ingram 1969: 133; Easterling 1985: 9.

[11] Cf. *El.* 1258–63; Sommerstein 1989: 2 f.

[12] With ἦλθεν ἐπί (495) compare ἐπελθεῖν (*Su.* 155, *Hel.* 165) meaning 'consult'. But there is also a suggestion of the more technical ἐπεξελθεῖν meaning 'prosecute'. Cf. Kells 1966: 52 n. 4.

[13] Willink 1986 (ad loc.) argues convincingly against the usual comma at the end of line 500, while West 1987a argues equally convincingly that Willink's interpretation makes the participle διώκοντ' (501) redundant. The ambiguity is carefully calculated.

prosecute for murder'). None of these expressions, however, is in the foreground, since δίκην depends much more obviously on ἐπιθεῖναι, and δίκην ἐπιθεῖναι is an established expression itself, not markedly technical (cf. 576 f., Hdt. 1. 120. 1), and with parallels in early poetry (H. *Od.* 2. 192; Hes. *Op.* 334). Tyndareus' strained syntax is designed to suggest as strongly as possible that Orestes should have prosecuted Clytaemestra, while at the same time avoiding any jarring anachronism. Tyndareus is making a rhetorical case, and there are problems in what he says, but his argument should not be dismissed as obviously and grotesquely anachronistic.

Similar points can be made about his argument that exile, and not death, is the traditional penalty for murder. He alleges that πατέρες οἱ πάλαι (512) ordained that killers should be purified by exile rather than killed.[14] This has some plausibility, but is in some respects exaggerated for rhetorical effect. Tyndareus frames his argument in terms of an appeal to a widely defined Panhellenic and ancestral authority (the laws of 495 and 512 are evidently the same), and it must be related both to Homeric and to Athenian practice. Homeric practice was that the murderer might first try to pay blood-money and, failing that, go into exile. Exile seems to have been the most common outcome, but less as a formal punishment than as a measure of prudence to escape revenge.[15] There was some formal control, as exemplified by the arbitration scene on the shield of Achilles in *Iliad* 19, but the onus of retribution lay on the relatives of the dead man. It is thus possible to say, speaking loosely, that exile was the punishment for homicide in Homer, but it would be an exaggeration to conclude that individual retaliation was ruled out. Homicides would not, in fact, have had any incentive to go into exile without the threat of such retaliation. Athenian homicide law seems to have prescribed death and exile as alternative penalties for homicide, and voluntary exile was at least always a way of avoiding punishment even if it is not admitted that exile was in itself a penalty.[16]

Tyndareus' argument demands a complex response. His suggestion that Orestes should have prosecuted Clytaemestra verges on the anachronistic, and this shocking and innovative aspect to it should not be ignored. He does, however, express his proposal in language which is vague and

[14] On exile as purification, see Parker 1983: 114, 121. Tyndareus never makes his overall argument clear enough for there to be any certainty about whether line 515 refers to a complete ban on the death penalty (di Benedetto) or only on vendetta killing (Paley).

[15] Cf. Glotz 1904: 51–9; Gagarin 1981: 6–10. On the transition from self-help to full legal control, see H. J. Wolff, 'The Origin of Judicial Litigation among the Greeks', *Traditio*, 4 (1946), 31–87.   [16] See Gagarin 1981: ch. 7.

ambiguous enough to make it intelligible within the context of the heroic world. There may not be courts as such, but it is easy to envisage a popular assembly of the kind to which Telemachus has recourse in *Odyssey* 2, or which is, indeed, described in the messenger speech in *Orestes*. Tyndareus' argument that exile is the appropriate penalty for homicide is plausible and humane, and is supported by a convincing argument against vendetta. There is also some justification for his statement that exile is the traditional Greek punishment for homicide, but there is no support, in either Homeric or Athenian practice, for his denial that death was also an accepted penalty. Revenge was always a possibility in Homer, while the more formal Athenian system certainly did not rule out the death penalty.[17]

Tyndareus emerges as a Euripidean character of a fairly typical kind, somewhat reminiscent of Hecuba in *Troades*, in putting forward an argument which combines traditional and advanced ideas in a superficially attractive way, but which is also in some respects inadequate to the strongly defined mythical world of the play. Hecuba used her striking and impressive ideas about the gods in the attempt to refute Helen's reliance on the details of the myth, while Tyndareus tries to minimize the unique and problematic features of Orestes' traditional predicament. His argument must be taken seriously, not least because it reflects the social and political dimension which is such a striking feature of the way in which the myth is treated in this play. The people of Argos evidently share his attitude and, although he is himself a Spartan, his verbal objections in the agon correspond to the physical force by which they put pressure on Orestes and Electra.[18]

Tyndareus' argument is consistent with the emphasis in the play on the social and political context of Orestes' crime. His case is thus not intrinsically absurd, but it remains to be seen whether it is actually valid. The main objection to it is that, even if there were legal processes to which Orestes might have resorted, they would have been of little use to him in prosecuting the reigning tyrants. He was a baby when Agamemnon sailed to Troy (377, cf. H. *Od.* 1. 41; 3. 304 f.; E. *El.* 14–18), and thus still a child at the time of Agamemnon's murder, and a powerless exile thereafter. Finally, the description of the popular assembly in the messenger speech gives no grounds for confidence in Argive justice. The people of Argos certainly took no steps to prosecute Clytaemestra and Aegisthus for the

---

[17] On Draco's homicide law, reinscribed in the agora in 409/8, see R. S. Stroud, *Drakon's Law on Homicide* (Berkeley, 1968). On the reinscription, see N. Robertson, 'The Laws of Athens, 410–399 B.C.: The Evidence for Review and Publication', *JHS* 110 (1990), 43–75.

[18] Cf. Conacher 1967: 218–20; Fuqua 1976: 73.

murder of Agamemnon.[19] The problem, therefore, is not so much that society intervenes in the administration of justice, but that it does not do so systematically. The Argive *polis* does nothing about the murder of Agamemnon, but then persecutes Orestes when he takes revenge himself. His tragedy is that it is unclear whether or not there are efficient legal processes, and justice is only one of several competing elements, along with power politics and self-interest. Euripides explodes the neat contrast in the *Oresteia* between private vendetta and the impeccably impartial justice of the *polis*, and his analysis of the inadequacies of the *polis* was no doubt prompted by contemporary Athenian politics.[20]

In the next section of his speech (518–25), Tyndareus concedes the wickedness of his daughters but affirms his desire to defend the law. This rhetorical *consensio* is designed to pre-empt criticism of his own part in the chain of events, about which Orestes will indeed comment (585–7, 750).[21] Tyndareus employs another rhetorical device, παρρησία, when he criticizes the judge Menelaus for his readiness to go to Troy for the sake of a bad wife.[22] Prosecutors commonly claim to be defending the law (e.g. Ant. 1. 31), but Tyndareus' language here is of particular interest. He is in some respects a traditionalist, with his appeal to ancestral authority (512) and to absolute standards of τὸ ὅσιον (481, 501, 515, 518) and τὸ δίκαιον (494, 538), but he also shows the influence of more advanced ideas. His regular appeals to νόμος have, on the whole, been in fairly traditional terms (487, 495, 503, 523), although his argument that Orestes should have prosecuted Clytaemestra is a novelty in the myth. Here, however, his implication that it is νόμος that separates humans from beasts reflects sophistic ideas of progress.[23] He argues that Orestes' 'bestiality' destroys cities (525), and this reflects his general attempt to treat the matricide in the context of the *polis*. Tyndareus thus resembles such characters as Theseus (*Supplices*), Hecuba (*Troades*), Jocasta (*Phoenissae*), and Tiresias (*Bacchae*) in his combination of traditional and advanced ideas, and in his confident

---

[19] Cf. Krieg 1934: 30; Eucken 1986: 158 f. The question whether, in Athenian law, murderers could be prosecuted by persons unrelated to the victim is discussed by M. Gagarin, 'The Prosecution of Homicide in Athens', *GRBS* 20 (1979), 301–23.

[20] On the political background, see especially Arrowsmith 1963; Rawson 1972; Burkert 1974; Longo 1975. Many scholars rightly stress the relevance of the *stasis* chapters in Thucydides, especially 3. 82.

[21] *Consensio*: Ant. 5. 27, 62; Lys. 12. 34. Cf. Quintilian 9. 2. 51.

[22] παρρησία: Dover 1974: 23–5; Macleod 1983: 92.

[23] Cf. Winnington-Ingram 1969; Longo 1975: 284 f.; West 1987a on 524. On the theme of bestiality in *Orestes*, see P. N. Boulter, 'The Theme of ἀγρία in Euripides' *Orestes*', *Phoenix*, 16 (1962), 102–6.

attempt to apply his theories to complex moral problems. His argument, in many ways so attractive, presupposes that recourse to the law will always be effective. The action of *Orestes* suggests that things are not so simple.

Tyndareus then turns to address Orestes directly, strictly in contradiction to his earlier interpretation of the pollution law, but with obvious dramatic effect (526–33). His speech comes to an emotional climax with his graphic evocation of the crime (526–9), and continues with the rhetorical denial that there is need of other witnesses (cf. *Hi.* 971 f.) because Orestes is visibly hated by the gods (cf. *Su* 494–505). This leads on to his final appeal to Menelaus (534–41), in which he exhorts him not to oppose the gods (cf. *Tro.* 964 f.), and concludes by saying that Clytaemestra deserved to die but not at Orestes' hand (cf. *El.* 1169–71, 1185–9).[24] This echoes Tyndareus' argument in the first section of his speech, but makes no allusion to his controversial proposal about what Orestes should actually have done.

In the transmitted text, Tyndareus demands, in this closing section of his speech, that Menelaus allows Orestes to be stoned by the Argives (536 f.). These two lines reappear as 625 f., and were accordingly deleted by Brunck.[25] Willink has supported Brunck's deletion, arguing that Tyndareus is only provoked to demand the death penalty by Orestes' infuriating defence.[26] There are, however, several arguments against the deletion of 536 f. In the first place, Orestes' statement (564) that Tyndareus has demanded stoning is *prima facie* evidence that he has done so, although certainly not conclusive (Hecuba misrepresents Helen at *Tro.* 998–1001). Secondly, as West (on 536–7) comments, 'one expects a positive injunction to complement the negative in 535'. More generally, one expects some positive demand at the end of a prosecution speech in order to make clear what the prosecutor actually wants to happen (contrast the precise demands of Hecuba at *Tro.* 1029–32 and of the Herald at *Hcld.* 175–8). Some parallel to a speech ending merely 'do not help him' is afforded by *Hec* 1233, but there Polymestor has already made it perfectly clear what help he wants (1127 f.). Willink (on 536–7) argues that the chorus would not have reacted so mildly (542 f.) if Tyndareus had demanded the death penalty at the end of his speech. The chorus is, however, reacting only to the last two lines of Tyndareus' speech, just as the chorus does to the last two lines of Polymestor's speech at *Hec.* 1183 f. Anodyne choral distichs follow ferocious speeches at *Hcld.* 179 f. and *El.* 1100 f.[27]

[24] On this formulation, see Xanthakis-Karamanos 1979: 70 f.
[25] On repeated lines in Euripides, see Barrett 1964 on *Hi.* 1049
[26] Willink 1986 on 470–629, 491–51, 544–601. Cf. Burnett 1971: 206.
[27] On the genuineness of *El.* 1100 f., see above, pp. 68 f.

Even without 536 f., it is difficult to believe that any audience would have supposed Tyndareus to be demanding anything other than the death penalty. It has already been made clear that this is what the Argives want (431–46), and Tyndareus, although he is a Spartan, seems in many ways to represent their views. Orestes' own reaction (564) can only confirm this impression. There is, however, no need to delete both lines. Hermann's deletion of 537 leaves the tolerable repetition of a single line (536 = 625), and even this repetition could be avoided with Wilamowitz' additional deletion of 625.

It would, in any case, be out of keeping with Euripides' normal practice in the agon for the style of a defence speech to make a significant difference to the action. He normally organizes the action in such a way that the participants can deploy a full range of contentious arguments without the distracting possibility that a more conciliatory manner might have been more effective. This is clearly the case, for example, in *Hippolytus* and *Andromache*, and the point is that these are tragic conflicts which cannot be solved merely by talking about them. Euripides uses the medium of a formal debate to represent the conflict, rather than to show a causal factor in the development of it.

One problem with Tyndareus' demand for the death penalty at 536 f. is that it seems inconsistent with his earlier argument that homicide should be punished with exile rather than death (512–15). A demand for Orestes' execution is, however, implied by other passages in Tyndareus' speech. He says that Clytaemestra died justly (538) and also that Orestes was worse than her (504–6). It could be argued that Orestes and Clytaemestra were worse than ordinary murderers, but Tyndareus does not make any such distinction.[28] These inconsistencies must be accepted as evidence of the inability of his argument to cope with the present situation.[29]

Orestes' speech is addressed entirely to Tyndareus, and ignores altogether the judge Menelaus. This is unusual in a three-person agon, but indicates that this debate is not really for Menelaus' benefit at all. When Orestes appeals to him later (640 ff.), he does so on quite different grounds.

Orestes begins his speech with a formal proem (544 f., 548–50).[30] This is a defensive proem of the type in which the speaker knows that he is likely to cause offence but tries to counteract this.[31] This proem, unlike some in Euripides, is highly appropriate to the character and situation of

---

[28] Cf. Wilamowitz 1924: 255.
[29] On Tyndareus' inconsistencies, see Krieg 1934: 31; Zeitlin 1980: 65, 75 n. 43.
[30] With Hartung's transposition of 546 f. to follow 550.   [31] See above, pp. 26 f.

the speaker. Orestes has already expressed his αἰδώς at even meeting Tyndareus (459–69), and the proem of his speech in the agon shows his unwillingness to engage in contentious debate with him. Orestes thus displays rhetorical skill in the wide sense of knowing what it is appropriate to say in a given situation.[32] Orestes has been criticized by some scholars for his contentious approach here, while others have defended him by pointing to the conventions of the agon.[33] The conventions are significant, of course, and it was argued above that it is in any case already too late for a more conciliatory approach to have any effect, but it is interesting that Euripides does something to naturalize Orestes' behaviour towards his grandfather.

The next section of Orestes' speech (546 f., 551–63) advances his most important arguments, the primacy of the father and the adultery of Clytaemestra. He summarizes the ambiguity of his position at the beginning (546 f.), and echoes this summary, in ring composition, in the concluding line of this section (563). He recognizes the unholiness of what he did, and his awareness of the dilemma is expressed by the anguished question τί χρῆν με δρᾶσαι; (551), the first of many rhetorical questions in this speech. He must, nevertheless, defend what he did, and he begins by echoing Apollo's argument at A. *Eum* 658–61 that the father is the only true parent.[34] The problem with this is not only that Apollo's argument is far from convincing even in *Eumenides*, but also that Tyndareus has tried to explode Orestes' dilemma by stating precisely what he ought to have done (500).[35] It is one of the main problems with Orestes' speech that he offers arguments of his own which are far from convincing, while making no attempt to criticize the numerous implausibilities in Tyndareus' attack on him. He could well have made a speech, perhaps in the style of Electra's rejection of the tokens in *Electra*, in which he pointed out that Tyndareus' proposal that he should have prosecuted Clytaemestra is totally impractical. Clytaemestra herself, at A. *Ag.* 1412 ff., puts forward arguments along the lines which Orestes might have adopted, asking why the people of Argos are taking steps to exile her when they did nothing about Agamemnon's

---

[32] Cf. Macleod 1983: 52.

[33] Criticism: Willink 1986 on 544–601; Winnington-Ingram 1969: 134. Defence: Krieg 1934: 15. For a well-balanced view, see Grube 1941: 384 f.

[34] J. Diggle, 'On the *Orestes* of Euripides', *CQ* 40 (1990), 100–23, at 101–5, argues for the deletion of 554 (Nauck) and 555 f. (Paley). 555 f. undoubtedly contain many difficulties, but something is needed to make explicit the implication of 553 that the mother's role is secondary.

[35] On the problems of Apollo's argument in *Eumenides*, see Sommerstein 1989 on *Eum.* 657–66.

murder of Iphigenia. Orestes, however, while he produces a variety of positive arguments to defend himself, puts forward none of the obvious negative arguments which could have undermined Tyndareus' case.[36]

It has been argued that it is a sign of Orestes' inadequacy that he keeps repeating the old arguments even though they have lost their validity.[37] There is, however, a good parallel for his approach in Theseus' speech in the democracy debate in *Supplices*. Theseus ignores the Herald's criticisms of democracy, and puts forward a defence entirely on his own terms. The point of this is clearly that Euripides wants to characterize two opposing positive views, and not to reduce the second speech to a mere denial of the first. In the present case, Orestes acted out his traditional role in the myth without even contemplating the possibilities raised by Tyndareus. He thus reiterates the considerations which influenced him at the time, and this is not unreasonable since it is far from clear that Tyndareus' proposal was practicable. It is important to note that Orestes is not in any sense opposed to the justice of the *polis*, and is not to be seen, at least in the context of the matricide, as a reactionary or oligarchic figure who does not believe in the democratic courts. It never even crossed his mind that anyone other than himself could have punished Clytaemestra, and this is shown by the way in which he conducts his defence in the agon. Euripides is exploiting the tensions and contradictions which occur when heroic myth is treated in the context of the fifth-century *polis*, and it is not merely a mistake by Orestes to suppose that his traditional tragic dilemma still has some validity.

Orestes concludes this section of his speech by drawing attention to the adultery of Clytaemestra (557–63). He employs a form of *praeteritio*, expressing hesitation about mentioning Aegisthus' name but then going ahead and doing so (compare *El.* 945–8, 1245 f. for a similar technique). He treats the murder of Clytaemestra as a mere by-product of the killing of Aegisthus, who was undeniably liable to death as an adulterer.

In the next section of his speech (564–71), Orestes claims to have put a stop to the νόμος of women killing their husbands. He may earlier have seemed to be ignoring Tyndareus' arguments, but his rebuttal here is carefully calculated. Tyndareus had blamed him for ignoring law, and he responds by saying that he is opposed only to the law of wives killing their husbands. He counters Tyndareus' *reductio ad absurdum* (507–11) with one of his own which also envisages an unchecked series of killings.[38]

---

[36] Cf. Grube 1941: 384; Krieg 1934: 30; Conacher 1967: 219.
[37] e.g. Zeitlin 1980: 58 f.   [38] Cf. O'Brien 1988: 187 f.

His scornful language (especially 568) is designed to defuse the pity which Tyndareus had tried to evoke (526–9).[39] Orestes' claim to be a public benefactor is a common rhetorical move, but also shows that he is aware of the social context of his actions.[40] The agon is not merely a conflict between private and communal views of justice, and the discussion of what is best for society at large is resumed in the assembly reported in the messenger speech where the αὐτουργός also argues that Orestes should be treated as a public benefactor. Orestes rebuts Tyndareus' accusation of having committed δεινά (571), and there are two problems with this. Tyndareus did not, in fact, use this word, but it is hard to deny that this is what he meant. Secondly, Orestes himself actually did use this word earlier when describing his actions to Menelaus (396).

This is one of a number of apparent contradictions in Orestes' attitude to his own actions at different points of the play, and various interpretations have been offered.[41] There are two plausible explanations of these contradictions, explanations which are complementary rather than mutually exclusive. In the first place, it is highly appropriate that Orestes should have contradictory reactions to what he has done. He himself recognizes that the matricide can correctly be evaluated with contradictory moral terms (546 f.), and it would be positively inappropriate for him to have consistent and well-integrated attitudes to the matter. Secondly, it is not surprising that different reactions should be provoked in Orestes by the various persons with whom he converses. It is quite in keeping with naturalistic characterization that he should feel guilty at one moment, but later emphasize his innocence when confronted with a death-demanding prosecutor who shows no signs of recognizing the complexities of the situation. This is also, of course, in keeping with the confrontational style of the agon. The demands of rhetoric and of character are perfectly complementary.

In the next section of his speech (572–8), Orestes argues that he killed Clytaemestra justly because she betrayed her husband while he was away fighting for Greece. This argument, reminiscent of A. *Eum.* 625–39, is also used by the αὐτουργός in the assembly (923–30). Orestes does not,

---

[39] On the ἐλέου ἐκβολή here, see E. B. Stevens, 'Some Attic Commonplaces of Pity', *AJP* 65 (1944), 1–25, at 13 f.

[40] Claims to be a public benefactor: *An.* 680–4, *Tro.* 924–37; Pl. *Ap.* 36c–d. Precedents: *Su.* 540 f.; C. Carey and R. Reid (eds.), *Demosthenes: Selected Private Speeches* (Cambridge, 1985), 10 f.

[41] Krieg 1934: 31 and Reinhardt 1960 argue that Orestes feels guilty but needs to defend himself against others. O'Brien 1988 argues convincingly that Orestes adopts different rhetorical strategies for different situations.

however, get to grips with Tyndareus' attack on him. Tyndareus conceded that Clytaemestra died justly (505, 538), and argued only that Orestes was not the person to kill her. Orestes is arguing on his own terms, as he does throughout the speech, assuming that Tyndareus' proposals were unrealistic and that no one other than himself could have punished Clytaemestra. In the last three lines of this section of his speech, he does, in fact, show that he has paid close attention to what Tyndareus has said (576–8). Tyndareus had blamed Orestes for ignoring τὸ δίκαιον and νόμος, and Orestes responds by saying that Clytaemestra, when she realized that she had done wrong, did not punish herself but punished Agamemnon instead.[42] This insistent legal language, with an especially striking echo of ἐπιθεῖναι δίκην (500), shows that Orestes takes a different view from Tyndareus of the operation of legal processes in this case. Orestes does not attack Tyndareus explicitly, but his adaptation of Tyndareus' legal language to describe a system of retribution confined to the family implies that only he could have punished Clytaemestra.

Orestes goes on to argue that he would have been persecuted by his father's Erinyes if he had not punished Clytaemestra (579–84).[43] This argument evokes Aeschylus (*Cho.* 283 f., 1029–33; *Eum.* 465–7), although Orestes here argues from probability rather than, as in the *Oresteia*, from the authority of Apollo. This does not, however, falsify his argument, any more than does the contradiction (of the kind discussed above) with his earlier statement that Agamemnon would have opposed the matricide (288–93). Orestes emphasizes the traditional supernatural aspects of the story, rather as Helen does in *Troades*, in contrast to Tyndareus' reliance on secular and social factors.[44] The tension in Orestes' speech derives partly from the fact that the continued relevance of Apollo and the Erinyes is still unclear.

A further reminiscence of Helen's speech in *Troades* comes in Orestes' next argument, when he blames Tyndareus for begetting Clytaemestra (585–7, cf. *Tro.* 919–22).[45] He goes on to contrast the virtuous wife

---

[42] Cf. Kells 1960.
[43] West 1987b: 283 n. 9 argues (against Willink) that there is no need for these lines to be transposed to follow 590. On φόνον δικάζων (580), see Willink 1986 ad loc., but his conjecture φόνου δικαστῶν (sc. τῶν Ἐρινύων) is unconvincing because Orestes has not mentioned the Erinyes at all. A line may have fallen out after 579, perhaps containing some mention of Apollo (cf. 164 f.). For the interrupted appeal to the gods, compare *Tro.* 469, 1280. Cf. Fraenkel 1957: 194.
[44] Tyndareus does refer to the gods (530–6) but only in vague and general terms.
[45] See above, pp. 101 f. With ἀπώλεσάς με (586) compare *Tro.* 920, *Cretes* fr. 82. 34 Austin. With *Or.* 595 compare *Tro.* 948.

of Odysseus, pointing out that Telemachus had no need to kill her (588–90). The contrast between Clytaemestra and Penelope is familiar from the *Odyssey*, but it is exploited here in a very feeble fashion and the authenticity of the lines has often been doubted.[46]

In the final section of his speech, Orestes refers his guilt to Apollo (591–9).[47] He takes a different attitude to the matricide here, conceding that it was wrong but blaming Apollo. This apparent inconsistency can be seen in rhetorical terms as a form of *consensio*, but is also (as was suggested above) intelligible in terms of character. Orestes' argument here goes back to Aeschylus (*Cho.* 269–305, etc.), and is undoubtedly valid in the context of the present play. Responsibility is regularly attributed to Apollo (28–31, 76, 121, 160–5, 191–4, 276, 285–7, 327–31, 416–20, 955 f.), who himself admits to it at the end of the play (1665).[48] There is, in fact, a marked contrast between the repeated references to Apollo's sanction of the matricide and his absence from most of the second half of the play, when Orestes acts on his own initiative.[49] Apollo's approval does not, however, make Orestes' deed unproblematic, and the moral and social problems remain the same whichever of them is to blame.

Orestes ends his speech with a two-line conclusion (600–1), in which he stresses his own suffering (cf. 586; *Tro.* 920, 935, 964), and in which εὐδαιμόνως (601) echoes εὐδαιμονῶ (541) at the end of Tyndareus' speech.[50]

The result of the agon is, as usual in Euripides, to intensify the antagonism, and Tyndareus announces his intention to rouse the Argive assembly to stone Orestes and Electra (607–14). This is a new development, but its significance should not be exaggerated since both Tyndareus and the Argives had favoured stoning even before

---

[46] Del. Dindorf. Cf. Fraenkel 1950: 814 n. 3; Page 1934: 53; Johansen 1959: 51 f. The lines are defended by Willink 1986 (ad loc.) and by West 1987a (ad loc., cf. 1987b: 283), but they do not fully face up to the problems of ἐπεγάμει (589). γαμεῖσθαι can be used offensively of a man (cf. Page 1938 on *Med.* 606), but there is no good parallel for the reverse insult, which would in any case be obscure and inappropriate here. *Trag. Adesp.* 194 is of uncertain date and context, while *Med.* 606 is a rhetorical question which is making a statement about Jason.

[47] The use of ὁρᾷς (591) is unusual, since it does not introduce an illustration of anything that has gone before. Cf. Johansen 1959: 50–5; Stevens 1976: 36 f.

[48] Cf. Krieg 1934: 27; Steidle 1968: 99; Erbse 1984: 251 ff.

[49] Cf. Schein 1975: 61 f. Apollo is only mentioned once (955 f.) between 591 and his appearance at 1625.

[50] On 602–4 (del. Herwerden), see Fraenkel 1946: 85 f. On *El.* 1097–9 (del. Hartung), see above, p. 68.

the agon.[51] Euripides often gives the impression of the dispute escalating in the course of an agon, while avoiding any suggestion that the agon itself has made any significant difference to what will happen. In *Phoenissae*, for example, the specific desire of the brothers to kill each other is only expressed at the end of the agon (622), but such an outcome has long been implicit in their actions even before the agon.

Menelaus' only reaction to the agon is to show uncertainty (632–5), and he makes no speech of judgement or decision. His response is distanced from the agon by a further speech by Orestes (640–79), which continues the supplication interrupted by the arrival of Tyndareus. He abandons the self-justification which was central to his speech in the agon, concedes that he acted unjustly, and makes his appeal on the grounds of Menelaus' obligation to Agamemnon and his duties as a φίλος. The contradictions in Orestes' attitude to his crime can be seen here at their most extreme. His admission of injustice at the beginning of this speech (646) can be seen at once as a rhetorical *consensio* and as an expression of one appropriate attitude to what he has done. It can also be argued that he adopts a style of argument calculated to appeal to Menelaus.[52] In dramatic terms, the agon is detached from any question of its influence on Menelaus by the interposition of an appeal which is not only made on different grounds but which positively rejects the defence put forward in the agon. Euripides thus makes clear that Menelaus' decision will not depend on his attitude to what Orestes has done, and that the issue now is the appropriate behaviour of φίλοι.

The Messenger Speech (866–956), describing the Argive assembly, is highly relevant to the agon. The assembly has a somewhat similar blend of heroic and modern elements to that which we have seen in Tyndareus' speech in the agon. Assemblies are familiar from the *Iliad*, but the most striking Homeric precedent is the assembly in *Odyssey* 2. In both cases the assembly assumes greater importance because of the lack of a king, but even in the *Odyssey* the presence of a king did not obviate the need for assemblies (*Od.* 2. 27).[53] The Argive assembly also has elements

---

[51] Willink 1986 (on 544–601) argues that Tyndareus would have had no answer if Orestes had pleaded for exile. The Argives, however, have positively prevented voluntary exile, so that the issue is life or death (50, 438–42, 758). Willink (on 704–7) over-stresses the likely effect of Tyndareus' intervention on the Argive assembly, and West's (1987a) interpretation of this passage is preferable.

[52] *Consensio*: Krieg 1934: 15; Biehl on 646. Argument to appeal to Menelaus: Smith 1967: 301; Falkner 1983: 295; O'Brien 1988: 188 f.

[53] Cf. M. I. Finley, *The World of Odysseus* (2nd revised edn., Harmondsworth, 1979), 78–83; Falkner 1983: 290.

reminiscent of the Athenian *ecclesia*, such as the Herald's introductory announcement (884–7) and the idea of voting (944, with Wecklein's χερῶν).⁵⁴ More generally, Euripides introduces some unattractive aspects of democracy which were doubtless inspired by the Athens of his own day.⁵⁵

Tyndareus' proposal that Orestes should have prosecuted Clytaemestra is not in principle absurd, and the Messenger Speech shows the process by which the *polis* might exercise some formal control over justice. The problem is that the assembly is portrayed in an unattractive light, as prey to mob-orators and special interest groups, and little confidence can be placed in its judgements. The contrast is no longer, as it was in the *Oresteia*, between vendetta and impartial justice, but between individual revenge and a justice which is neither trustworthy nor comprehensive in its scope.⁵⁶

The messenger's description of the assembly shows that no adequate discussion of Orestes' deed can take place there. One reason for this is the factionalism and the influence of demagogues, but more generally it becomes clear that justice ceases to be a factor in such a context. The aims of deliberation should be τὸ δίκαιον and τὸ συμφέρον,⁵⁷ but the Argive assembly ignores the former and does not even pursue the latter in any systematic way. Talthybius is portrayed unsympathetically as evasive and opportunistic, and he seems to have no firm principles whatever (887–97). Diomedes' proposal of exile has been treated by some scholars as being clearly correct,⁵⁸ but if this were so it would be very surprising that it should be so unemphatically presented (898–902). Exile seems here to be no more than a compromise solution, which may preserve the city's εὐσέβεια, but which evades the important issues. The mob-orator who proposes Tyndareus' view that Orestes and Electra should be stoned is naturally (in view of the messenger's sympathies) described in the most hostile terms (902–16).⁵⁹ More serious problems arise with the speech of the αὐτουργός, proposing that Orestes should be garlanded for avenging his father and for vindicating the rights of the soldier away on campaign (917–30). The messenger describes this character in the most enthusiastic

---

⁵⁴ Cf. West 1987a on 612, 885; Willink 1986 on 884–7; Schein 1975: 60. On the 5th-century connotations of voting, see Easterling 1985: 2 f.
⁵⁵ See Willink 1986 on 887–97, 902–16.
⁵⁶ Cf. Eucken 1986: 163; de Romilly 1972: 249 f.   ⁵⁷ See above, pp. 73 f.
⁵⁸ e.g. Willink 1986 on 844–956, 887–930, 898–902.
⁵⁹ On the messenger's bias, see Wedd 1895: p. xxviii; Rawson 1972: 159; Heath 1987: 149 f. Generally: Taplin 1977: 82.

terms, and he is the type of person who is highly regarded elsewhere in Euripides.[60] The problem is that he describes Orestes' deed in a way that does no justice to the complexity of the issues. Clytaemestra may have deserved to die, and Orestes himself was placed in an impossible position, but the play has done nothing to prepare us for the idea that the matricide was a straightforwardly admirable act. On the other hand, the play offers little support to such views as that of Zeitlin that the αὐτουργός is 'clearly anachronistic' in his support of 'male values'.[61]

One possible explanation of this contradiction between the sympathetic way in which the αὐτουργός is presented and the manifest inadequacy of the views which he advances is that the whole context of the assembly makes it impossible even for an admirable character to do justice to a case like that of Orestes. This explanation gains some support from the final speech which the messenger describes, that of Orestes himself (931–42).[62] Orestes has expressed a variety of attitudes to the matricide earlier in the play, and revealed a good understanding of the significance of what he has done. The speech which he addresses to the assembly does, however, express none of this understanding, but appeals in the crudest terms to the misogyny of his audience. We may have no evidence that the αὐτουργός would express more enlightened views even in a more favourable context, but there is good reason to suppose that Orestes is adapting his arguments to suit his audience.[63] The whole description of the Argive assembly makes it clear that no serious discussion of Orestes' case can take place there, and that even sympathetic characters must express their arguments in crude terms.

The agon in *Orestes* resembles that in *Troades* in confronting two speeches which are in many ways convincing on their own terms but which also have internal difficulties and inconsistencies. Tyndareus' idea that exile is the best punishment for homicide is broadly compatible with both epic and Athenian practice, and he argues his case in a sophisticated manner. The just enforcement of law by society is manifestly preferable to vendetta, and this is the conclusion of Aeschylus' *Oresteia*. Orestes does, however, have some reason to ignore Tyndareus' proposal, since it was clearly impracticable for him to prosecute Clytaemestra. The Argive people did nothing to bring her to justice, and it is not clear that a helpless exile

---

[60] Cf. Dover 1974: 112–14; Collard 1975*b* on *Su.* 238–45; Goossens 1962: 645–7.
[61] Zeitlin 1980: 63. Cf. Burnett 1971: 208; Schein 1975: 61.
[62] Wecklein rightly deleted 938–42, but there is no need for Willink's (1986) additional deletion of 932–7.
[63] Cf. O'Brien 1988: 192 f.

could have brought the reigning tyrants to court. Orestes does not point to the difficulties in Tyndareus' case, but instead gives an eloquent statement of the best positive arguments that were available to him.

The agon gives a serious statement of a tragic dilemma. Each side has a case with strong and weak points, and there is no obvious compromise between them. The lack of contact between the two speeches vividly expresses a situation in which different modes of reasoning conflict but cannot come to terms with each other. The contrast is no longer, as it was in *Eumenides*, between vendetta and ideal justice. Society now has some interest in enforcing justice, but does not do so consistently or fairly. Euripides challenges the ideal solution of the *Oresteia* by confronting the myth of Orestes with a realistic portrayal of the justice of the *polis*.

Conclusion

EURIPIDES' last agon, in *Iphigenia in Aulis*, provides a salutary warning against trying to sketch any straightforward development in his use of the agon form. The three agones before this one, in *Troades*, *Phoenissae*, and *Orestes*, may have indicated a tendency in his later agones to complexity and abstraction. The agon in *Iphigenia in Aulis*, on the other hand, is a quarrel in which the contestants concentrate on points of an essentially personal nature, and in this respect it recalls the agon in *Alcestis*. This suggests that there was no linear development in Euripides' style, and also that similarities between the thirteen agones may be more striking than the differences. This is not to deny that the agon in *Iphigenia in Aulis* shows some differences in style from that in *Alcestis*, and it is both more formal and more elaborately rhetorical. Menelaus resembles Hecuba in *Troades* and Tyndareus in *Orestes* in describing his opponent's position in down-to-earth terms, ignoring its traditional mythical context.

The patchy nature of our evidence makes it difficult to detect any continuous development in Euripides' use of the agon form. The dozen or so years between *Medea* and *Electra* account for eight of the thirteen agones, which means that the plays of a comparatively short period are disproportionately represented. Four agones survive from the last decade of Euripides' life, and the unparalleled complexity of the agones in *Troades* and *Orestes* may owe less to any significant development in his style than to the elaborate literary and rhetorical background to discussions of the guilt of Helen and Orestes. A repertoire of arguments existed, for refutation or emulation, which was not available for such an issue as the guilt of Hippolytus. At the beginning of Euripides' career, there is a temptation to regard the agon in *Alcestis* as being in some way typical of his earlier style. *Alcestis* is not, however, a typical tragedy, and far-reaching conclusions should not in any case be drawn from a single play.

If a continuous development cannot be discerned in Euripides' agones, some contrasts can, nevertheless, be made between earlier and later plays. In the earlier extant agones, rhetorical expertise is related to character, at least in broad terms. In his later plays, on the other hand, Euripides' whole style becomes more elaborately rhetorical, and participants in the later agones are equipped with whatever skill in speaking is necessary to make their case. Euripides seems to have responded to rhetorical influences with particular immediacy in the 420s, and the whole question of rhetorical expertise is itself a prominent subject in the plays of this period. This can be seen most clearly in Hecuba's speech in the agon of *Hecuba*, which does nothing to advance our understanding of the issues but which is a compendium of rhetorical devices. The whole point of this speech is that it shows Hecuba's ability to use rhetorical skill to gain her ends. In Euripides' later plays, rhetorical skill attracts less attention in itself, and interest is focused more on the ideas which these highly articulate characters use their verbal skills to express.

This contrast is perhaps related to the fact that the arguments in the later plays are much more finely balanced. In the earlier agones, with the sole exception of that in *Alcestis*, it is obvious which side is in the right, and tension derives from uncertainty about whether an obviously sympathetic character will win his or her case. In the later agones, there are usually good arguments on both sides, and *Troades* and *Orestes* are especially notable in confronting complex speeches which make good points but also contain contradictions within themselves. The agon form is at its most powerful when there is right on both sides, and the agones in *Troades* and *Orestes* are also interesting for the broad scope of their treatment of philosophical, political, and religious issues.

These contrasts between Euripides' use of the agon at different periods of his career are outweighed by the continuities and similarities. He evidently found the agon form, as it appears as early as *Alcestis*, highly satisfactory for his dramatic purposes, and he saw no reason to make significant changes to the pattern. Much the same is true of his use of the prologue speech, the messenger speech, and the *deus ex machina*. The agon, from *Alcestis* to *Iphigenia in Aulis*, retains the same basic form in which conflicting formal speeches, balancing each other in length as well as in other ways, are followed by angry dialogue. Euripides saw little need to disguise the formality of the agon, and formal markers do, if anything, become more noticeable as his career progresses.

The function of the agon in Euripides remained as consistent as its form. There are many ways of expressing conflict in drama, and Euripides' preferred method was to concentrate the conflict between two important characters so that it could be isolated and expressed formally in a single scene. This is not a naturalistic method, but it has the advantage of allowing a conflict to be represented with clarity and explicitness.

These are tragic conflicts, which cannot be resolved merely by talking about them, and it is thus not surprising that the agon rarely achieves anything in the narrower sense of influencing the action. Sometimes there is a dramatic point in the futility of rational discussion, but more often the agon is subtly detached even from the possibility of having any effect. It exists in a kind of equilibrium, separated from the sequence of events which constitutes the action of the play, so that neither can it influence the action nor is any significance attached to its inability to do so. We have seen how Euripides goes to considerable lengths to achieve this in *Hippolytus, Andromache, Electra, Troades, Orestes,* and *Iphigenia in Aulis.* The point of the agon is to depict the main conflict of the play, and not to represent the expression of that conflict on a particular occasion.

Euripides' agones contain some of his most characteristic features as a dramatist, notably formalism of structure and interest in argument and debate. Different readers and spectators will inevitably react in different ways to these aspects of his style, and he has often been criticized because of them. The main advantage of the agon form for Euripides was that it enabled him to give the fullest and subtlest possible account of a given point of view, and this might not have been possible through the medium of a more fluid and naturalistic style. The fixed form of the agon gave Euripides a mould into which every kind of argument and rhetorical technique could be poured.

He would not have reverted so frequently to this dramatic form if his concern had been merely with the illusion of genuine debate and not with its substance, and it is essential that the actual arguments in the agones be taken seriously. Fifth-century Athenians were notorious connoisseurs of debate, as Cleon complains (Thuc. 3. 38), and the arguments in Euripides' agones are rarely less than subtle and ingenious. Often they are much more than that, and encompass serious religious, political, and philosophical themes. We have little enough contemporary rhetoric and philosophy with which to compare Euripides' agones, but there is no reason to suppose that the level of argument which they contain was not as high as anything then available. The speeches in Thucydides afford the best parallel for these scenes in which the glories and the limitations of human reason are analysed in the context of tragic conflict.

Bibliography

ADKINS, A. W. H. (1960), *Merit and Responsibility: A Study in Greek Values* (Oxford).
AÉLION, R. (1983), *Euripide héritier d'Eschyle* (Paris).
ARNOTT, W. G. (1981), 'Double the Vision: A Reading of Euripides' *Electra*', *G&R* 28: 179–92.
ARROWSMITH, W. (1963), 'A Greek Theater of Ideas', *Arion*, 2: 32–56.
ARTHUR, M. B. (1975), 'Euripides' *Phoenissae* and the Politics of Justice' (dissertation, Yale University).
—— (1977), 'The Curse of Civilization: The Choral Odes of the *Phoenissae*', *HSCP* 81: 163–85.
AUSTIN, C. (1968) (ed.), *Nova Fragmenta Euripidea in Papyris Reperta* (Berlin).
BAIN, D. (1977), *Actors and Audience: A Study of Asides and Related Conventions in Greek Drama* (Oxford).
—— (1987), 'Some Reflections on the Illusion in Greek Tragedy', *BICS* 34: 1–14.
BARRETT, W. S. (1964) (ed.), *Euripides: Hippolytos* (Oxford).
BATEMAN, J. J. (1962), 'Some Aspects of Lysias' Argumentation', *Phoenix*, 16: 157–77.
BOND, G. W. (1981) (ed.), *Euripides: Heracles* (Oxford).
BROCK, R. (1989), 'Athenian Oligarchs: The Numbers Game', *JHS* 109: 160–4.
BURIAN, P. (1977), 'Euripides' *Heraclidae*: An Interpretation', *CP* 72: 1–21.
BURKERT, W. (1974), 'Die Absurdität der Gewalt und das Ende der Tragödie: Euripides' *Orestes*', *A&A* 20: 97–109.
BURNETT, A. P. (1971), *Catastrophe Survived: Euripides' Plays of Mixed Reversal* (Oxford).
BUXTON, R. G. A. (1982), *Persuasion in Greek Tragedy: A Study of Peitho* (Cambridge).
CAIZZI, F. D. (1969) (ed.), *Antiphontis Tetralogiae* (Milan).
CAREY, C. (1989) (ed.), *Lysias: Selected Speeches* (Cambridge).
COLLARD, C. (1975*a*), 'Formal Debates in Euripides' Drama', *G&R* 22: 58–71.
—— (1975*b*) (ed.), *Euripides: Supplices* (Groningen).
CONACHER, D. J. (1967), *Euripidean Drama: Myth, Theme and Structure* (Toronto).
—— (1972), 'Some Questions of Probability and Relevance in Euripidean Drama', *Maia*, 24: 199–207.
—— (1981), 'Rhetoric and Relevance in Euripidean Drama', *AJP* 102: 3–25.
—— (1986), *Greek Tragedy and Its Legacy: Essays Presented to D. J. Conacher*, ed. M. Cropp, E. Fantham, and S. E. Scully (Calgary).
—— (1988) (ed.), *Euripides: Alcestis* (Warminster).
CRAIK, E. M. (1988) (ed.), *Euripides: Phoenician Women* (Warminster).
CROPP, M. J. (1982), 'Euripides *Elektra* 1013–7 and 1041–4', *LCM* 7: 51–4.
—— (1988) (ed.), *Euripides: Electra* (Warminster).

DALE, A. M. (1954) (ed.), *Euripides: Alcestis* (Oxford).
—— (1969), *Collected Papers* (Cambridge).
DAUBE, B. (1938), *Zu den Rechtsproblemen in Aischylos' Agamemnon* (Zurich/Leipzig).
DENNISTON, J. D. (1939) (ed.), *Euripides: Electra* (Oxford).
—— (1954), *The Greek Particles*[2] (Oxford).
DESCH, W. (1985/1986), 'Die Hauptgestalten in Euripides' Troerinnen', *Grazer Beiträge*, 12/13: 65–100.
DODDS, E. R. (1959) (ed.), *Plato: Gorgias* (Oxford).
—— (1960) (ed.), *Euripides: Bacchae*[2] (Oxford).
DONZELLI, G. B. (1978), *Studio sull'Elettra di Euripide* (Catania).
DOVER, K. J. (1968), *Lysias and the Corpus Lysiacum* (Berkeley/Los Angeles).
—— (1974), *Greek Popular Morality in the Time of Plato and Aristotle* (Oxford).
—— (1980) (ed.), *Plato: Symposium* (Cambridge).
—— (1983), 'The Portrayal of Moral Evaluation in Greek Poetry', *JHS* 103: 35–48 (= Dover 1987: 77–96).
—— (1987), *Greek and the Greeks (Collected Papers, i. Language, Poetry, Drama)* (Oxford).
DUCHEMIN, J. (1968), *L'ΑΓΩΝ dans la tragédie grecque*[2] (Paris).
DUE, B. (1980), *Antiphon: A Study in Argumentation* (Copenhagen).
DYSON, M. (1988), 'Alcestis' Children and the Character of Admetus', *JHS* 108:13–23.
EASTERLING, P. E. (1985), 'Anachronism in Greek Tragedy', *JHS* 105: 1–10.
EDWARDS, M., and USHER, S. (1985) (eds.), *Greek Orators, i. Antiphon and Lysias* (Warminster).
EHRENBERG, V. (1947), 'Polypragmosyne: A Study in Greek Politics', *JHS* 67: 46–67.
Entretiens sur l'Antiquité classique (1958) (Fondation Hardt), 6. *Euripide* (Geneva, published 1960).
EPKE, E. (1951), 'Über die Streitszenen und ihre Entwicklung in der griechischen Tragödie' (dissertation, University of Hamburg).
ERBSE, H. (1984), *Studien zum Prolog der euripideischen Tragödie* (Berlin/New York).
EUCKEN, C. (1986), 'Das Rechtsproblem im euripideischen *Orest*', *MH* 43: 155–68.
FALKNER, T. M. (1983), 'Coming of Age in Argos: Physis and Paideia in Euripides' *Orestes*', *CJ* 78: 289–300.
FINLEY, J. H. (1967), *Three Essays on Thucydides* (Cambridge, Mass.).
FITTON, J. W. (1961), 'The *Suppliant Women* and the *Herakleidai* of Euripides', *Hermes*, 89: 430–61.
FOLEY, H. P. (1985), *Ritual Irony: Poetry and Sacrifice in Euripides* (Ithaca, NY).
FRAENKEL, E. (1946), 'A Passage in the *Phoenissae*', *Eranos*, 44: 81–9.
—— (1950) (ed.), *Aeschylus: Agamemnon* (Oxford).
—— (1957), *Horace* (Oxford).
FRIEDRICH, W.-H. (1953), *Euripides und Diphilos: zur Dramaturgie der Spätformen* (Munich).

FRITZ, K. VON (1962), *Antike und moderne Tragödie: Neun Abhandlungen* (Berlin).
FROLEYKS, W. J. (1973), 'Der ΑΓΩΝ ΛΟΓΩΝ in der antiken Literatur' (dissertation, University of Bonn).
FUQUA, C. (1976), 'Studies in the Use of Myth in Sophocles' *Philoctetes* and the *Orestes* of Euripides', *Traditio*, 32: 29–95.
—— (1978), 'The World of Myth in Euripides' *Orestes*', *Traditio*, 34: 1–28.
GAGARIN, M. (1981), *Drakon and Early Athenian Homicide Law* (New Haven/London).
—— (1990), 'The Nature of Proofs in Antiphon', *CP* 85: 22–32.
GARTON, C. (1957), 'Characterisation in Greek Tragedy', *JHS* 77: 247–54.
—— (1972), 'The "Chameleon Trail" in the Criticism of Greek Tragedy', *Stud. Philol.*, 69: 389–413.
GARVIE, A. F. (1986) (ed.), *Aeschylus: Choephori* (Oxford).
GLOTZ, G. (1904), *La Solidarité de la famille dans le droit criminel en Grèce* (Paris).
GOEBEL, G. H. (1983), 'Early Greek Rhetorical Theory and Practice: Proof and Arrangement in the Speeches of Antiphon and Euripides' (dissertation, University of Wisconsin at Madison).
—— (1989), '*Andromache* 192–204: The Pattern of Argument', *CP* 84: 32–5.
GOFF, B. E. (1988), 'The Shields of *Phoenissae*', *GRBS* 29: 135–52.
—— (1990), *The Noose of Words: Readings of Desire, Violence and Language in Euripides' Hippolytos* (Cambridge).
GOLDHILL, S. D. (1986), *Reading Greek Tragedy* (Cambridge).
GOMME, A. W. (1956), *A Historical Commentary on Thucydides*, i (Oxford).
GOOSSENS, R. (1962), *Euripide et Athènes* (Brussels).
GOULD, J. P. (1978), 'Dramatic Character and "Human Intelligibility" in Greek Tragedy', *PCPS*, NS 24: 43–67.
GRAF, G. (1950), 'Die Agonszenen bei Euripides' (dissertation, University of Göttingen).
GRIFFIN, J. (1980), *Homer on Life and Death* (Oxford).
GRUBE, G. M. A. (1941), *The Drama of Euripides* (London).
GUTHRIE, W. K. C. (1971), *The Sophists* (Cambridge), first published as Part 1 of *A History of Greek Philosophy*, iii (Cambridge, 1969).
HALL, E. (1989), *Inventing the Barbarian: Greek Self-Definition through Tragedy* (Oxford).
HAMILTON, R. (1985), 'Slings and Arrows: The Debate with Lycus in the *Heracles*', *TAPA* 115: 19–25.
HEATH, M. (1987), *The Poetics of Greek Tragedy* (London).
HORNBLOWER, S. (1987), *Thucydides* (London).
HUDSON-WILLIAMS, H. L. (1950), 'Conventional Forms of Debate and the Melian Dialogue', *AJP* 71: 156–69.
HUNTER, R. L. (1985), *The New Comedy of Greece and Rome* (Cambridge).
HUSSEY, E. (1972), *The Presocratics* (London).
HUTCHINSON, G. O. (1985) (ed.), *Aeschylus: Septem contra Thebas* (Oxford).

JOHANSEN, H. F. (1959), *General Reflection in Tragic Rhesis: A Study of Form* (Copenhagen).
JOUAN, F. (1966), *Euripide et les légendes des chants cypriens* (Paris).
—— (1984), 'Euripide et la rhétorique', *LEC* 52: 3–13.
KAMERBEEK, J. C. (1958), 'Mythe et réalité dans l'œuvre d'Euripide', *Entretiens sur l'Antiquité classique* (Fondation Hardt), 6. 1–41.
KANNICHT, R. (1969) (ed.), *Euripides: Helena* (Heidelberg).
KELLS, J. H. (1960), 'Euripides, *Electra* 1093–5, and Some Uses of δικάζειν', *CQ*, NS 10: 129–34.
—— (1966), 'More Notes on Euripides' *Electra*', *CQ*, NS 16: 51–4.
—— (1967), 'Euripides, *Hippolytus* 1009–16, and Greek Women's Property', *CQ*, NS 17: 181–3.
KENNEDY, G. (1959), 'The Earliest Rhetorical Handbooks', *AJP* 80: 169–78.
—— (1963), *The Art of Persuasion in Greece* (Princeton).
KERFERD, G. B. (1981), *The Sophistic Movement* (Cambridge).
KIRKWOOD, G. M. (1947), 'Hecuba and Nomos', *TAPA* 78: 61–8.
KNOX, B. M. W. (1979), *Word and Action: Essays on the Ancient Theater* (Baltimore/London).
KOVACS, P. D. (1982), 'Tyrants and Demagogues in Tragic Interpolation', *GRBS* 23: 31–50.
—— (1987), *The Heroic Muse: Studies in the Hippolytus and Hecuba of Euripides* (Baltimore/London).
KRIEG, W. (1934), 'De Euripidis Oreste' (dissertation, University of Halle).
KROLL, W. (1940), 'Rhetorik', *Paulys Real-Encyclopädie der classischen Altertumswissenschaft*, Suppl. 7 (Stuttgart).
LANZA, D. (1963), 'Νόμος e Ἴσον in Euripide', *RFIC* 91: 416–39.
LAVENCY, M. (1964), *Aspects de la logographie judiciaire attique* (Louvain).
LECHNER, M. (1874), *De Euripide Rhetorum Discipulo* (Anspach).
LEE, K. H. (1976) (ed.), *Euripides: Troades* (London).
LEES, J. T. (1891), 'ΔΙΚΑΝΙΚΟΣ ΛΟΓΟΣ in Euripides' (dissertation, Johns Hopkins University).
LESKY, A. (1958), 'Psychologie bei Euripides', *Entretiens sur l'Antiquité classique* (Fondation Hardt), 6. 123–68.
—— (1966), *Gesammelte Schriften* (Bern).
LLOYD, G. E. R. (1979), *Magic, Reason and Experience: Studies in the Origin and Development of Greek Science* (Cambridge).
LLOYD, M. A. (1984), 'The Helen Scene in Euripides' *Troades*', *CQ*, NS 34: 303–13.
—— (1985), 'Euripides' *Alcestis*', *G&R* 32: 119–31.
—— (1986), 'Realism and Character in Euripides' *Electra*', *Phoenix*, 40: 1–19.
LLOYD-JONES, H. (1965), review of Barrett 1964, *JHS* 85: 164–71 (= *Greek Epic, Lyric, and Tragedy* (Oxford, 1990), 419–35).
—— (1971), *The Justice of Zeus* (Berkeley/Los Angeles).
LONG, A. A. (1968), *Language and Thought in Sophocles: A Study of Abstract Nouns and Poetic Technique* (London).

LONGO, O. (1975), 'Proposte di lettura per l'*Oreste* di Euripide', *Maia*, 27: 265–87.
LORAUX, N. (1986), *The Invention of Athens: The Funeral Oration in the Classical City* (Cambridge, Mass./London); Eng. tr. of *L'Invention d'Athènes: Histoire de l'oraison funèbre dans la 'cité classique'* (Paris, 1981).
LUDWIG, W. (1957), 'Sapheneia: Ein Beitrag zur Formkunst im Spätwerk des Euripides' (dissertation, University of Tübingen).
MACLEOD, C. W. (1983), *Collected Essays* (Oxford).
MARTIN, J. (1974), *Antike Rhetorik: Technik und Methode* (Munich).
MASTRONARDE, D. J. (1974), 'Studies in Euripides' *Phoinissai*' (dissertation, University of Toronto).
—— (1979), *Contact and Discontinuity: Some Conventions of Speech and Action on the Greek Tragic Stage* (Berkeley/Los Angeles).
—— (1986), 'The Optimistic Rationalist in Euripides: Theseus, Jocasta, Tiresias', in Conacher 1986: 201–11.
MATTHIESEN, K. (1964), *Elektra, Taurische Iphigenie und Helena: Untersuchungen zur Chronologie und zur dramatischen Form im Spätwerk des Euripides* (Göttingen).
MICHELINI, A. N. (1987), *Euripides and the Tragic Tradition* (Wisconsin).
MILLER, T. (1887), 'Euripides Rhetoricus' (dissertation, University of Göttingen).
MORRISON, J. S. (1941), 'The Place of Protagoras in Athenian Public Life (460–415 B.C.)', *CQ* 35: 1–16.
MUELLER-GOLDINGEN, C. (1985), *Untersuchungen zu den Phönissen des Euripides* (Stuttgart).
MURRAY, R. L. (1964), 'Persuasion in Euripides' (dissertation, Cornell University).
NAVARRE, O. (1900). *Essai sur la rhétorique grecque avant Aristotle* (Paris).
NORDEN, E. (1898), *Die antike Kunstprosa* (Leipzig/Berlin).
NORTH, H. F. (1988), 'Socrates Deinos Legein', in *Language and the Tragic Hero: Essays on Greek Tragedy in Honor of Gordon M. Kirkwood*, ed. P. Pucci (Atlanta), 121–30.
NUCHELMANS, J. C. F. (1971), *De ΑΓΩΝ of ΑΜΙΛΛΑ ΛΟΓΩΝ in de Tragedies van Euripides* (Nijmegen).
O'BRIEN, M. J. (1964), 'Orestes and the Gorgon: Euripides' *Electra*', *AJP* 85: 13–39.
—— (1988), 'Character, Action and Rhetoric in the *Agon* of the *Orestes*', in *Filologia e forma letterarie: Studi offerti a Francesco della Corte* (Urbino), i. 183–99.
OSTWALD, M. (1986), *From Popular Sovereignty to the Sovereignty of Law: Law, Society and Politics in Fifth-Century Athens* (Berkeley/Los Angeles/London).
PAGE, D. L. (1934), *Actors' Interpolations in Greek Tragedy* (Oxford).
—— (1938) (ed.), *Euripides: Medea* (Oxford).
PARKER, R. C. T. (1983), *Miasma: Pollution and Purification in Early Greek Religion* (Oxford).
PELLICCIA, H. N. (1987), 'Pindarus Homericus: Pythian 3.1–80', *HSCP* 91: 39–63.
POHLENZ, M. (1954), *Die griechische Tragödie*[2] (Göttingen).
POWELL, A. (1990) (ed.), *Euripides, Women, and Sexuality* (London/New York).

RADERMACHER, L. (1951), 'Artium Scriptores: Reste der voraristotelischen Rhetorik', *SAWW* 227: 3.
RAWSON, E. (1970), 'Family and Fatherland in Euripides' *Phoenissae*', *GRBS* 11: 109—27.
—— (1972), 'Aspects of Euripides' *Orestes*', *Arethusa*, 5: 155—67.
REINHARDT, K. (1960), 'Die Sinneskrise bei Euripides', in *Tradition und Geist* (Göttingen), 223—56.
RITCHIE, W. (1964), *The Authenticity of the Rhesus of Euripides* (Cambridge).
ROHDICH, H. (1968), *Die euripideische Tragödie: Untersuchungen zu ihre Tragik* (Heidelberg).
ROMILLY, J. DE (1951), *Thucydide et l'impérialisme athénien²* (Paris).
—— (1965), 'Les *Phéniciennes* d'Euripide, ou l'actualité dans la tragédie grecque', *R. Ph.* 39: 28—47.
—— (1967), *Histoire et raison chez Thucydide²* (Paris).
—— (1972), 'L'Assemblée du peuple dans l'*Oreste* d'Euripide', in *Studi classici in onore di Quintino Cataudella* (Catania), i. 237—51.
—— (1975), *Magic and Rhetoric in Ancient Greece* (Cambridge, Mass.).
—— (1983), 'Les Réflexions générales d'Euripide', *CRAI* 1983: 405—18.
SCHADEWALDT, W. (1926), *Monolog und Selbstgespräch: Untersuchungen zur Formgeschichte der griechischen Tragödie* (Berlin).
SCHEIDWEILER, F. (1966), 'Antiphons Rede über den Mord an Herodes', *Rh. M* 109: 319—38.
SCHEIN, S. L. (1975), 'Mythical Illusion and Historical Reality in Euripides' *Orestes*', *WS*, NS 9: 49—66.
SCHLEGEL, A. W. (1909), *Lectures on Dramatic Art and Literature* (Eng. tr., 2nd edn., London).
SCHMALZRIEDT, E. (1980), 'Sophokles und die Rhetorik', *Rhetorik*, 1: 89—110.
SCHWARTZ, E. (1887—1891) (ed.), *Scholia in Euripidem* (Berlin).
SCHWINGE, E.-R. (1968), *Die Verwendung der Stichomythie in den Dramen des Euripides* (Heidelberg).
SCODEL, R. (1980), *The Trojan Trilogy of Euripides* (Göttingen).
SEAFORD, R. (1984) (ed.), *Euripides: Cyclops* (Oxford).
SEGAL, C. P. (1970), 'Shame and Purity in Euripides' *Hippolytus*', *Hermes*, 98: 278—99.
—— (1972), 'Curse and Oath in Euripides' *Hippolytus*', *Ramus*, 1: 165—80.
—— (1986), *Interpreting Greek Tragedy: Myth, Poetry, Text* (Ithaca/London).
SEIDENSTICKER, B. (1982), *Palintonos Harmonia: Studien zu komischen Elementen in der griechischen Tragödie* (Göttingen).
SENONER, R. (1960), 'Der Rede-Agon im euripideischen Drama' (dissertation, University of Vienna).
SMITH, W. D. (1967), 'Disease in Euripides' *Orestes*', *Hermes*, 95: 291—307.
SOLMSEN, F. (1931), *Antiphonstudien* (Berlin).
—— (1975), *Intellectual Experiments of the Greek Enlightenment* (Princeton).
SOMMERSTEIN, A. H. (1989) (ed.), *Aeschylus: Eumenides* (Cambridge).

STEIDLE, W. (1968), *Studien zum antiken Drama: unter besonderer Berücksichtigung des Bühnenspiels* (Munich).
STEPHANOPOULOS, T. K. (1980), *Umgestaltung des Mythos durch Euripides* (Athens).
STEVENS, P. T (1971) (ed.), *Euripides: Andromache* (Oxford).
—— (1976), *Colloquial Expressions in Euripides* (Wiesbaden).
STINTON, T. C. W. (1965), *Euripides and the Judgement of Paris* (London) (= Stinton 1990: 17–75).
—— (1976), '"Si credere dignum est": Some Expressions of Disbelief in Euripides and Others', *PCPS* NS 22: 60–89 (= Stinton 1990: 236–64).
—— (1986), 'The Scope and Limits of Allusion in Greek Tragedy', in Conacher 1986: 67–102 (= Stinton 1990: 454–92).
—— (1990), *Collected Papers on Greek Tragedy* (Oxford).
STROHM, H. (1957), *Euripides: Interpretationen zur dramatischen Form* (Munich).
SÜSS, W. (1910), *Ethos: Studien zur älteren griechischen Rhetorik* (Leipzig).
TAPLIN, O. (1977), *The Stagecraft of Aeschylus: The Dramatic Use of Exits and Entrances in Greek Tragedy* (Oxford).
—— (1986), 'Fifth-Century Tragedy and Comedy: A *Synkrisis*', *JHS* 106: 163–74.
TIERNEY, M. (1946) (ed.), *Euripides: Hecuba* (Dublin).
TIETZE, F. (1933), 'Die euripideischen Reden und ihre Bedeutung' (dissertation, University of Breslau).
USHER, S. (1965), 'Individual Characterisation in Lysias', *Eranos*, 63: 99–119.
—— (1985), see M. Edwards and S. Usher (1985).
VAHLEN, J. (1891), 'Zu Sophokles' und Euripides' *Elektra*', *Hermes*, 26: 351–65.
VERNANT, J.-P., and VIDAL-NAQUET, P. (1972), *Mythe et tragédie en Grèce ancienne*, i (Paris).
—— —— (1986), *Mythe et tragédie en Grèce ancienne*, ii (Paris).
—— —— (1988), *Myth and Tragedy in Ancient Greece* (New York); Eng. tr. of Vernant and Vidal-Naquet 1972, 1986.
VICKERS, B. (1973), *Towards Greek Tragedy: Drama, Myth, Society* (London).
VLASTOS, G. (1947), 'Equality and Justice in Early Greek Cosmologies', *CP* 42: 156–78.
VÖGLER, A. (1967), *Vergleichende Studien zur sophokleischen und euripideischen Elektra* (Heidelberg).
VOLKMANN, R. (1885), *Die Rhetorik der Griechen und Römer in systematischer Übersicht*[2] (Leipzig).
WEDD, N. (1895) (ed.), *Euripides: Orestes* (Cambridge).
WEIL, H. (1879) (ed.), *Sept tragédies d'Euripide*[2] (Paris).
WEST, M. L. (1987a) (ed.), *Euripides: Orestes* (Warminster).
—— (1987b), 'Problems in Euripides' *Orestes*', *CQ*, NS 37: 281–93.
WILAMOWITZ-MOELLENDORFF, U. VON (1883), 'Die beiden *Elektren*', *Hermes*, 18: 214–63.
—— (1895) (ed.), *Euripides: Herakles*[2] (Berlin).
—— (1924), 'Lesefrüchte', *Hermes*, 59: 249–73.
WILL, F. (1961), 'Tyndareus in the *Orestes*', *SO* 37: 96–9.

WILLINK, C. W. (1986) (ed.), *Euripides: Orestes* (Oxford).
WINNINGTON-INGRAM, R. P. (1948), *Euripides and Dionysus: An Interpretation of the Bacchae* (Cambridge).
—— (1958), '*Hippolytus*: A Study in Causation', *Entretiens sur l'antiquité classique* (Fondation Hardt), 6. 169–97.
—— (1969), 'Euripides: Poiêtês Sophos', *Arethusa*, 2: 127–42.
—— (1980), *Sophocles: An Interpretation* (Cambridge).
XANTHAKIS-KARAMANOS, G. (1979), 'The Influence of Rhetoric on Fourth-Century Tragedy', *CQ*, NS 29: 66–76.
ZEITLIN, F. I. (1980), 'The Closet of Masks: Role-Playing and Myth-Making in the *Orestes* of Euripides', *Ramus*, 9: 51–77.
ZUNTZ, G. (1955), *The Political Plays of Euripides* (Manchester).

GENERAL INDEX

action, agon detached from 17, 43 f., 51 f., 54, 59 f., 96 f., 110–12, 120, 126, 131 f.
adultery 63 f., 67
Aeschylus:
   Agamemnon 60, 61, 62, 64, 66 n., 68 n., 69
   Choephori 58 f., 70, 124, 125
   Eumenides 13 f., 22, 118, 121, 128 f.
   Septem contra Thebas 84 f.
   Supplices 73, 76
a fortiori argument 33, 103 f.
agonistic terminology 4 f., 47, 72, 83, 85, 114
Alcmaeon 91
ambiguity 87 f., 114, 115 n., 116 n.
Anaxagoras 108
Anonymus Iamblichi 91
Antiphon 21, 22, 29, 30, 32, 34 n., 102
antithesis 34, 86
arbitration:
   in agones of *Hcld., Su., Pho.* 71, 84, 85
   in Athenian law 31
argument (section of a speech) 21, 24 f.
Aristophanes 19, 20 n., 91
Aristotle:
   Metaphysics 108
   Politics 92 n.
   Rhetoric 21, 22, 26, 28, 73, 103 f.
   Rhetorica ad Alexandrum 21, 23, 25, 26, 28, 73
Athenians:
   assembly of 82, 126 f.
   as connoisseurs of debate 22 f., 132
   criticism of their empire 93
   enterprising spirit of 78, 80
   law of 49, 116 f.
   in Melian Dialogue (Thuc. 5. 85–111) 89 f., 91

pious response to supplication of 72, 73
see also democracy
authority, appeal to 68 n.

barbarians 53, 54, 98, 103

character, argument from 48 f.
characterization *see* rhetoric, significance for character in E.
chorus 5, 14, 37 f., 60 f., 65 f., 68 f., 119
Cleon 81, 132
conflict, agon compared/contrasted with other types of 2, 4 f., 13–15, 71, 83, 85, 114
consensio 118, 125, 126
Corax and Tisias 20–2
'couldn't/wouldn't' argument 50, 53
Cratinus 21 n.
cross-examination 14
Cypria 102, 103

deliberative oratory 20, 71, 73 f., 127
democracy:
   debated (*Su.*) 79–81
   defended by Jocasta (*Pho.*) 90–3
   persuasion as feature of 75, 79
   unattractive aspects of (*Or.*) 127
   see also tyranny
deus ex machina 1, 67, 76, 131
dilemma, arguments from, *see* disjunctive arguments
Diogenes of Apollonia 107 f.
disjunctive arguments 30, 92, 98
Draco 117 n.

Eleatics 30 f.
Empedocles 91
entrances:
   extended announcement of 58

entrances (cont.)
  lyric announcement of 85 n.
  marking beginning of agon 3, 12, 41, 43, 79, 97, 99 f., 113
Ephialtes 22
epideixis scenes 10 f., 90
epilogue 21, 27 f., 119
  balancing proem 65, 86, 87
  echoing adversary's epilogue 68, 125
  gnomic 28, 38, 42, 82, 97
equality 80 f., 87 f., 90−3
Euripides:
  Alcestis 8, 36−41
  Alexandros 106
  Andromache 10, 15, 51−4, 64, 79, 99
  Antiope 18
  Bacchae 10, 107
  Cretes 24, 29, 50, 103, 104 f., 124 n.
  Cyclops 9
  Electra 1, 55−70
  Hecuba 8 f., 33, 35, 94−9, 112, 131
  Helen 9
  Heracles 10 f., 104
  Heraclidae 7, 71−6, 88, 98, 105
  Hippolytus 34, 42 n., 43−51, 55
  Ion 10
  Iphigenia in Aulis 3 f., 5, 9, 15 f., 67, 87 n., 130
  Medea 7, 24, 32 f., 41−3, 76
  Orestes 33, 98, 104, 113−29
  Phoenissae 24, 28, 71 f., 83−93, 126
  Rhesus 7 f.
  Supplices 9, 35, 71 f., 76−83
  Troades 35, 88, 94 f., 99−112, 117, 124
exile, as penalty for homicide 115−17, 126 n.
exit, marking end of agon 3 f., 8 f., 12, 39, 76
expediency:
  as a factor in deliberative oratory 73 f., 127
  contrasted with justice in Melian Dialogue (Thuc. 5. 85−111) 89 f.

factual questions, unresolved 63 n., 67, 98, 105, 109
formalism 1, 2, 4, 5, 13, 36, 73, 131

Gorgias 22, 34, 51
  Helen 30, 100 f.
  Palamedes 21, 29, 30

heiresses 49 f.
Helen 66 f., 99−112 *passim*, 118
Homer:
  assemblies in 126
  on guilt of Helen 101, 104 f., 109
  as inventor of rhetoric 19
  Judgement of Paris in 106
  'not A, or B, but C' as a formula in 111 n.
  oath challenge in (*Il.* 23. 581−5) 22
  penalties for homicide in 116 f.
homicide 114−18
hyperbole 49 n.
hypophora 29 f., 49 f., 53, 98
hypothetical role-reversal 32 n., 64 f.
hypothetical syllogism 32 f., 98 f.

judge, in agon 27 f., 72, 76, 90, 98, 99, 110−12, 114, 126
justice:
  contrasted with expediency in Melian Dialogue (Thuc. 5. 85−111) 89 f.
  as a factor in deliberative oratory 71, 73 f., 127
  in Hecuba's supplication of Agamemnon (*Hec.*) 95 f.
  in Polynices' speech (*Pho.*) 89
  in Tyndareus' speech (*Or.*) 118

law 62, 81, 95, 114−19, 122
  Athenian 49, 116 f.
  Panhellenic 76, 78, 79, 83, 114−17
  prosecutors claim to defend 34, 118
lawcourts, evoked in E.'s agones 2, 13 f., 33 f., 47−51, 104, 114, 124

see also rhetoric
Lysias 31, 32 f.

messenger speeches 1, 56 f., 97, 126–8, 131
mini-agon 13
misogyny 47, 128

narratio 21, 24 f., 38, 42
near-agon 6–8, 76

oaths 22, 34, 46, 50 f.
'optimistic rationalists' 78, 90–2, 108, 117–19
oxymoron 86

personalization, absurd 115 n.
personification 88
persuasion:
    as feature of democracy 75, 79
    in Gorgias' *Helen* 100
    in *Hec.* 95 f., 99
Pindar (*Pyth.* 11. 22–4) 67 n.
pity 77, 123
Plato:
    Apology 30, 48, 101
    Gorgias 89, 91
    Phaedrus 21 n., 22 n.
    Protagoras 81
    Republic 89
points of view 28, 73 f.
praeteritio 122
precedent 110 n., 123 n.
probability, argument from 22, 29, 46, 53, 98, 103, 106
proem 21, 25–7
    absent 25, 97, 105
    balancing epilogue 86, 87
    connected with rest of speech by relative clause 66, 81
    in Sophocles 27
    typical elements in: abuse 26, 42, 66; disadvantages of speaker 26 f., 47 f., 53, 61, 101, 120; dismissal of opponent's speech 39, 87 f.; establishing right to speak 27, 39, 52 f., 75; fine words contrasted with truth 26, 47, 86, 97; headline 25 f., 61, 81, 114; 'I have often observed' 77 n.; need for clever speaking 27, 43; need to defend oneself 47, 53; 'unaccustomed as I am' 27, 47 f.; undermining opponent's right to reply 38, 42, 52 f.
proofs, natural/artificial 22
    see also oaths; probability, argument from; witnesses
Protagoras 23, 89
public benefactor, claim by speaker to be 123 n.

realism 1, 56 f., 104, 122, 126 f.
reductio ad absurdum 31 f., 64 f., 122 f.
relativism 89
rhetoric 19–36 *passim*
    date of impact of on E., 23, 35, 36
    defined 19 n.
    deliberative, epideictic, forensic distinguished 20, 73 f.
    E. as evidence for development of 20
    Sicilian, *see* Corax and Tisias
    significance for character in E. 36, 42 f., 50 f., 54, 55, 94 f., 101, 109, 130 f.
Rhetorica ad Alexandrum, *see under* Aristotle

self-consciousness, rhetorical 34 f., 42 f., 80, 81, 101
Solon 107
Sophocles:
    agon in 11–13
    argument from probability in 29
    hypophora in 29 f.
    proems in 27
    works:
        Ajax 12; *Antigone* 12 f., 82; *Electra* 11 f., 17, 55–70 *saepe*

speeches, in agon:
  addressee of 98
  balance of 5 f., 9
  length of 5
  order of 17, 101
  structure of 21 f., 24–8, 38, 42
Stesichorus 84
stichomythia 1, 6, 7, 10 n., 39, 54, 72, 76, 85, 93, 95, 113
suppliant plays 52, 73, 78, 83 f.
supplication scenes 8 f., 13 n., 77 f., 95 f., 113 f., 126

Thebes, as negative counterpart to Athens? 72 n.
Thucydides:
  1. 32–43: 74
  2. 35–46: 81, 91 f.
  3. 9–14: 74
  3. 37–48: 39, 74, 132

3. 53. 2: 101
3. 82: 88, 118 n.
5. 85–111: 89 f., 91
6. 38 f.: 92
6. 76–80: 74
Tisias, see Corax and Tisias
tricolon 111 n.
tyranny
  Aegisthus (*El.*) exemplifies 58
  contrasted with democracy (*Su.*) 80 f.
  pursued by Eteocles (*Pho.*) 88–90
  rejected 49, 92
  see also democracy

vendetta 115, 127
victory, in agon 15 f.

witnesses 22, 33 f., 46, 47, 50, 109, 119

Xenophanes 107

INDEX OF GREEK WORDS

ἀγών 4–5, 13, 85, 114
ἄκουσον 35
ἅμιλλα λόγων 4–5
ἀντικατηγορία 102
ἄτεχνος/ἔντεχνος 22

βοή 109

γαμεῖσθαι 125
γόης 51

διαβολή 26, 81
διδάσκω 35
δίκην ἐπιθεῖναι 115–16, 124

ἐλέου ἐκβολή 123
ἐν μέρει 80, 92

ἐπελθεῖν 115
ἐπίκληρος 49
εὐλάβεια 82, 88

ἥσυχος/ἡσυχία 82

ἵν' εἰδῇς 110

καιρός 86

λέγοιμ' ἄν 25

νόμος/φύσις 91

ὅδε 86
ὁρᾶς 125
ὅστις 66
ὄχλος 48, 81

Index of Greek Words

παρρησία 34, 48, 118
πλεονεξία 91, 92, 93
πολλῶν μίαν ὕπερ 62
πολυπραγμοσύνη 93
πόνος 79, 82
προκατάληψις 21, 30–1, 38, 46
προκατασκευή 21
προοίμιον 25, 66

σκέψασθε 45
σοφός/σοφία 28, 48, 85, 87, 89, 114

σωτηρία 92
σώφρων/σωφροσύνη 48–9

τάξις 34, 35, 43, 50, 98
τεκμήριον 22
τελικὰ κεφάλαια 28, 73

φίλος/φιλία 28, 65, 98, 113, 126
φιλότιμος/φιλοτιμία 90, 92, 93

χάρις 75, 96, 98